OKANAGAN COLLEGE LIBRARY

01423854

F 2537 .D52 1991
Diacon, Todd A.
    Millenarian vision,
capitalist reality :

DATE DUE

MAY 0 1 1997	
JUL 3 1997	
JAN - 2 1998	
JUN 1 3 2001	
FEB 2 9 2003	
MAR 1 3 2003	

BRODART, INC.   Cat. No. 23-221

Millenarian Vision,
Capitalist Reality

Colonists at Cruz Machado Colony general store

OKANAGAN COLLEGE LIBRARY
BRITISH COLUMBIA

Millenarian Vision, Capitalist Reality

BRAZIL'S CONTESTADO REBELLION, 1912–1916

TODD A. DIACON

Duke University Press

Durham and London

1991

OKANAGAN COLLEGE LIBRARY
BRITISH COLUMBIA

© 1991 Duke University Press
All rights reserved
Printed in the United States of America
on acid-free paper ∞
Library of Congress Cataloging-in-Publication Data
appear on the last page of this book.

For Dorothy Hoch Diacon (1929–1977)
and Nathan Diacon-Furtado

Contents

List of Tables
and Figures

Tables

Figures

Acknowledgments

This is a book about Brazil, and as such I wish to thank the many Brazilians responsible for its completion. First on this list are the elderly Contestado residents who graciously agreed to speak about what was a painful event for them. I met these wonderful people with the help of four committed journalists from Florianópolis, Santa Catarina. Ênio Staub, Jurandir Píres de Camargo, Sérgio Antonio Flores, and Dario de Almeida Prado Jr. graciously invited me to join with them as they tracked down and interviewed the few remaining rebel survivors. Special thanks goes to Ênio Staub, whose kindness was exceeded only by his willingness to share his special knowledge of Brazil past and present.

For their help in locating valuable materials, I wish to recognize the staffs of the Arquivo Nacional and the Biblioteca Nacional, both in Rio de Janeiro. Thanks also to the staffs at the Arquivo Público do Paraná (Curitiba, Paraná), and the Arquivo do Estado de Santa Catarina (Florianópolis, Santa Catarina). I owe a special debt to the staffs of the municipal and parish archives in Rio Negro and União da Vitória, Paraná, and Três Barras, Canoinhas, and Campos Novos, Santa Catarina. Friendly people there took time out of their busy days to answer questions about what to me was an absolutely confusing land registration process. Thanks also to Professor Cecília Maria Westphalen, of the Federal University of Paraná, and David Carneiro, of Curitiba, Paraná, for their advice on what to look for, and where.

For their hospitality and support in Brasília I sincerely thank Wriggberto Câmara Furtado and Jovita Lacerda Furtado. Moema Lacerda Furtado also provided special support, and was especially helpful with Portuguese translations. In São Paulo, Fernando Ravinet provided room, board, and stimulating conversation. I also wish to thank Dona Dorileia Gustaverson of Rio de Janeiro.

Of course, my debts are equally numerous here in the United States. In 1980, Thomas E. Skidmore took a chance on a student from an unknown small college in Kansas. I had never taken a course in Latin American history, yet Tom invited me to join the graduate program at the University of Wisconsin–Madison. In this sense, and in many other ways, he is the person most responsible for my graduate education. His knowledge, kindness, and ongoing friendship are most appreciated. Also at Wisconsin, Forencia E. Mallon taught me how to better analyze both primary documents and secondary works. Her special literary ability encouraged me to enliven my own prose; I hope I succeeded. Steve J. Stern provided patient advice and cogent criticism. Always one to ask especially probing questions, he literally shaped this book. The Tinker and Doherty foundations funded my research.

A special thanks goes to my graduate school classmates at Wisconsin. Judith Allen, Joel Wolfe, Teresa Veccia, Luiz Pinero, Doug Cope, and Jonathan Glassman offered helpful advice and much needed friendship. At the University of Tennessee my colleagues in the History Department have done the same. Larry Malley, director of Duke University Press, was quick to offer his support and friendship. Tom Campbell brought a refreshing degree of sympathy and professionalism to his job as copyeditor. The very helpful comments of Barbara Weinstein and John Tutino made this a better book. I, of course, am solely responsible for any problems that remain.

In closing, I wish to note that it was my grandmother, Evelyn Cox Hoch, who encouraged me to become a historian. Now approaching her one hundredth birthday, in 1916 Grandma enrolled in her first Latin American history course at the University of Kansas, just as the Contestado Rebellion drew to a close. Whether by reading to me when I was a youngster, or by recounting family history as I grew older, she never let me forget about the past.

Finally, thanks Dad, for surviving.

Knoxville, Tennessee
May 1991

Millenarian Vision,
Capitalist Reality

1

The Contestado
Rebellion

On the night of 7 February 1915, Domingos Crespo ordered his 200-man elite guard to the rim of the valley. Below them, well hidden beneath the thick pine forest canopy, some 10,000 men, women, and children prayed and prepared for the coming battle. At dawn the cannon fire began, and soon the Brazilian army officers ordered the first charge of their 1,000-man strike force. The members of the Crespo guard were crack shots, however, and from their positions behind trees and boulders they beat back the Brazilian army's every advance. By the end of the day the officers had had enough, and they barked the orders for a general retreat. Members of the Crespo guard immediately congratulated themselves on the victory. Below them, 10,000 voices rose in a deafening chorus of "Praise be to God," "Long live the monarchy," and "Viva José Maria."[1]

In early 1912 a mysterious man began wandering around the backlands of the Brazilian states of Paraná and Santa Catarina in the so-called "Contestado" region. Soon he gained fame as a powerful *curandeiro* (healer), a man who, with his supply of herbs, could heal virtually any ill. He moved from *fazenda* (ranch) to *fazenda*, where residents would greet him with pleas for help.[2]

This mysterious man, whose name was Miguel Lucena Boaventura, had earlier deserted from the Paraná security force. A literate man of around forty years of age, he soon adopted the name José Maria, presumably to take advantage of the fame of João Maria, a popular healer who had lived in the region some twenty years earlier. Local legend tells that José Maria brought a small boy back to life a few months after arriving in the area. By doing so he solidified his fame as a powerful healer, and some people began to follow him on his journeys throughout the backlands.[3]

In addition to his medicinal activities, José Maria began preaching to those gathered about him. He spoke frequently of the evil of the Brazilian Republic (declared in 1889) and argued that monarchy was God's true, and holiest, form of government. At night he read aloud passages from *The History of Charlemagne* to his growing audience, which numbered 300 followers. At these readings he dwelled on Charlemagne's personal courage and on the holy war he waged against the infidel Moors in Spain.[4]

José Maria's popularity alarmed local officials, especially given that the memory of the bloody Canudos millenarian revolt was still fresh in their memory.[5] Fighting began in Irani, Paraná, on 22 October 1912, when a hundred-man unit of the Paraná state militia attacked the people they called *fanáticos*. José Maria died in the clash, but to the horror of most urban Brazilians the rebels defeated this force, killing its commander, Colonel João Gualberto. Calm soon prevailed, however, for José Maria's followers dispersed throughout the area.[6]

Sometime during mid-1913, a rumor swept through the Contestado claiming that José Maria was not dead. Instead, he was waiting in heaven for the moment to return and establish a "holy city" in the *sertão* (interior). Not only would José Maria return but so too would all those believers killed at Irani. Together they would form the army of St. Sebastian and prepare for the 1,000-year war of Charlemagne.[7]

Euzébio Ferreira dos Santos, the religious landowner who in 1912 had invited José Maria to preach at the patron saint celebration of the village of Perdizes Grandes, now traveled throughout the area preaching of the return of the mystic healer. Soon, Euzébio's son Manoel began having visions in which José Maria appeared. In one vision, José Maria ordered Euzébio, via Manoel, to sell all his goods and move to the rugged area of Taquaraçu (Taquarassu). Others were to do likewise, and once at Taquaraçu they were to share their wealth.[8]

João Paes de Farias remembers watching the "rebirth" of the millenarian movement at the home of his father, Francisco Paes de Farias (nicknamed Chico Ventura). One night in December 1913, Euzébio and his daughter Teodora arrived at the Paes de Farias home in Perdizes Grandes. Euzébio spoke wildly of the return of José Maria and of the visions of his son Manoel. He and Teodora then fell to the floor, wrapped themselves in a white sheet, and later emerged, in João's words, fanaticized. At that point Euzébio gave the order to settle the holy city of Taquaraçu.[9]

By December 1913, some 200 people lived at Taquaraçu. Local officials once again considered their presence a threat, and on 29 December 1913, government soldiers advanced on the redoubt. Once within visual distance the soldiers witnessed an unbelievable sight, one that caused the most jittery of the men to desert immediately: before them stood twenty-four rebel soldiers, dressed in white astride white horses, their white banners snapping in the breeze. These were the *Pares de França* (Peers of France), Charlemagne's imperial guard, now come to Taquaraçu to protect the holy city.[10]

It was not much of a battle. Shots from well-hidden rebels ripped through army ranks. Officers panicked, and both officers and soldiers fled the scene in an anarchic retreat. José Maria had protected his followers. The *fanáticos* had defended Taquaraçu.[11]

The December victory convinced larger numbers of Contestado residents of the power of the millenarian movement. Daily they arrived at the gates of the city, some with a few head of cattle, others with nothing. In February 1914, government soldiers massacred rebel women and children in an unguarded camp. In response, the *fanáticos* adopted a more aggressive strategy of attacks against local *fazendeiros* (landowners), the holdings of the American-owned Brazil Railway Company, and European immigrant colonies.[12] In early April 1914, 200 *fazendeiros* signed an angry petition demanding government protection.[13] On 5 September 1914, a band of 300 rebels destroyed two Brazil Railway station houses, along with a company sawmill and sections of railroad track. The rebels killed 100 people. They then ambushed the federal force sent to oppose them, killing its commander, Captain João Teixeira de Matos Costa.[14]

The millenarian rebels now dominated the rugged border area between the states of Paraná and Santa Catarina. One army official estimated that they controlled a 30-square-kilometer area and were able to move freely within a 28,000-square-kilometer area.[15] Some 20,000 men, women, and children now lived in the several redoubts spread throughout the region.[16] The rebels had killed the regional army commander and destroyed the facilities of the Brazil Railway Company. Their power now reached mythical proportions among both believers and nonbelievers alike.[17]

In response, Brazilian federal authorities named General Fernando Setembrino de Carvalho to lead an intensified campaign against the rebels. Carvalho arrived from the state of Ceará, where he fought against the millenarian-political rebellion led by the famous Padre Cícero.[18] General Setembrino de Carvalho demanded, and received, a large influx of men and matériel. He began his campaign backed by 7,000 soldiers.[19]

Given rebel numbers, their complete mastery of the region's rugged terrain, and the failures of his predecessors, Setembrino de Carvalho opted for a war of attrition. He surrounded the entire region, began a scorched-earth policy, and gradually narrowed the rebels' field of operations.[20] As early as December 1914, starving women and children straggled into the federal camps, but "rarely did armed and healthy men appear."[21] In late January the trickle turned into a flood, with more than 2,000 people surrendering. At that time emaciated women began giving their starving, lice-ridden children to any town dweller willing to accept them.[22]

Weakened by starvation and sickness, various smaller rebel redoubts fell to government forces in early 1915. In February, soldiers captured the Santo Antonio redoubt and burned the settlement's 500 wooden shacks. Redoubts at Pinheiros, Reichardt, Marcello, and Josephina were also destroyed.[23] Those rebels who did not surrender now made their way to the newly formed redoubt of Santa Maria, whose population soon ballooned to more than 10,000. There starvation continued to plague the rebels. Boiled cowskins became the staple of the rebel diet, and one ex-resident of Santa Maria remembers how children rushed to drink the blood of freshly slaughtered cattle. To avoid such tumult, Santa Maria's leaders began slaughtering cattle only late at night.[24]

On 8 February 1915, General Setembrino de Carvalho ordered the 1,800-man Southern Division to attack Santa Maria. This was the attack so incredibly repelled by the 200-man Crespo family guard. Faced with this defeat, Setembrino de Carvalho returned to the strategy that had served him so well: siege and starvation. To block rebel supply lines he deployed his 7,000 soldiers, who at that time represented nearly one-half of the entire Brazilian army! He then ordered his artillery units to begin daily shellings of the redoubt. Finally, in early April 1915, Captain Potiguara and his force pierced the center of the redoubt, killed nearly 600 rebels, and burned 5,000 houses. Santa Maria had fallen after a siege of nearly two months.[25]

As government troops concluded operations in late 1915 and early 1916, crowds cheered General Setembrino de Carvalho's return to Rio de Janeiro. Army officials praised his efforts, although the rebellion's US $250,000 price tag no doubt tempered their spirits.[26] In the Contestado, however, no one celebrated. There, both the victors and the vanquished faced a countryside in ruins, and both wondered where their next meal would come from.[27]

The Contestado Region

Bordered by the Iguaçu and Negro rivers to the north and the Uruguay River to the south, the Contestado region fits between 26° and 28° southern latitudes and 50° and 52° western longitudes. In the east the

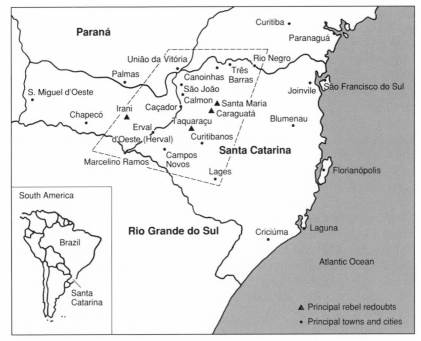

Figure 1   The Contestado Rebellion Zone

rugged mountains of the Serra Geral do Mar dominate the landscape. There, peaks over one mile high give way to long narrow valleys. Moving to the west, rolling hills appear, but the elevation never drops below 2,500 feet. In all areas the Paraná pine (*Araucaria augustifolia*) spreads out its umbrellalike canopy, providing the region with its distinctive "fresh air" smell. To the east the forest becomes so thick as to be virtually impenetrable. In the west the forest gives way to grasslands suitable for grazing.

During the Contestado Rebellion, one army officer complained of the difficulties of operating in the region. Narrow mountain and forest footpaths forced soldiers to march single file. Wagon traffic was impossible in many areas. Cold rains soaked uniforms and forced soldiers to discard their heavy boots when they stuck in the mud. At that time the Contestado was an isolated region, and it continues to be so to some extent today. A footpath connecting the area with the coast did not open until 1787. Not until after 1945 did a paved road open between the Contestado and Florianópolis, the state capital of Santa Catarina. Even today no paved road directly links Florianópolis with Lajes (Lages), the largest city in the Contestado region.[28]

The term "Contestado" as used throughout this book refers to a region that was the object of a long-standing border dispute between the states of Santa Catarina and Paraná. The dispute, which involved half of present-day Santa Catarina, began in the colonial era. It acquired new importance with the creation of the province of Paraná in 1853 and the occupation of the contested lands by that province. In 1904 the Brazilian Supreme Court ruled in favor of Santa Catarina in the dispute, but Paraná officials refused to recognize the judgment.[29]

In 1905 the government of Santa Catarina organized the first of several invasions of the border zone. Armed with Winchester rifles, the Santa Catarina force seized control of the Canoinhas area. Later, in 1911, the Santa Catarina government created the municipality of Canoinhas to secure its hold on the region. Between these years, partisans clashed numerous times, especially in the Canoinhas–Rio Negro area. The dispute ended in 1916 with an accord recognizing the Santa Catarina claim.[30]

Historians continue to discuss the relationship of the border dispute with the outbreak of the rebellion. At the time, each state accused the other of using the rebellion as a means to win control of the contested zone.[31] It is true that several Santa Catarina citizens involved in the Canoinhas incursion later joined the millenarian movement. Chief among these was Aleixo Gonçalves, who became one of the most important leaders of the millenarian movement. In the end, however, this border dispute between elites did not influence the majority of the millenarian movement's participants. As noted by one soldier at the time, "The true inhabitant of the Contestado, the often ignored peasant, is indifferent to competing jurisdiction claims." On this point historian Marli Auras agrees, arguing that for the Contestado peasantry, the state simply did not exist.[32]

Millenarianism in Brazil and the Contestado

Mention the Contestado Rebellion, and most scholars think of the Canudos Rebellion, made famous by Euclydes da Cunha and, more recently, Mario Vargas Llosa.[33] This confusion occurs both in Brazil and, to a larger extent, in the United States. Within Brazil, many of those who have heard of the Canudos Rebellion or of the famous millenarian movement led by Padre Cícero in Joaseiro (Juàzeiro do Norte), Ceará, know nothing about the Contestado Rebellion. In southern Brazil, most people know of the Contestado but only in the sketchiest sense. Why, then, study such an apparently insignificant rebellion?

The reasons are many. As we have seen, the sheer size of the rebellion merits study in itself. At one point some 20,000 rebels controlled 28,000 square kilometers of territory, that is, roughly 3 percent of Brazil's national territory. This was clearly an unacceptable threat to a national elite attempting to impose its vision of a nation. As such the rebellion is an important example of the ways people in the periphery resisted the process of nation building and consolidation, a process that threatened their way of life.[34]

Indeed, the appearance of two massive millenarian movements (Joaseiro and Canudos) at the beginning of the Old Republic (1889) has led some scholars to focus on political events as a key to understanding millenarianism in Brazil.[35] The 1889 miracle of Joaseiro brought tens of thousands of pilgrims to Padre Cícero's church, and this ability to attract a large following made him an important figure to regional elites bent on consolidation under Brazil's new federal system.[36] In turn, battles with ecclesiastical authorities over the authenticity of the miracle led Padre Cícero to cooperate with these elites, thereby explaining why his movement was never violently repressed by federal authorities. Likewise, partisan political struggles explain why local and regional elites first cooperated with, and then attacked, Antonio Conselheiro and his followers at Canudos.

Other scholars explain the timing of Brazil's massive millenarian movements largely in terms of the material changes taking place in Brazil at the turn of this century.[37] In the Brazilian Northeast, a series of devastating droughts stripped peasants of their subsistence, thereby increasing the prestige of millenarian leaders who offered food and shelter. In the Contestado, peasants joined a movement dedicated to destroying the railroad company that stripped them of their land. Millenarianism became the vehicle of peasant protest, it is argued, because religion generated the kind of high exaltation and fever necessary to organize an illiterate and isolated peasantry.[38]

Clearly the Contestado Rebellion included these kinds of material and political issues. The Contestado rebels sought the return of the monarchy as God's chosen form of government, a fact that guaranteed a violent reaction on the part of national leaders as the movement grew. National policies and concerns also prompted the construction of a railroad in the region. Thus, the study of the Contestado Rebellion is significant because it suggests how rural concerns shaped the actions of urban-based politicians in the Old Republic.

At the same time, it is important to study the Contestado Rebellion because it erupted in reaction to the transition to capitalism in the region. In searching for the origins of the movement, we are thus forced to take a detailed look at how capitalism transformed the area. As we shall see, this process produced the loss of land, new forms of violence, and the breakdown of established socioeconomic relations. Such changes are important to describe if we are ever accurately to write the rural history of Brazil, for out of these changes the present rural structure was born.

Today in Santa Catarina large farmers and corporations dominate the countryside. Squatters faced with the constant threat of eviction are now mobilizing, along with rural landless workers, to gain a secure access to land of their own.[39] In 1984 such people invaded three *fazendas* in the interior of the state. In June 1985 over a thousand of "those without land" (*os sem terras*) invaded the *fazenda* Paupuã in western Santa Catarina, where today they still occupy and till the land.[40] No doubt some of these people are descendants of the thousands who lost their access to land at the time of the Contestado Rebellion.

The issue is resistance—resistance to the present-day situation and resistance to the changes brought by the transition to capitalism at the turn of the century. We study the Contestado Rebellion as such an example of peasant mobilization and rebellion. But this was a millenarian rebellion, and herein rests its ultimate significance. By millenarian, what is meant is a religious movement obsessed with salvation and the moral regeneration of a society. This is a movement that viewed the world as "dominated by an evil, tyrannous power," a power that could be defeated only by a holy war sanctioned by God.[41]

Because of its millenarian character, the Contestado Rebellion represents a special case of peasant mobilization and resistance. Yet, in spite of all the religious imagery associated with millenarian movements, most scholars choose to ignore precisely this element. Those who focus mainly on class relations, or only on national and regional politics, deal with why a rebellion occurred, but they fail to explain satisfactorily the millenarian nature of certain movements. By contrast, the interesting question here is not only why a rebellion erupted, but also why a specifically millenarian rebellion emerged in the Contestado.

Because the idea of millenarianism as a cultural and religious phenomenon has received precious little attention, this study seeks to link the material and cultural sources of millenarianism in the Contestado.[42] The argument presented here is that millenarian movements emerge from, and respond directly to, the material *and* spiritual transformations gripping a society. That is, millenarian movements emerge when a society is suffering from a spiritual as well as material crisis. It is by understanding the nature of this spiritual crisis that we can understand the special appeal of the millenarian vision.

The transition to capitalism in the Contestado was not a wholly external force that negatively affected all members of the local society. Rather, external pressures became internalized as key local elites cooperated with the extralocal forces to the detriment of nonelites. By doing so these elites broke with responsibilities and norms mandated by religious tradition and practice.

With its emphasis on moral regeneration, the millenarian vision promised salvation to those suffering from the self-doubt and guilt associated with events that questioned the validity of shared cultural assumptions. It promised to re-create an idealized past where elites would reassume their culturally mandated responsibility to guarantee the subsistence of "their people." The internal crisis thus resolved, it then called for the destruction of the external pressures that prompted the crisis. It was this powerful promise to heal problems both within and outside of the local society that made the movement uniquely attuned to the particular needs of a people in crisis.

We can better understand millenarianism in Brazil (and beyond) by focusing not only on millenarian leaders and political elites, but also on the tens of thousands of poor peasants who joined these movements. Yes, material conditions are important, but while they might explain the outbreak of a rebellion in the Contestado, they do not explain its millenarian features. For this reason we also need to know more about how followers interpreted the preachings and images associated with millenarianism. In this spirit this book seeks to answer one deceptively simple question: Why did peasants join a millenarian movement in the Contestado?

2

The Contestado

Backwater Economy,

Patriarchal Society

The patron-client complex dominated social and material relations in the Contestado. Landowners granted peasants usufruct rights to land, born of the need to claim and control their vast holdings. In return, clients worked cattle roundups for the *patrão* (patron), in addition to performing various personal services. Chief among the latter, patrons often called upon their clients to form a personal army during clashes with other regional bosses.

In the Contestado, co-godparenthood relations colored the entire patron-client complex. Here the large landowner's position as both patron *and* godfather placed him in control of both the material and spiritual aspects of local life. As such, the co-godparenthood complex sanctified the patron's material dominance. At the same time, however, the special ties created between godfather and godchild provided clients with a moral claim to patron reciprocity.

Violence was an ever-present aspect of life in the Contestado region. Individual acts of violence took place regularly between patrons and clients. In addition, the defense of a male code of honor contributed to the area's level of violence. To understand these aspects of the Contestado society fully, however, we must first place the region in its prerebellion economic and historical contexts. Was the Contestado an area already industrialized and densely populated? The answer is no. It was a pastoral, subsistence-oriented frontier region in which Europeans gradually encroached on indigenous communities. And, far from the situation of São Paulo at the turn of the century, where coffee earnings fueled industrialization, the Contestado zone was an economic backwater. A look first at the state of Santa Catarina, and then at the Contestado region, well illustrates this point.[1]

Santa Catarina and the Contestado
as Economic Backwaters

In 1900, Brazil contained nearly 18 million inhabitants. The greatest population concentrations were in the Northeast (38.7 percent) and Southeast (44.9 percent). The South (Paraná, Santa Catarina, and Rio Grande do Sul) held 10.3 percent of the total population. Within this region, the fellow southern states dwarfed Santa Catarina in populational and geographical terms. São Paulo, with a total area of 290,876 square kilometers, contained 3,397,000 inhabitants in 1908. In that same year nearly 1.5 million people lived in Rio Grande do Sul. By contrast, the state of Santa Catarina, with a total area of 65,000 square kilometers, counted only 353,000 in its population. In the realm of population growth, São Paulo grew 5 percent per year between 1890 and 1900, Paraná 2.8 percent, and Rio Grande do Sul 2.5 percent. The figure for the country as a whole was 1.9 percent. Santa Catarina lagged behind with an annual growth rate of just 1.2 percent.[2]

These population figures give us a clue as to Santa Catarina's socioeconomic position at the turn of the century. State industry figures for 1907 further define and confirm the state's position as an economic backwater. In that year São Paulo contained 326 industries, employing 24,186 workers, for an average of 74 workers per industry. In Rio Grande do Sul, 314 industrial establishments employed 15,426 workers, for an average of 49 laborers per unit. Paraná contained 297 industries and 4,724 workers.

Compared with these southern states, Santa Catarina was home to a diminutive industrial sector in 1907. Its 173 industries employed just 2,102 workers, for a paltry average of 12 workers per unit. Its industrial production was seven times smaller than that of Rio Grande do Sul (99,779 contos to 14,144 contos*). Even more telling is a comparison with Sergipe, the smallest state in the country. With a total area of 30,000 square kilometers (half that of Santa Catarina) and a 1910 population of 400,000, Sergipe contained 103 industries employing 3,327 workers. Its average of 29 workers per industry easily doubled the Santa Catarina figure. In Santa Catarina, the first modern industries did not open until the late nineteenth century. At that time German immigrants opened the first textile mill (1880) and steel works (1886).[3]

Export figures provide a final example of Santa Catarina's inferior

---

*Until 1942, the Brazilian currency was based on reis, milreis, and contos. One thousand reis equaled one milreis. One thousand milreis equaled one conto. Thus, 3 contos, 482 milreis, 182 reis was written 3:482$182.

economic position to its neighboring states at the turn of the century. In 1912 Santa Catarina exports (mainly mandioca flour and *erva mate*) amounted to 3,410 *contos*. In that same year São Paulo exports were valued at 381,475 *contos*, Rio Grande do Sul exports at 30,535 *contos*, and Paraná exports at 24,765 *contos*. At that time, then, Santa Catarina was a nonindustrialized, sparsely populated state, with few exports and virtually no infrastructure development.[4]

The state of Santa Catarina was an economic backwater in comparison with its neighbors, and so was the interior of the state in comparison with the coast. In the 1820s the famous French traveler Auguste de Saint-Hilaire noted that in Santa Catarina, "Except for the district of Lages and the margins of a few rivers, the population . . . had not penetrated more than three leagues [from the coast]."[5] Saint-Hilaire refers to the cow town of Lajes, which, until the late 1800s, was the only *município* (roughly, the equivalent of a U.S. county) in the central plateau region. The settlement of the interior will be discussed below. At this point it should be noted only that the imposing mountains of the Serra Geral completely isolated the interior from the coast. The first road connecting the two areas was not completed until 1873. To this day no paved road directly connects Florianópolis with Lajes.

In 1872 the sprawling Lajes district contained 8,488 residents. On the coast, the district of Florianópolis held 25,619 residents. The only other towns near Lajes were Curitibanos (2,191 residents) and Campos Novos (2,136 inhabitants), giving the central plateau region the lowest population density in the state. In 1890, in the northern portion of the Contestado zone, the Rio Negro district held 13,628 people and União da Vitória 2,533. In 1915 the Brazil Railway Company estimated that of all the areas served by its southern railroads, the Contestado zone was the least populated. Station agents estimated 426 inhabitants per mile of railroad line along the Estrada de Ferro São Paulo–Rio Grande. In São Paulo, the figure was 1,645 along the company's Sorocaba line.

As with the state of Santa Catarina in comparison with its neighbors, export figures, industry figures, and comments on the level of infrastructure development within the state confirm the view of the Contestado zone as a regional economic backwater. In 1850 Lajes produced only 1.1 percent (five *contos*) of the state's export earnings. In that same year Florianópolis produced 65 percent (298 *contos*) of the export earnings. Industrial development did not begin in Santa Catarina until the 1880s, and then it was located near the coast. Indeed, in 1907 the thirteen largest industrial enterprises in Santa Catarina were all located in Blumenau, Joinvile, and Florianópolis.[6]

Portuguese Colonization
of the Contestado

The settlement of the Contestado region was directly dependent on the emergence of a cattle, mule, and horse trade in southern Brazil. In the early eighteenth century the expansion of the mining industry in Minas Gerais created a great demand for mules and horses. Rio Grande do Sul contained large herds of both, and the famous Caminho do Sul (Southern Road) opened to facilitate the transport of these animals north. Use of the road increased in the mid-eighteenth century when the Rio de Janeiro coffee boom boosted the demand for pack animals. The road stretched from Rio Grande do Sul, through what is today Santa Catarina and Paraná, to Sorocaba, São Paulo. There the mules and horses were sold in the large market and then sent to the cities of São Paulo and Minas Gerais.[7]

As the Caminho do Sul increased in importance, the Portuguese crown took steps to secure it against Indian and Spanish attack. In 1770 a group of crown-sponsored settlers founded the village of Nossa Senhora dos Prazeres das Lagens, or simply Lages (later Lajes). This was the first Portuguese settlement in what was later to become the Contestado zone. In 1777, 257 freemen and 144 slaves lived in the village. In 1808 the figures were 723 freemen and 155 slaves.[8]

The village of Rio Negro was the second interior settlement to emerge due to the Caminho do Sul. In the early eighteenth century the crown created a fiscal station on the road at the Rio Negro river. Again to protect against attack, the crown sent fifty Portuguese couples to settle the area in 1816. In 1829, 108 people lived there, and in 1833 the village was named Rio Negro. By the 1870s settlers from the other parts of Paraná began hewing out ranches on lands surrounding the town.[9]

The growth of the mule, horse, and cattle trade continued to prompt the settlement of the Santa Catarina–southern Paraná interior. Between the 1770s and 1830s, cattle ranchers out of Lajes expanded their holdings in search of new grazing lands. Out of this expansion grew the villages of Curitibanos and Campos Novos. After 1830, settlers coming south from Rio Negro and northwest from Lajes occupied the pastures of the Palmas area. These *campos de Palmas* contained thirty-seven cattle ranches in 1840, with 36,000 estimated head of cattle grazing there in the late 1850s.[10]

The expansion of Portuguese settlement was a very gradual affair in the entire Contestado area. The first settlers did not arrive in the Canoinhas area (approximately 60 kilometers west of Rio Negro) until the late 1860s, some fifty years after the initial arrivals in Rio

Negro. Closer to Lajes, 100 years elapsed between the first occupation of the Curitibanos pastures and that area's attainment of municipal status in 1869. Population densities remained low in the entire area throughout the nineteenth century.[11]

As one might imagine, the Portuguese accomplished the settlement of the Contestado region at the expense of the Indian peoples living there. Until the eighteenth century the Xokleng people occupied the entire southern interior region, from Paraná to the *sertão* of Rio Grande do Sul.[12] The Xokleng were a hunting and gathering society and pursued a life-style that required easy access to large areas of land. During the 1700s colonization of Rio Grande do Sul and Paraná forced the Xokleng out of these two provinces, concentrating them in the central plateau of Santa Catarina. The Portuguese settlement of the central plateau (Lajes, Palmas, Curitibanos, Rio Negro) then forced yet another move. In the mid- to late nineteenth century new settlements continually pushed the Xokleng out of the central plateau and into the mountains of the Serra Geral. Typical of the colonist's view of both the Indians and the settlement process, one settler commented that his land claim "was without any sign of another inhabitant, except for ferocious Indians and animals."[13] The Xokleng had never lived in the mountains, and one anthropologist found in the 1930s that Xokleng legend spoke "with nostalgia of the time long ago when they lived [on the central plateau]."[14]

As noted by Sílvio Coelho dos Santos, in the mid-nineteenth century, "The progress of the nation could not be harmed by a group of 'savages.'"[15] The settlement of the central plateau now threatened the Xokleng with extermination. They fought back. In the Palmas area, a government surveyor noted that on one *fazenda* "the crop lands are now abandoned because, located in the *sertão*, they are continually invaded by *índios bravos* . . . for years there has been virtually no crop production because the crops are always destroyed by the Indians." During various attacks in 1907, Indians killed and/or stole several head of cattle from the Campo Alto *fazenda*. Indians killed four men in an attack against a neighboring *fazenda* one year earlier. As late as 1912 Indians attacked a *fazenda* near Curitibanos, killing seventy cattle.[16] These were the final attempts of the Xokleng to stop the advances of the settlers. From the 1870s on, the government of Santa Catarina sponsored armed expeditions against the Xokleng, which virtually wiped out the population. In 1914 the Serviço de Proteção dos Indios (SPI) announced the "pacification" of the Xokleng.[17]

A Ranching Economy
and Society

Upon arriving in the interior of the Contestado region, settlers created a society based on cattle ranching. Virtually self-sufficient *fazendas* of differing sizes produced crops for internal consumption and cattle and mules to be sold on the market. Locals employed an open range system, where cattle roamed over large distances and were rounded up periodically by ranch hands. In the summer and fall, large landowners often organized cattle and mule drives to Sorocaba, São Paulo, where they sold their animals in the local market.

Until the mid-nineteenth century, slaves performed much of the labor on the *fazendas*. In the 1860s owners began selling their slaves to the owners of expanding São Paulo coffee plantations. After abolition, the ex-slaves that remained in the interior often fled to the cities. People of mixed European and Indian descent (*caboclos*) filled the space left by slave migration and abolition.[18]

A few scholars have written about the cattle economy of both the Contestado region and the whole of southern Brazil.[19] Most of the literature, however, deals with the topic in a very broad manner. Fortunately, in the case of the Contestado, government survey records provide a much more detailed account of the interior cattle ranches. Using these *processos* we gain a clearer picture as to the size, products, and labor relations of the ranches. But here a word of caution is in order, for landowners were not always interested in providing accurate information to local officials. It is quite possible that owners deflated the estimates of their cattle herds to avoid increased taxation. As for their land claims, here they often inflated their holdings, for they could purchase land deemed in excess of their title for a nominal per hectare price.[20]

Inflated or not, pioneers established their claims in much of the Contestado in the 1840s and 1850s. They did not purchase the land but merely occupied it as the first whites in the area. In later years continued low land values allowed descendants to inexpensively expand holdings. For example, in the 1840s members of the Carneiro family migrated from central Paraná to the *campos* of Palmas. There the family settled near the village of São João, some 50 kilometers south of União da Vitória. Located along both banks of the Rio do Peixe, various family members established cattle ranches in the surrounding hills. Half a century later, in 1898, the government of Paraná ordered the survey of Carneiro family properties.

The size of the Carneiro holdings varied from 5,000 to 13,000 hectares. José Antonio Carneiro's Capão Alto *fazenda* covered

10,118 hectares, 6,000 of which were suitable for grazing. At the Rio do Peixe holding, João Simeão Carneiro claimed 5,289 hectares. Antonio dos Santos Carneiro, Manoel dos Santos Carneiro, and Maria Prudencia de Souza controlled 7,141 hectares at the Merim Doce *fazenda*. Finally, Absalão Carneiro owned the Cruzeiro (5,012 hectares) and Faixinal dos Pobres (13,234 hectares) properties, although at least part of this latter holding had previously been set aside as a donation to the church. Together, the Carneiros owned 40,794 hectares along the Rio do Peixe. These *fazendas* all shared common borders, but it is not known how much the owners cooperated with one another.[21]

Holdings in the *município* of Rio Negro, in the northern Contestado region, were of similar sizes. Nicolau Bley Netto owned 10,018 hectares at the Invernada das Pombas *fazenda* and 2,202 hectares at the Salto de Itajahy *fazenda*. By 1924 one publication listed Bley Netto as the most powerful man in Rio Negro. The Pacheco family also dominated the Rio Negro scene and was, perhaps, the largest landowning group in the area. Upon his death in 1907, *coronel* (an honorific term applied to important landowners) João Pacheco left nearly 14,000 hectares composed of six different holdings. The average *fazenda* holding in Rio Negro was around 3,000 hectares.[22]

A review of the same land documents provides valuable information on the produce and labor arrangements of the Contestado *fazendas*. The Carneiro documents list cattle as the main *fazenda* product, as do the Rio Negro documents. José Antonio Carneiro claimed 600 cattle on his 10,000-hectare Capão Alto holding. Absalão Antonio Carneiro claimed 700 cattle on the 5,000-hectare Cruzeiro *fazenda*. These were probably grossly low estimates, aimed at manipulating tax liabilities. One old-timer, for example, claims that his father kept 1,500 head of cattle on 800 hectares, and Maurício Vinhas de Queiroz adds that some large *fazendeiros* owned as many as 20,000 head of cattle. In addition to cattle, virtually all of the ranches contained pigs, mules, and horses.[23]

The *processos* support the claim of the general literature as to the near self-sufficiency of the interior *fazendas*. All the owners mentioned grew corn and beans, and the Capão Alto *processo* specifically mentioned that these were grown for internal consumption. None of the *processos* mentioned the sale of these crops. On the Capão Alto holding, 150 of the total 10,000 hectares were devoted to crops.

In addition to cattle and subsistence crops, *fazendeiros* around Rio Negro also harvested, prepared, and sold *erva mate*, a type of tea that grew wild in the area. The first Portuguese settlers in the area adopted the use of *erva mate* from the Guaraní Indians. For years the product was for internal consumption only. In the late nineteenth century, increased demand for the product in Argentina and Uruguay prompted the first Brazilian *erva mate* exports. By 1907 *erva mate* was the largest export item of Santa Catarina.[24]

In Rio Negro, most *fazendeiros* produced *erva mate*. Nicolau Bley Netto and *coronel* João Pacheco both listed it among their *fazendas'* products. Two other members of the Pacheco family, the brothers Francisco and Joaquim, were especially involved in *erva mate* production. Joaquim claimed an average production of 7 *arrobas* per year (1 *arroba* equals 14.4 kilograms).[25]

On the Pacheco brothers' property, as on most *fazendas*, workers first stripped the *erva* trees of their leaves. They then dried the leaves over a low fire in a process known as the *barbaquá*. The drying took six to eight hours, with one man, the *Urú*, responsible for stirring the leaves. The exhausting nature of the work led one contemporary observer to note that "there are only a few people who are able to meet the challenge of being an *Urú*." After curing, workers bagged the *erva mate* for transport and storage. Joaquim and Francisco owned a warehouse and dock on the Rio Negro, where boats arrived to take the product to the port of São Francisco.[26]

Erva mate harvesting did not take place solely on private holdings. Some *fazendeiros* purchased government contracts to harvest the tea where it grew wild on public lands. In 1906 Manoel Fabrício Vieira purchased such collection rights from the state of Santa Catarina. After agreeing to pay the state 200 *reis* per 15 kilos of *erva mate* harvested, Vieira received sole collection rights on public lands in the *municípios* of Curitibanos, Campos Novos, and Lajes. Two years later he purchased a Paraná concession to harvest *erva mate* on public lands in the *município* of Clevelândia. It appears that Vieira prospered from these contracts, for in 1910 one local newspaper reported that "there are various labor gangs employed in the harvesting of *erva mate* by, and under the direction of, Col. [*coronel*] Fabrício Vieira."[27]

So far we have concentrated on the elites of the Contestado society. But what of those among the lower echelons of that society? When slavery declined in the region, two main groups emerged to perform labor on the *fazendas: camaradas* (peons) and *agregados* (sharecroppers). These two groups differed from one another by their access to land. *Camaradas* had little or no access to land. Sometimes they received wages, but these were usually negated by the room and board charges of the *fazendeiros*. They lived in shacks provided by the landowner and performed all types of duties. *Agregados*, by contrast, received usufruct rights to a piece of land in return for services rendered to the owner. In addition to growing crops, *agregados* usually raised a few head of cattle.²⁸

Let us construct a more detailed description of labor relations in the Contestado. According to Francisco Pacheco, grandson of *coronel* João Pacheco, *agregados* were people of confidence who raised their families on the *fazenda*. They grew crops and always raised a few pigs and cows. Each year Francisco's grandfather "gave" his *agregados* presents of free seeds and in some years a cow or pig. Most important, stressed Francisco, the *agregados* received the protection of his father and grandfather. *Agregados* were *always* (Francisco's emphasis) related to his grandfather and father by co-godparenthood ties. When Francisco was young, his playmates were the children of the *agregados*.²⁹

Eight *agregados*, that is to say eight *agregados* and their families, lived on the 1,200-hectare *fazenda* owned by Francisco's father. Virtually all of the land *processos* for the Palmas and Rio Negro areas mention their presence. João Simeão claimed in 1900 that four *agregados* (and their families?) resided on his 5,000-hectare Rio do Peixe *fazenda*. On the Merim Doce holding, *agregados* "exploit[ed] for their own benefit a small portion of the land."³⁰

Given the nature of the ranching economy, *patrões* called their *agregados* into service only during certain times of the year. In the summer, *agregados* rounded up pregnant cows and delivered the calves. In spring and summer, herds were moved between pastures. The winter brought the general roundup, where branding and the treatment of sick animals took place. Finally, at various times *agregados* gathered fattened cattle for sale. Beyond these services they were free to tend their own crops and herds.³¹

At this point, Mario Góngora's work on the *inquilinos* of central Chile provides a useful comparison with the life-style of the Contestado *agregados*. In the late seventeenth century, when the commodification of land was low, Chilean landowners gave *prestamos*, or usufruct land grants, to poorer individuals. Little or no labor was required in return from the land recipient. Instead, the landowner viewed the grant as the cheapest means to populate his holding and thus establish a valid claim.

For years then, *inquilinos* lived a life similar to their Contestado counterparts. *Inquilinos* resided on isolated portions of large landholdings and participated infrequently in cattle roundups. With the commercialization of the Chilean economy, however, this semi-independent life-style began to change. As wheat exports to Peru began, land values soared, and *inquilinos* were drawn into increasingly onerous labor relations. In addition to ranching duties, they

now had to provide crop labor to the patron. By the end of the
eighteenth century the Chilean *inquilino* was no longer comparable
to the Contestado *agregado* of the late nineteenth century. In the
latter case land commodification remained low, and Contestado
agregados retained their semi-independent life-style.[32]

As opposed to the *agregados*, Francisco Pacheco claims that
camaradas were not people of confidence, even though they were
usually also linked to the owner by co-godparenthood bonds. Here
the interview with Francisco, combined with information gleaned
from the *processos*, establishes that two different types of *camaradas* actually worked on the *fazendas*. First were those who lived
permanently on the estate. Whether they received a wage or simply
room and board for their services is not clear. Several of the *processos*
mention a wage of two or three *milreis* per day, from which the
owners always deducted the cost of room and board.

Permanent *camaradas* did not enjoy the usufruct right to land. In
the *processos*, the houses of the *agregados* are often referred to as
casas, while the *camaradas* were said to live in *ranchos*. This
semantic difference reflected a very real material difference. In various *processos*, the *casas* of the *agregados* are sometimes listed as
having a small value to the *fazendeiro*, while no such value was ever
assigned to the *ranchos*.[33]

In addition to permanent *camaradas*, landowners also hired temporary *camaradas* to help with crop harvests. Again, their salary
varied between two and three *milreis* per day, with room and board
deducted from this amount. These were the people that Francisco
Pacheco's father and grandfather did not trust, because "they came
and went with the harvest." Nevertheless, the son and grandson of
two different *fazendeiros* claimed that all area residents established
co-godparenthood bonds with the large landowners. Unfortunately,
the *processos* do not mention the numbers of either permanent or
temporary *camaradas*.[34]

Some temporary *camaradas* in the Contestado were no doubt
"cowboy" types along the lines of the Argentine *gaucho* and Mexican
vaqueiro. Given, however, that *camarada* work most often involved
crop harvesting, it would seem that many were drawn from the ranks
of the area's independent peasantry. These peasants, known as *posseiros* because they took possession of the land without legal title,
were people who cleared a spot in the forest and began cultivating
subsistence crops. Stuart Schwartz has written about the emergence
of this group in late colonial Brazil. Schwartz concentrates, however,
on the Northeast, with one brief reference to São Paulo. He argues
that it was in the Northeast, especially in Bahia and Pernambuco,

where the largest growth of a free peasantry took place.[35] For the Contestado, little information exists on this group. Nevertheless, numerous government documents make passing references to *posseiros*, and taken together they create an important portrait of this independent peasantry.

Posseiros often occupied lands on the periphery of a large landowner's claim. At times the landowners seemed willing to accept their presence. In 1893 Nicolau Bley Netto of Rio Negro did not measure his lands right up to the edge of the Itajaí River "so as to not enter into conflict with the nationals living there." In 1899 a government surveyor noted that Manoel Lourenço Araujo of Palmas/São João "allow[ed] nearby poor residents to cultivate plots for their consumption." Perhaps these *fazendeiros* accepted the presence of *posseiros* because it was from their ranks that harvest help was hired. Here, at any rate, low commodification of land made the costs of such a presence quite low from the *fazendeiro*'s standpoint.[36]

Besides occupying lands claimed by *fazendeiros*, *posseiros* also inhabited state-owned lands. These public lands were known as *terras devolutas*, because these once national lands became the property of the states after the declaration of the Republic in 1889. A few *posseiros* eventually registered their claims with the state governments.

The obstacles to the registration of claims were enormous, and not the least of them was the requirement that these poor and generally cash-starved peasants *purchase* their claims. The fact that a few registrations nonetheless took place points to the existence of many more *posseiros*. Perhaps a typical case was that of Sebastião Pereira de Lima of the Canoinhas municipality. Sebastião claimed to have occupied his 50-hectare plot for many years, and he noted that he grew a variety of crops and had a few animals. Because of his poverty, Sebastião requested the minimum government land price for his claim. Other registrations speak of claims for 30 and 60 hectares.[37]

The existence of *posseiros* on public lands sometimes unnerved officials from Paraná and Santa Catarina. In 1900, one official complained that in the Peixe River valley "one finds many residents on *terras devolutas*. Near the [river] there already exists a small settlement, and the number of [land] invasions grows day by day, causing grave damages to the State." Three years later the government of Santa Catarina lamented that there was "still a lot to do to rid the public lands . . . of the intruders that use [the land], devastating it, without any desire to obtain legal title." Such government complaints soon grew in both number and intensity as the development of the Contestado caused land values to soar.[38]

The hardest part of a *posseiro's* life was not, at first, government opposition, but the threat of Indian attack. *Posseiros* usually lived somewhat removed from the large landowners, and thus away from the very protection that many have posited as a fundamental factor in the establishment of patron-client bonds.[39] As the white settlement of the interior progressed, Indian attacks became frequent. Many *posseiros* complained bitterly of these attacks in their land title petitions. In 1911 José Souza Cabral of the Lajes municipality complained of the damages he had suffered from Indian attacks throughout the years. Also in 1911, Aureo João Cabral of Lajes made a similar complaint and claimed that he should be given the minimum government land purchase price because of these damages. These applicants no doubt overstated this danger to lessen the purchase price of their claims. Nevertheless, their use of this tactic and the government's willingness to listen to their claims illustrates that the threat of Indian attack was a daily reality for poor peasants.[40]

In the northern *erva mate* zone of the Contestado, it appears that some peasant-*posseiros* harvested and sold *erva mate*. This product grew wild in the interior, and for two or three months a year local *caboclos* fanned out to harvest the leaves of the *erva* trees. They would then sell the leaves to local landowners such as the Pacheco family. By doing so they could meet their meager cash needs.[41]

In addition to these small tracts worked by independent peasants, larger *posseiro*-cultivated tracts could also be found in the Contestado. In the general literature, both Emília Viotti da Costa and Warren Dean point to the existence of large *posseiro* tracts throughout Brazil. As with their small, subsistence-oriented counterparts, these *posseiros* squatted on unclaimed public lands instead of holding legal title to the land through a royal grant (*sesmaria*).[42]

According to Dean, by the late nineteenth century "there were many squatters who held claims as large as, or larger than, the formal grants." He also states that these "were squatters in the Australian usage, *latifundists* [large estate holders] on a scale even beyond that of the *sesmaria* holders, and unrestrained by any legal obligation to cultivate their claims." In the Contestado, the largest claims by *posseiros* were on a similar scale, along the lines of 200 to 500 hectares. In the Santa Catarina land documents, there are no *posseiro* registrations for over 500 hectares. Thus, in addition to families like the Carneiros, Bleys, and Pachecos, all of whom held legal title to their lands, there were also those larger *posseiro* holdings in the Contestado used for raising cattle and harvesting *erva mate*.[43]

Life in the Contestado revolved around cattle ranching. It was the opening of the mule, cattle, and horse trade that first brought settlers into the area. The non-Indian population grew as *fazendeiros* searched for new pastures. After the founding of Lajes and Rio Negro came Curitibanos, Campos Novos, and Canoinhas. The Xokleng bore witness to this expansion process and suffered in its wake.

With the decline of slavery, *agregados* and *camaradas* provided the bulk of the labor on the Contestado *fazendas*, although in the predominantly cattle-grazing economy such labor requirements were not very heavy. Often related to the *fazendeiros* by co-godparenthood ties, these two groups normally received little or no monetary compensation for their work. Temporary harvest workers and small subsistence peasants joined with the *agregados* and *camaradas* to form the lower echelons of the society.

As the harvesting, preparation, and transportation of *erva mate* expanded in the Contestado region, both large landowners and "large" *posseiros* participated in the *erva mate* economy. "Small" *posseiros, agregados,* and *camaradas* harvested wild growths of the tea, thereby earning enough cash to meet their meager monetary requirements. Everywhere people grew corn, beans, and mandioca to meet their subsistence requirements. Some *agregados* and small peasants were also able to raise a few cows and pigs.

As demonstrated by various indicators, the Contestado zone was an economic backwater within the larger backwater that was the state of Santa Catarina. And in spite of the production for market that went on in the area, a precapitalistic mode of production dominated. *Fazendeiros* appropriated surplus in noneconomic ways, relying on established relations of dependence, while most of those in the lower strata managed to maintain some access to the means of production.

Patrons and Clients:
Material Pressures and Spiritual Needs

The status of the Contestado as an economic backwater began to change at the close of the nineteenth century. Indeed, the area underwent a dramatic transformation with the entrance of international capitalism in the twentieth century. But to understand the ramifications of this transformation, we must first further examine social relations in the Contestado. In particular, we must understand the relations of dominance in the region, which entails an examination of not only the material relations between patrons and clients, but of spiritual ties as well, for religious tradition and practice helped shape the patron-client complex. Who were the Contestado *patrões,* who were their clients, and what ties bound them together?

When the German immigrant Henrique Rupp arrived in Campos Novos in the late 1800s, he did so with a large sum of money and the area's first wood-burning stove. The stove was soon a local novelty, and Rupp became one of the most powerful men in the region.[44] Between 1895 and 1908 Rupp made nineteen land purchases at a cost of over US $9,800.[45] Rupp's landholdings were such that in 1940 it still took two hours to traverse the family Monte Alto *fazenda* by car. Mule trader, cattle rancher, land dealer, newspaper owner, entrepreneur, municipal official, national guard officer—Rupp was a man of many titles at the time of his death in 1915.

In 1907 Francisco Ferreira de Albuquerque led a forty-man expedition to transport a large printing press from Blumenau, Santa Catarina, to his hometown of Curitibanos. Once in operation, Albuquerque used the printing press to defend his interests via the newspaper *O Trabalho*. Like Rupp, Albuquerque was a man with many interests to defend.

Born in Lajes, *coronel* Albuquerque, as he came to be known, lived in Campos Novos before moving to Curitibanos in the early 1890s. There he opened a small store. He began buying land, and soon he established a *fazenda* on the outskirts of town. As his holdings increased, so too did his prestige and power. In 1902 he began his first of many terms as the municipal superintendent of Curitibanos. From there he served as a deputy in the state legislature. Embroiled in political and personal battles all his life, Albuquerque was ambushed and killed near his *fazenda* in 1917.[46]

To the north of Rupp and Albuquerque, *coronel* Arthur de Paula e Souza owned large amounts of land near União da Vitória. Paula e Souza founded his Santa Leocadia *fazenda* on the banks of the Iguaçu River in 1897. On this land he raised cattle and collected *erva mate*. Area records show that Paula e Souza continued to add to his holdings throughout his lifetime. In addition to the Santa Leocadia holding, he also owned the 15,000-hectare São Zacharias *fazenda* near the village of São João. Between 1897 and 1912, Paula e Souza made at least eleven land purchases in the União da Vitória area, spending over sixteen *contos*, or approximately US $4,000. He then began to colonize these lands with European immigrants.[47]

Like so many others, Paula e Souza participated in much more than the management of his *fazendas*. According to one historian, he owned a large store in the town of União da Vitória. In addition, he owned the steamship *Vitória*, which transported goods along the Iguaçu and Negro rivers. In the political arena Paula e Souza served on the first jury ever assembled in União da Vitória, and in 1911 he became the police commissioner. As with *coronel* Albuquerque,

Arthur de Paula e Souza met a violent death in an attack against his Santa Leocadia *fazenda* during the Contestado Rebellion.[48]

Henrique Rupp, Francisco Ferreira de Albuquerque, and Arthur de Paula e Souza were three of the large landowners who dominated the Contestado area. There were others, such as Amazonas Marcondes of União da Vitória, Manoel Fabrício Vieira, and various members of the Pacheco family. In addition to their various other dealings, these men gained a reputation as *patrões* in the ranching economy of the Contestado. All, as the documents attest, cultivated patron-client relations with those who lived on or near their holdings.

Patron-Client Relations:
Theoretical Background

To understand the actions of the *patrões*, and to understand the sources of their control, we will examine the patron-client relationship as it is treated in the general literature. Such an examination is important, for it was the nature of the patron-client relationship, and its eventual transformation, that led to a specifically millenarian revolt in the Contestado. First, however, one must remember that not all *patrões* exercised the power of the three landowners mentioned. The resources controlled by *patrões* ranged from the enormous power held by an Henrique Rupp to the meager possessions of the peddler/*patrão* with whom a single young boy worked and lived at the beginning of the century.[49] Large patron or small, controlling many clients or but a few, the patron-client relationship pervaded everyday life in the Contestado.

Any study of patron-client relationships in the Contestado is limited by a paucity of data on the subject. Duglas Teixeira Monteiro provides an interesting sociological discussion on the relationship in his book on the Contestado Rebellion. Nevertheless, this discussion includes little data actually drawn from the Contestado region. Likewise, Maurício Vinhas de Queiroz relies on generalities when he discusses the mechanics of the patron-client relationship. Because of this lack of detail, it is even more important to discuss the general literature on the patron-client complex to provide a better feel for the dynamics of the relation. We can then compare this general view with the available evidence from the Contestado to gain a more sophisticated understanding of the patron-client complex as it operated in this particular case.[50]

The past twenty years have witnessed an explosion in the study of the patron-client relationship. Beginning especially with the work of

George Foster, others, such as S. N. Eisenstadt and James Scott, have contributed enormously to the understanding of the patron-client relationship.[51] Studies range from examinations of patrons and clients on a local or regional level to discussions of politics and party patronage on a national scale.[52] Geographically, these studies cover such diverse areas as Mexico and Southeast Asia, Italy and West Africa.[53] More recently, historians have begun to tread where once only anthropologists and political scientists entered. To this end, Florencia Mallon's work on Peru sheds new light on how the patron-client relationship operated in that area.[54]

A number of defining characteristics of the patron-client relationship emerge from a review of the literature. The first is the asymmetrical nature of the relationship, that is, the fact that it ties together people of different economic groups. Most scholars have viewed it as a dyadic "contract," creating strong links between patron and client while preventing such strong links between peasants. The emphasis is on the vertical ties inherent to the patron-client relationship.

Patron-client relationships exist because patrons control key resources in the society. Chief among such resources is land. By controlling the access to land, patrons force peasants into their unequal position. Patrons provide certain necessities such as seeds and tools, plus items such as rudimentary medical care. In addition, patrons usually control the means of defense in an area. Peasants are thus forced to rely on the patron for protection from bandit or Indian attacks. In a slightly different manner, patrons represent authority. Not only can patrons mediate between peasants and regional powers, but they can also protect their clients from persecution by those same regional powers.

Although the patron-client relationship is an unequal one, it is a reciprocal relationship. Inherent is the exchange of goods and services. We have seen how patrons "provide" land, seeds, and protection to their clients, as well as occasional gifts of a cow or some other material good. In return they "receive" the labor services of their clients, some of the goods produced by these clients, and the use of these peasants in armed encounters with other elites. Patrons "need" their clients just as the clients depend on their patrons.

The example of rice growing in premechanized Malaysian paddies is a case in point. There, access to labor was perhaps the crucial element in a successful harvest, for any delays in planting, weeding, or harvesting could reduce yields. As such, James C. Scott argues, "It made eminent sense for large farmers to develop a loyal workforce by means of material and symbolic acts of social consideration and friendship."[55]

The provision of agricultural imputs for a client's personal use is one example of such an act, and it implied a sense of obligation between patron and client. Marcel Mauss, in his classic study *The Gift*, argues just this, that under certain circumstances the offering of a gift "is based on obligation and economic self interest."[56] Pierre Bourdieu contrasts such gift giving to swapping, "which . . . telescopes gift and counter-gift into the same instant," and to lending, "in which the return of the loan is explicitly guaranteed by a juridical act."[57]

This element of reciprocity should not, however, blind us to the fundamentally violent and exploitative nature of the patron-client relationship. Some scholars unfortunately gloss over, if not completely ignore, this aspect of the patron-client tie. E. Bradford Burns speaks of past rural relations as an "inorganic democracy" and glorifies the historical roles of rural *caudillos*.[58] Even James C. Scott and Benedict J. Kerkvliet ignored this violent and exploitative side when they defined the patron-client link as

an exchange relationship or instrumental friendship between two individuals of different status in which the patron uses his own influence and resources to provide for the protection and material welfare of his lower status client and his family who, for his part, reciprocates by offering general support and assistance, including personal services, to the patron.[59]

Let us not, however, forget that the patron-client relationship is the means by which one group extracts a surplus from another. Patrons often employ violence, or the threat of violence, to force the surrender of peasant labor and goods.

S. N. Eisenstadt and Luis Roniger were probably closer to the mark when they described the patron-client tie as "a combination of potential coercion and exploitation with voluntary relations and mutual obligations."[60] Scott also now places more emphasis on violence or the threat of violence. Specifically, he rejects the idea that a lack of public protest means that peasants accept relations of domination as legitimate. In other words, he rejects the argument that "dominant classes can persuade subordinate classes to adopt their self-serving view of existing social relations" and that this "will in turn block the perception of conflicting interests."[61] Instead, peasants are keenly aware of their exploitation, but material conditions (lack of access to land, for example) and "the knowledge of probable repression" limit action to a subculture of opposition which is rarely made public.[62]

Patrons and Clients in
the Contestado

Patron-client relations in the nineteenth-century Contestado evidenced many of the characteristics mentioned in the general literature. As noted by Duglas Teixeira Monteiro, social roles and expectations in the Contestado were well defined and followed.[63] The patron-client tie was asymmetrical, linking powerful landowners with their *agregados*. Henrique Rupp, Francisco Ferreira de Albuquerque, the Pacheco family, and Arthur de Paula e Souza all maintained patron-client relations with numerous people.

In the Contestado, as in rural areas in general, the key to the power of the *patrões* was their control over resources. The most important resource was land. To be sure, many *caboclos* lived well beyond the authority of local landowners. But many, and probably most, *caboclos* lived on lands claimed by a *patrão*. This residence no doubt involved these people in a patron-client relationship to one degree or another. In the case of the Pacheco family the ties were close, with *agregados* regularly working for the patrons in return for the use of Pacheco land. In the case of the *fazendeiro* Manoel Lourenço de Araujo, we only know that he allowed "friends and poor people living in the area to use his land for their own benefit." Perhaps the ties here were not so close, but nevertheless it is not hard to imagine that some form of labor commitment accompanied this access to land.[64]

In the Contestado, patrons controlled the resources necessary to protect a local population. As mentioned earlier, Indian attacks were a regular part of life. The threat of these attacks no doubt limited the possibilities of settlement in isolated areas. Living alone, a *caboclo* family did not possess the means to protect themselves from a group of attacking Indians. The patrons, given their control over the workforce and firearms, provided such protection.[65]

It was not just that patrons protected peasants, but that peasants also protected their patrons. During Indian attacks, *agregados* were called upon to defend the *fazendeiro*. At other times, patrons gathered their clients into small armies to battle rival patrons. During a particularly intense period of political battles, twenty *capangas* (hired thugs), including "godchildren by baptism," accompanied *coronel* Albuquerque of Curitibanos. In 1914 a group of Manoel Fabrício Vieira's men murdered José Lyro Santi and seventeen of his *camaradas* in a land dispute near Vieira's Chapéu do Sol *fazenda*.[66]

Patrons also gathered their armed clients to express their displeasure with public land surveys. In February 1900, the Cardoso brothers and their clients, all of them "armed to the teeth," prevented the government land agent of Curitibanos from completing a land survey near the Cardosos' Fazenda do Serrado.[67]

Patrões sometimes extended offers of protection to other bosses. One such case involved Manoel Fabrício Vieira. During the Contestado Rebellion, Vieira, under contract from the federal government, led his own force of *vaqueiros* into various battles. By that time he was a powerful landowner who, in addition to his Chapéu do Sol *fazenda*, organized labor gangs to harvest *erva mate* in the region.

At the end of the Contestado Rebellion, the federal government decided in favor of Santa Catarina in its long-standing border dispute with Paraná. Vieira, always a supporter of the Paraná claim, quickly organized a rebellion against the decision, and led this force in several attacks against towns controlled by Santa Catarina.

To recruit followers, Vieira visited the homes of local soldiers who had fought in the army during the Contestado Rebellion. To tempt them, he offered a percentage of the loot they would amass during their attacks. The remaining federal troops in the area quickly quelled the revolt, and local and national authorities began a manhunt for Vieira. At this point the Pacheco family, longtime friends of Vieira, intervened on the latter's behalf. They escorted him to their land, where they helped him build a shack in the middle of the forest. The Pachecos prevented authorities from entering their land to search for the rebellious *patrão*. Vieira lived in the shack for some time, leaving only when the calls for his arrest had subsided.[68] If patrons and peasants protected each other, *patrões* sometimes protected members of their own group.[69]

In the Contestado, at least, one cannot ignore the element of violence and coercion in the patron-client relationship. Unfortunately, evidence of this violence, or the threat of such violence, is hard to obtain. Of course Francisco Pacheco, the son of a powerful *patrão*, did not mention this violent aspect of the patron-client relationship. But given the patron's control over vital resources, clients found themselves in an unenviable bargaining position. Perhaps clients were able to play one patron against another as a strategy of resistance to patron demands.[70] But aside from this strategy, the alternative in the Contestado was to flee to an isolated area and take one's chances with the possibility of Indian attacks.

Two examples illustrate that violence and resistance figured into the patron-client relationship in the Contestado. The first involves the case of a boy who lived and worked in the house of *fazendeiro* João Thibes. While Thibes was away one day, the boy fled and allegedly sought shelter in the cabin of the *agregado* José Domingos Soares. Upon his return, Thibes went to Soares's hut to inquire about the boy. Soares denied any knowledge of the runaway, and for this he was beaten by a group of Thibes's men. Thibes himself then allegedly entered Soares's hut and raped the *agregado*'s wife. On a lighter note, the second case involves Manoel, an *agregado* of the *fazendeiro* Manoel Pedro Kemer, who took advantage of the latter's absence to steal his patron's wool dress suits, boots, and silver coins. Guards later arrested Manoel at a train station for selling the stolen clothes to passengers in transit![71]

Ties between patrons and clients created a complex web of relations that produced contradictory attitudes and norms. Along with patron violence there existed a rustic kind of equality in the Contestado. This is the argument of Brazilian scholar Maria Isaura Pereira de Queiroz, who writes that the harshness of life in the interior assured that "differences of resources [among patrons and clients] did not lead to serious differences in the standard of life."[72]

The rugged life of the Contestado, its isolation, and its limited participation in the commercial economy prevented large landowners from leading life-styles similar to their brethren elsewhere in Brazil. Comparisons of Contestado photographs to those taken in Vassouras, Rio de Janeiro, during the coffee boom illustrate this point. In the Contestado, Joaquim dos Santos Pacheco's house was a small, simple wooden structure. Yet Pacheco was one of the largest *fazendeiros* in the Rio Negro, Paraná, region. By contrast, photographs from Vassouras show impressive white mansions dominating the *Carioca* countryside.[73]

Consider further the meager luxury goods included in the inventories of two wealthy Contestado *fazendeiros*. Upon his death in 1854, Caetano Couto left what was described as an "enormous" *fazenda*, with 35 slaves, 2,000 head of cattle, and 300 mules. A few silver horse reins and stirrups, however, were the only luxury goods left by the *fazendeiro*. Likewise, the inventory of dona Vicência de Almeida, widow of Curitibanos *fazendeiro* Elias de Almeida Leite, included a large area of land, "a large number of cattle, and a few slaves." Nevertheless, a wall clock, a music box, and a few small silver objects comprised the total of dona Vicência's luxury items. Finally, Pereira de Queiroz notes that in the Contestado "the rudimentary standards of men considered large landowners amazed the officers sent there to combat the [Contestado] insurrection." Differences in wealth did not lead to significantly different styles of life in the Contestado.[74]

In support of this idea, Duglas Teixeira Monteiro argues further that the "male code" of the interior society emphasized the value and importance of cattle-working abilities. This code, states Monteiro, applied to all male members of the society, including the most powerful patrons. Such an emphasis on the manliness of cattle work meant that patrons often worked cattle alongside their clients, promoting an idea of equality.[75] In the Contestado we know that *coronel* Henrique Rupp regularly worked cattle alongside his clients.[76] The fact that such a powerful *fazendeiro* did so implies that other *fazendeiros* of equal and lesser status did the same.

Further evidence of a rustic form of equality comes from a 1912 editorial of an interior newspaper. In this piece, *A Notícia* attacked wealthy interior *fazendeiros* for leading an isolated existence void of culture and grace: "Removed from the confines of civilization, [these wealthy *fazendeiros*] live like beggars: with coarse, patched clothing, . . . a straw hat, [and] many times without shoes because they don't like superfluous clothing and unnecessary footwear." To *A Notícia*, this planter backwardness was unacceptable in an age of advancing civilization. Thus, "without any notion of the world, without realizing that the well-being of the people comes from the Nation, *without any notion of the division of labor* [emphasis added]. . . . They take care of themselves, only entering into relations with area residents when they see a chance for immediate gain."[77]

In addition to this rustic form of equality between *patrões* and *agregados*, the latter also held onto a semi-independent life-style. As noted earlier in the work of Mario Góngora, low land commodification made the granting of usufruct land rights to *agregados* the cheapest method of insuring a *fazendeiro*'s claim to a particular section of land. *Agregados* seized full advantage of this opening to raise their own cattle and grow their own crops in isolated areas of a large claim. They had time to do both, since the landowner's ranching activities were not labor intensive. Again, suffice it to compare this situation with Chile to note that the adoption of wheat production in that country sharply curtailed the independence of a "cowboy class."[78]

To make sense of the contradictory aspects of the patron-client relationship, that is, of patron violence on one side and equality and independence on the other, we must further examine the nature of rural violence. Here it is argued that in many ways violence acted as a *cohesive* factor in the patron-client relationship. As Amaury de Souza notes, violence in rural Brazil "was a common denominator in the disputes between the dominant families or classes." In a similar fashion, Maria Isaura Pereira de Queiroz argues that violence between *coronéis* was ever-present in pre-1930s Brazil. Indeed, she continues, such violence was the norm in the rural society.[79]

Both de Souza and Pereira de Queiroz argue that this violence, and the mutual defense needs it created, tied patrons and clients together. *Patrões* relied on their armed clients in battles with other rural bosses. In return, clients relied on the landowners for protection from these attacks by other elites and from the actions of public authorities. As Pereira de Queiroz points out, violence and solidarity thus became "two sides of the same coin." Amaury de Souza agrees, noting that because of the reciprocal nature of landlord violence, "it is safe to assume that at least in colonial and imperial Brazil, violence was a cultural norm shared by all members of the patriarchal community."[80]

In a society without marked differences in wealth, perhaps *patrões* relied even more heavily on violence to confirm their positions of power. Here it helps to think in terms of the use of violence to defend a code of manliness. Like intraelite violence, violence to confirm manliness also acted to bond landowners and male clients. This defense of male honor, and hence the use of patriarchy to unite men across class lines, appears clearly in the character of Rufino in Mario Vargas Llosa's novel of rural Brazil, *The War of the End of the World*.[81] Rufino seeks to avenge his honor when his wife abandons him in favor of the journalist Galileo Gall. Rufino's mother inquires, "'You'll clear your name of the filth they've heaped upon it, won't you?'" She then exclaims, "'It's worse than if they plucked out your eyes, worse than if they killed me.'"[82] Rufino must kill his wife and the journalist to defend his manliness. First, however, he takes pains to approach his *patrão*, his godfather, for permission to act. The latter reluctantly agrees, thus reaffirming the link violence in defense of manhood creates between patron and client.

In the Contestado, *patrões* committed acts of violence against their *agregados*. How is it possible, then, to reconcile the idea of a rustic equality with the notion of an underlying violence inherent in patron-client relations? We have seen how violence could also act in a cohesive fashion, when it emerged from landowners and clients involved in mutual defense networks, and when violence in defense of manhood united men across class lines. Returning to our earlier discussion of a rustic equality and the degree of *agregado* independence in the Contestado, we see that these worked to limit further the disruptive potential of patron violence against their followers.

Duglas Teixeira Monteiro addresses these potentially contradictory themes of patron violence and patron-client solidarity with his concept of "customary" versus "innovative" violence.[83] According to this sociologist, patron violence and patron-client solidarity are actually mutually reinforcing. A rustic form of equality, he argues, allowed for certain types of violence to occur without that violence threatening the logic of the patron-client relationship. Here Monteiro speaks not just of an *actual* equality but of the *potential* equality between patrons and clients created by the co-godparenthood tie.

Violence was ever-present in the Contestado of the nineteenth century. People killed each other over questions of honor. Powerful *fazendeiros* fought each other with the aid of their personal armies. Patrons committed acts of violence against their *agregados*. Such events, however, were thought of as individual acts of violence, acts that did not threaten the functioning of the patron-client relationship. What could (and later did) cause a fundamental crisis was a new type of patron violence that would threaten the continued existence of the client class. Such a violence, directed against the client class as a whole, would question the assumed level of equality. But for years in the Contestado, a rustic form of equality, *agregado* independence, and the nature of rural violence itself operated to limit the rebellious potential of patron-client violence.

Co-Godparenthood:
Theoretical Background

To understand further the rustic egalitarianism that existed in the Contestado we need to examine not only the material aspects, but also the social aspects of the patron-client tie. An understanding of the roles fictive kinship and other popular religious rituals play in cementing the bonds between patrons and clients is crucial, because the breakdown of these roles, and thus the breakdown of patron-client relations, provoked a specifically millenarian rebellion in the Contestado region.

Unfortunately for the Contestado, however, a paucity of data threatens the discussion of *compadrío* (co-godparenthood) in the region. Duglas Teixeira Monteiro includes a fine sociological discussion of co-godparenthood in *Os errantes do novo século,* but he relies entirely on the secondary literature, all of it drawn from other areas of Brazil. Maurício Vinhas de Queiroz altogether ignores the co-godparenthood aspect of the patron-client relationship. To appreciate the importance of co-godparenthood then, we must turn to the general literature on the subject. By doing so we can then compare this information with what we do know about the Contestado in order to better understand the importance of *compadrío* in the interior society.[84]

The term "co-godparenthood" (*compadrazgo* in Spanish, *compadrío* in Portuguese) refers to the relationships created by baptismal sponsorship in the Catholic religion. According to Sidney Mintz and Eric Wolf in their classic article "An Analysis of Ritual Co-parenthood (*Compadrazgo*)," these relationships involve "an initi-ate, usually a child; . . . the parents of the initiate; . . . [and] the ceremonial sponsor or sponsors of the initiate."[85] Within this com-plex, relationships are thus established between (a) the godparents and the child and (b) the godparents and the parents of the child.

After presenting the historical development of co-godparenthood, Mintz and Wolf proceed with what they themselves call a "func-tional analysis" of *compadrazgo* (*compadrío*). The authors briefly mention the spiritual significance of the institution, claiming that "baptism was a sacrament designed to remove the stigma of original sin," and that "the mechanism of godparenthood took shape origi-nally as a means for guaranteeing religious education and guidance to the Catholic child." They quickly point out, however, that "the most important modern social result of the baptismal ceremony in practice [is] the creation of a security network of ritual kinfolk."[86]

Given their orientation, Mintz and Wolf devote their time to examining the functional roles assumed by co-godparenthood in a given society. By now we are well familiar with these roles. In general, it is through co-godparenthood that people often seek some type of social insurance. On a more particular level, co-godparent-hood ties are sometimes used, for example, to forestall sexual aggres-sions, since sexual relations are prohibited in the wider *compadre* relation. In a similar vein, *compadrío* relations are often established to avoid aggression between two people. Finally, Mintz and Wolf write that the co-godparenthood institution is utilized to solidify ties between members of different classes.[87]

Beginning in the 1970s a group of scholars began to criticize certain aspects of the Mintz-Wolf view of *compadrío*. The Brazilian Antonio Augusto Arantes Neto noted that this view virtually ignores the symbolic aspect of *compadrío* in favor of a detailed analysis of the *material exchanges* that occur between *compadres*. According to Arantes Neto, "This type of explanation takes the scholar outside of the institution that he is studying, because these forms of solidarity are also present in institutions such as the family, friends, etc."[88] What Arantes Neto seeks is an analysis of the spiritual relationships within the *compadrío* institution. This is also what Stephen Gude-man seeks in his work on co-godparenthood, that is, the recognition that co-godparenthood is *both* "a sacred and social set of relation-ships."[89] The concern here is with the *meaning*, and not just the functioning of, the *compadrío* institution. Thus, as Raymond T. Smith noted in regards to Gudeman, "Instead of seeing ritual co-godparenthood as some kind of functional mechanism for advancing individual material interests or repairing holes in the social fabric, he [Gudeman] examine[s] the context of the beliefs . . . of the institution."[90]

At this point we must examine the spiritual side of *compadrío*, for "although godparenthood is projected into social domains, the institution never loses its fundamental spiritual resonance and rooting."[91] This spiritual rooting comes from the rite of baptism, a rite that signifies the cleansing of original sin. The godparents are chosen to validate the baptism, and by doing so they become the spiritual parents of the child.[92]

The key distinction is between the natural and spiritual realms. Childbirth is of the natural realm, co-godparenthood of the spiritual: "Through baptism the passage from the state of Original Sin to the state of grace is achieved. Man is thought to be conceived by the sin of Adam: he is regenerated when his sin is "washed away" during baptism and he is reborn to Christ and a second set of parents."[93] Godparent ties are of the spiritual realm; they are said to have been created by God. In this sense they are thought of as superior to natural kinship. Canon law thus requires the godparents to supervise the moral and religious growth of the child. The significance of *compadrío* becomes a moral one, because it is a religious institution that emphasizes the duties of all involved.[94]

If we further examine this idea of the sacred versus the profane, we come to important conclusions about the co-godparenthood complex, patron-client relations, and the transmission of ideology. Parents are responsible for the material (profane) life, godparents for the religious (sacred, moral) life. Key is the concept of original sin and the spiritual rebirth that occurs with baptism. Together, the concepts of original sin, and of the sacred versus the profane,

form an element in the building of ideology: the symbolic allocation to those in authority of the power to create people as legitimate members of society. Godparenthood and *compadrazgo* links are therefore seen as part of the building of an ideological view of society, in that they are based on the replacement of dirty, natural birth by clean, legitimate second birth.[95]

The idea proposed in the work of Bloch and Gudeman is that natural childbirth is seen as something "dirty" and profane. Baptism replaces the natural, "dirty" birth with a clean, spiritual rebirth. In the patron-client relationship, it is the patron who most often serves as the godparent. The patron is thus identified with the sacred side of life. The ideology of the superiority of the patron has now been *sanctified* by religious ritual. This "institutionalized superiority" is

what Arantes Neto referred to when he noted that "the ties of
compadrío sanctify the ties upon which they are located, and establish . . . the moral superiority of the godparent relative to the father."[96]

The argument that the ideology of patron superiority is transmit-
ted via compadrío is strengthened by Bloch's and Gudeman's discussion of male dominance and the co-godparenthood complex. Again
the key is the concept of a natural, "dirty" childbirth versus spiritual
rebirth. As baptism devaluates the natural birth, it is used not only to
justify patron dominance in the patron-client relationship but also to
legitimate and insure male dominance in the general society.

Thus, the birth that baptism effects and the social relationships thereby
formed are under the control of men, because it is a birth into and by the
religious-political community, a birth which involves the symbolic denial of
the value of the procreative power of birth by women. . . . Vilification of
biological reproduction is thus the first step in the legitimation of an
alternative community based on other principles of reproduction: holier,
cleaner and controlled by legitimate authority.[97]

Biological reproduction, motherhood, and clients are all thought of as
inferior, while spiritual reproduction, controlled by men (and quite
often male patrons), is superior. The point is that compadrío legitimates male dominance and patron control, for "the creativity made
available by second birth rituals can be used to legitimate all kinds of
situations. Yet it always legitimates it in the same way: by making
these other people . . . the repository of the ability to create social/
spiritual people."[98]

This point illustrates the importance of not only cross-class compadrío but also of co-godparenthood ties between members of the
dominant class. On one level such ties insured the continuation of
patriarchy within the dominant class. In addition, such relations
allowed elites to capitalize on a region's material and social opportunities. Co-godparenthood relations between, say, a large landowner
and local merchant could benefit both parties. For the merchant,
such ties earned him the backing of an area's most powerful resident.
For the patrão, the relationship opened access to various material
goods, greater influence in the urban setting, and, with the onset of
capitalism, benefits such as access to loans for the purchase of ever-
increasing amounts of land. In addition, examples of patron religiosity clearly demonstrate that compadrío and other religious practices assumed a spiritual importance in the lives of Contestado elites.

Nevertheless, it is cross-class compadrío that is of most concern
in this book, for its use to insure patron control is crucial for an

understanding of patron-client relations. But here the situation is more complex, for the use of co-godparenthood to insure patron control can be a double-edged sword. To be sure, the position of godfather legitimates patron control. But responsibilities come with this position, as we shall see from examples taken from the Contestado. As godparents, patrons are required to oversee the religious and moral education of the child. A special relationship exists then between the godparent/patron and the godchild. And as various authors have noted, a special relationship also develops between the godparent/patron and client/parents of the child.[99] A special significance of the institution of *compadrío* is that it emphasizes everyone's duties.

The argument thus far is that in sanctifying patron control *compadrío* also establishes a required reciprocity between patrons and clients. This reciprocity is closely related to the idea of the "moral economy," as put forth by scholars such as James C. Scott, E. P. Thompson, and Eric Wolf.[100] We are speaking of peasant claims on the patron, of "a consistent traditional view of social norms and obligations of proper economic functions . . . within the community."[101] On a material level, patrons are forced into a degree of reciprocity with their clients to insure their access to labor. But on another level the focus switches to the peasantry's "moral requirement of reciprocity" to insure subsistence.[102] Through *compadrío*, the patron legitimates his control, but at the price of becoming morally responsible for the subsistence of his clients. In a rustic economy this price is not high, but in a commercialized setting it may rise.

One way to view the special tie created by the co-godparenthood complex is to examine a relationship where this connection rarely existed. Stuart Schwartz and Stephen Gudeman provide such an example with their examination of slavery in colonial Bahia, Brazil. According to these authors, slaveowners were never godparents to their slaves in colonial Bahia.[103]

Schwartz and Gudeman begin their discussion by reminding us that "baptism, above all, creates a spiritual relationship . . . [a] bond that unites the baptized and the sponsors."[104] The master-slave tie, however, involved property ownership. Indeed, "masters held the right to the labor effort of their slaves; they had the right to discipline, to sell, to dispose of, and kill their slaves. A slave was a piece of property, a kind of tool, or a piece of equipment, albeit a living one."[105] Such a relationship of property was fundamentally opposed to the bonds created by co-godparenthood. Baptism recognizes the humanity of individuals, it recognizes their freedom from sin. Yet one way of justifying slavery was to claim that slaves were sinners.[106] Thus, according to an English administrator of a Brazilian plantation, "I never heard of the master in Brazil being likewise the god-father; nor do I think that this ever happens; for such is the connection between two persons which this is supposed to produce, that the master would never think of ordering the slave to be chastised."[107]

As opposed to Gudeman and Schwartz, Eul Soo Pang argues that slave masters did establish fictive kinship ties with their slaves. In fact, he argues that masters went so far as to free their godchildren. Pang notes, however, that in such cases it is likely that the godfather was the real father of the slave, or that the master arranged free godparents for his illegitimate child. The child of an especially esteemed slave (most probably a house servant?) might also be baptized, but here the master-slave tie may have approached a kind of patron-client relationship between free people.[108]

The fact that slaveowners rarely served as godparents to their slaves sheds important light on the institution of co-godparenthood and on the patron-client relationship. Through *compadrío,* patrons recognize the humanity of their clients and assume at least some responsibility for the life of the godchild and his or her parents. This slave example helps us to understand that, at least symbolically, a "special" (i.e., spiritual and moral) relationship links the *compadres,* one that encourages, indeed mandates, patron-client reciprocity. It is in the patron's interest to extend material benefits to gain access to peasant labor. But via co-godparenthood ties, clients are also able to exert a moral claim to these benefits.

The theoretical work of symbolic anthropologists places meaning, and hence peasant conciousness, firmly at the center of analysis. For the historian, however, the problem of historical accuracy remains. Do theories based on ethnographic data drawn from other regions of Brazil and Latin America apply to the Contestado? Does evidence from earlier periods still apply to Brazil in the twentieth century? Fortunately, archival materials and interviews with local residents address the meaning *compadrío* and other types of religious ritual held for Contestado patrons and clients.

Co-Godparenthood in the Contestado

How important was the institution of co-godparenthood in the Contestado? One can gain a partial answer from baptismal records, in this case the baptismal records of the parish of Rio Negro, Paraná, for the years 1904–14. A review of these records uncovered a web of co-godparenthood ties among the elite of the area. The various members of the Pacheco family appear thirty-seven times as godparents. Nicolau Bley Netto, the recognized political boss of the area, served as godfather on eighteen different occasions during the ten-year span.[109] In one case a member of the Bley family served as the godparent of a Pacheco, and this same entry points to further co-godparenthood relationships between these two powerful families.[110]

Of the baptismal registrations surveyed in Rio Negro, it was possible to acertain the profession of the parents in only five cases. Given that professions were never noted in the baptismal records, these five cases resulted from checks with the Rio Negro birth and marriage records. Even this small sample illustrates the importance of elite *compadrío* ties. Bley Netto was the godfather to the children of both a large landowner and a businessman.[111] These elite ties led one local official to complain in 1910 that Rio Negro constituted

one large family united by material, moral, co-godparent, and kinship . . . ties, with this family having in its hands all of the power. To resolve any disputes this family is gathered . . . and thus, whenever a criminal (who has often already confessed) is judged, the sentence has to take in to account that the accused is the godchild of political boss "A," or the *compadre* of "B," a customer of his business, or son of "C," . . . thus the absolution [of the criminal] is resolved *a priori*, no matter how flagrant the act.[112]

Such could be the importance of co-godparenthood ties within the dominant class.

But what of cross-class *compadrío* relations in the Contestado? These are virtually impossible to find in the baptismal registers. Given the isolation of many of the *fazendas*, and the utter shortage of priests in the area, many baptisms were simply never recorded. What is more, given these conditions, landowners (patrons) often performed the baptismal ceremony themselves. This placed the patron in the dual role of priest *and* godfather, something that no doubt added even more force to the sanctity and validity of patron rule.[113]

Two recorded baptisms involving members of the Bley and Pacheco families do point to cross-class *compadrío* ties. In 1913 Nicolau Bley Netto and his wife, Amanda Bley Zorning, served as the godparents of the infant Leopoldo Egnácio Nirz. Leopoldo's father, Leão Nirz, listed his occupation as "lavrador," that is, peasant, or worker.[114] In 1914 Bemvindo Pacheco and his wife Maria served as the godparents of Diomedes Linhares, son of Didio and Maria Joanna Linhares. Didio listed his profession as that of an "industrial worker" in Três Barras, Paraná. Given that this was the home of the mammoth Brazil Lumber Company sawmill, it is likely that Didio labored at the sawmill. This is highly significant, since the Pachecos acted as labor contractors for the Brazil Lumber Company![115]

Three interviews with descendants of large *fazendeiros* confirm the existence of cross-class *compadrío* in the Contestado. At the onset of the rebellion, Sebastião Colomeno's uncle was an important *fazendeiro* near Curitibanos, Santa Catarina. According to Sebastião, "it was the norm for *agregados* and *fazendeiros* to be *compadres.*" His uncle "provided protection for the *agregados*" and gave presents to his godchildren. Sebastião also remembers that all his uncle's *agregados* occupied land on which they grew crops and raised cattle.[116]

Henrique Rupp, the important *fazendeiro* of Campos Novos, was the *compadre* and godfather to many area residents. According to his grandson, co-godparenthood ties connected Rupp with all of his *agregados* and *camaradas*. Francisco Pacheco remembers that *compadrío* relations were important for both his father and other members of the Pacheco family. In his very religious family, said Francisco, his father viewed the establishment of such ties "as a type of testimony that the little ones had received the faith."[117]

During the Contestado Rebellion, Brazilian army officials quickly recognized the importance of *compadrío* ties in the area. Sometimes they worried about the use of these ties by rebel spies. Such was the case of Captain Esperidião de Almeida, who complained that "at times the fanatics know even the most insignificant details about us." This led him to conclude that "if a fanatic came to our camp—he would be welcomed by many locals as a cousin [or] *compadre.*"[118]

At other times the army sought to use *compadrío* relations to their advantage. In one such instance, before an attack on the rebel Rio Timbó redoubt, the army turned to Second Lieutenant Antonio Pereira Campos, a Timbó village native who was a *compadre* with many local residents. Indeed, "in only one day he had once made thirty baptisms in a single country ceremony."[119] For their part the army commanders assumed that Campos's co-godparenthood ties would allow him to negotiate with the rebels. Campos himself was "confident in the absolute sincerity of these . . . relations, [and] he assumed that he could take advantage of them for the common good. . . . He thus supposed that in this rustic setting small interests would not destroy the strong ties of friendship which had operated for many years."[120] Both outsiders (army officials) and insiders (Campos) alike fully recognized the importance of cross-class *compadrío* ties in the Contestado.

A particularly graphic example of the importance of *compadrío/* patron-client ties in the Contestado comes from an interview with Rufino Ferreira da Silva. Rufino, eighty-three years old in 1984, was eleven years old at the beginning of the Contestado Rebellion. As a boy Rufino accompanied his *patrão* as the latter transported various cargos in the Santa Catarina interior. It is not clear what kind of relationship existed between Rufino's parents and his *patrão.*

One day Rufino's *patrão* said, "Let's go," and man and boy headed for the rebel encampment at Taquaraçu. According to Rufino, his *patrão* joined the rebels because army troops had just destroyed his cargo. And what of Rufino? To begin with, his parents did *not* join the rebellion. But Rufino did indeed join, stating that "I went because I was the *camarada* of my *patrão.*" Faced with the choice of loyalty between parents and patron, Rufino chose the latter. Rufino's father in fact joined the fight against the rebels and died in the failed army attack against the very same Taquaraçu redoubt! Patron-client ties could be that strong in the Contestado.[121]

As mentioned, a particular source of strength of the patron-client tie was the responsibility patrons assumed for the material welfare of their clients. In the Contestado several examples of patron paternalism confirm that a reciprocal relationship operated between patrons and clients. As we have seen, Contestado patrons made land and seeds available to their *agregados.* In addition, informants note that patrons periodically gave presents to their godchildren. For his part, Francisco Pacheco did not see any larger significance in the gifts his father gave to *agregados.*[122] Earlier, however, we saw how such patron gifts confirmed client labor obligations to the *patrão.*

Perhaps actions in the religious sphere best illustrate the paternalism of the Contestado *fazendeiros.* By the late nineteenth century the Carneiro family owned nearly 30,000 hectares of land in the southern interior. Each family member employed *agregados* and *camaradas* in food production. Within their vast holdings the Carneiros included the Faixinal dos Pobres, a 13,000-hectare tract near the village of São João.

The Faixinal dos Pobres was a peculiar sort of property. In 1851 an ancestor donated the use, and a portion of the revenue, of the land to the chapel at São João. By the late 1890s thirty families lived there, each growing corn and beans and raising some cattle. Two plots were tilled in exclusive benefit of the chapel, while the thirty families were forced to donate ten *milreis* per year to the chapel.[123]

The creation of the Faixinal dos Pobres is a classic example of patron paternalism. The Carneiro ancestor felt some duty to establish, and insure the existence of, the São João chapel. That person also felt the need to give several families an access to land. Granted, in 1851 the establishment of such a holding did not entail much economic sacrifice, since land was plentiful and cheap. Nevertheless, it does speak to the importance of the paternal responsibilities of interior *fazendeiros*, for 13,000 hectares was a lot of land to donate to a chapel's upkeep. As for the lack of economic sacrifice, this would later change, for by 1897 one government surveyor realized that "within a few years this land will have, with the construction of the railroad, easy access to all points served by the line."[124]

Other examples further confirm the connection between paternalism and patron religiosity in the Contestado. As noted, Francisco Pacheco remembers that his father was a very religious man, so much so that he built a chapel on the *fazenda* and ordered *agregados* to the Sunday services. Today Francisco feels that this religious zeal was a backward trait in his father.[125] Nor was Francisco's father alone in the importance he placed on religion. On the *fazenda* of his neighbor Seraphim José Portes, an important *fazendeiro* in Rio Negro, there was a "modest church . . . dedicated to Saint John [whose day was] celebrated on the 24th of June . . . [and] every Sunday the *fazenda* population [awoke] to there receive lessons of morality and of the catechism, and all of the spiritual comforts."[126] In addition to these *fazendeiros*, others in the area built chapels where religious services and celebrations took place.[127]

The mention of the feast of Saint John suggests that patron saint celebrations further regulated patron-client relations. Such celebrations consist of a procession of the saint's image followed by a feast offered by the local *patrão*. Anthropologists argue that sponsorship of such events confirms, or even sacralizes, landowner authority, because it identifies him with the patron saint. Furthermore, peasants demonstrate their loyalty as clients by attending the celebration. However, the sponsorship of the feast also confirms peasant expectations of landowner paternalism and reciprocity.[128] Thus, "If the ruler and patron are secular versions of God and the saints, it is incumbent upon them to uphold the patriarchal duties they share with their sacred counterparts, that is to provide material security, spiritual growth, and physical protection for the poor."[129]

This reference to Seraphim José Portes confirms that Contestado landowners sponsored saints' feasts. Others did so as well. For example, Euzébio Ferreira dos Santos, a Contestado landowner of some means and a member of the Republican party, built a chapel and a number of shacks to be used during the annual Bom Jesus procession and feast at Perdizes Grandes. Dos Santos sponsored the annual event, going as far as to invite the millenarian prophet José Maria to preach at the saint's feast of 1912. It was this event, in fact, that led to the first battle of the rebellion![130]

This evidence drawn from the Contestado demonstrates the fundamental importance of the patron-client relationship in the region. For years the patron-client relationship functioned as the mechanism by which *fazendeiros* gained access to an oftentimes scarce labor supply. Given the abundance of land, patrons offered this access in return for client services. These services included not only labor in food production, but also clients were called upon to defend their patron in clashes with other members of the elite.

For their part clients maintained an access to land in return for participation in an unequal exchange relationship. From the patron they received tools, seeds, and sometimes a cow. In case of a problem with a public official, they could often count on their patron for protection. But most important, clients and patrons worked together to guard against Indian attacks. In the Contestado this was a daily threat, and it no doubt prevented many *caboclos* from establishing isolated subsistence holdings in the forest.

The patron-client relationship in the Contestado was not a completely nonviolent institution whereby clients happily submitted to a relationship of unequal exchange. Clients no doubt suffered from patron violence, or, perhaps more important, the threat of such violence. Sometimes they reacted simply by flight, or, as demonstrated in this chapter, by stealing from the patron and then fleeing. But in this context we need to recall Duglas Teixeira Monteiro's thoughts on "customary violence." Thus it seems that clients recognized and perhaps grudgingly accepted a certain type of planter violence in the Contestado. We need also recall the limits that life in the interior placed on the possibilities for differentiation between patrons and clients. Indeed, it is hard to imagine the São Paulo or Rio de Janeiro coffee planters working the fields alongside the slave or *colono* (immigrant plantation worker), as Contestado patrons did in the ranching economy. In the end, however, severe troubles did emerge when the nature of patron violence began to change.

A key argument of this chapter concerns the *compadrío* complex, popular religious ritual, and patron-client relations in the Contestado. Local interviews and documents clearly demonstrate the crucial role *compadrío* played in both the creation and regulation of patron-client ties in the interior. Descendants of powerful landowners speak of *compadrío* in terms of *agregado* loyalty and patron responsibilities. Military officers thought such ties would provide an opening into the otherwise closed world of the rebel opposition.

Evidence of Contestado patron paternalism and religiosity speaks to the ideological and spiritual aspects of the patron-client complex. This evidence, when combined with the theoretical work of symbolic anthropologists, suggests that, on the one hand, popular religious ritual acted to sanctify *fazendeiro* dominance in the society. It served as a conduit for an ideology that preached *fazendeiro* control, one placing the *patrão* at the head of both the material *and* spiritual realms. On the other hand, the establishment of *compadrío* ties and the sponsorship of saints' feasts created a moral responsibility for exchange between patrons and clients.

In the isolated interior of the Contestado the patrons' need for labor forced them to extend certain material benefits to their clients. The precariousness of life in the Contestado forced many peasants to accept this unequal exchange. The *compadrío* tie validated the operation of this system, embellishing it with a spiritual and moral tone. For many years the patrons' need for services corresponded with the peasantry's moral claim to reciprocity. But events in the Contestado would soon bring about a fundamental change in this situation, drawing patrons and clients into a sharp and ultimately irrevocable conflict. For on the horizon international capital, in the form of a massive railroad construction plan, prepared to invade the area and transform the isolated *sertão* into the center of one of the world's most modern enterprises.

3

Capitalists and Colonists

In 1906 Percival Farquhar, a Quaker capitalist from Pennsylvania, purchased the valuable railroad concession that would finally link central and southern Brazil. Backed by French and English capital, Farquhar hoped to add to his already enormous railroad holdings in Brazil. Following British railroad investment strategy in Argentina, Farquhar aimed to construct this southern line and develop the surrounding lands. As one associate put it:

His plan . . . was to get control of a port, a railroad and much land in the interior, and then establish working industries there. Thus his companies would get four sources of profit: 1st port profits, 2nd railroad profits, 3rd profits from lumbering, cattle or manufacturing, and finally from rising land values from increases in population and economic activity.[1]

For its part the security-conscious Brazilian government eagerly promoted the completion of a southern line. The line, which would link São Paulo with Pôrto Alegre, would facilitate the movement of troops in case of Argentine attack. As the minister of war, Hermes da Fonseca issued a report detailing the needs for such a strategic line, while one southern newspaper claimed that "in reality there is no national defense in the south . . . without a railroad with which to rapidly mobilize troops."[2] After the completion of the line, another Farquhar associate noted in 1914 that "from a purely strategical standpoint, the Federal Government has . . . a military line of the highest value, over which it can move troops from the Capital by its own line, the Central of Brazil, to São Paulo, and thence directly over the lines of the Brazil Railway Company."[3]

Thus began the process destined to transform the entire Contestado region. What was once a sparsely populated area, dominated by a few large cattle ranches, now became the construction site of a railroad as technically advanced as any other on the continent. Before the railroad, a horseback ride to Florianópolis was a grueling five-day experience. With its completion, Contestado residents, and the agricultural goods they shipped, could now reach São Paulo, Brazil's new industrial beacon, in less than half that time.

At the same moment that the Brazil Railway Company began its transformation of the Contestado region, the states of Paraná and Santa Catarina began to act on an equally revolutionary plan. At their invitation, thousands of European immigrants invaded the region, settling on thousands of the area's most fertile hectares. Determined to transform their interiors from economic backwaters to powerful agricultural breadbaskets, the two states marked off vast sections of once-public lands, sold them to the immigrants, and provided them with free transportation, tools, and seeds. With the railroad opening up the São Paulo market, state officials were certain their plans would not fail.

What follows is a detailed examination of this two-sided process, which shook the Contestado region at the turn of this century. It was a whirlwind affair, one that uprooted the foundations of the Contestado society in less than a decade. In its wake it left ecological destruction, a revolution in land tenure, and a millenarian rebellion the size of which rivaled that of Canudos. Here, however, we are getting ahead of the story, for first we must confront and understand the details of railroad construction and colonization in the Contestado.

The Brazil Railway Company
in the Contestado

Percival Farquhar purchased the rights to complete construction of a line from Itararé, São Paulo, to Marcelino Ramos, on the Rio Grande do Sul–Santa Catarina border (see figure 2). This stretch would then connect with a number of other Farquhar-owned railroads in São Paulo, Paraná, and Rio Grande do Sul. Together, these railroads comprised the Brazil Railway Company, a holding company that Farquhar created in November 1906. By 1914 this mammoth outfit owned nearly 3,000 miles of track in Brazil. In addition, the company held significant stock interests in another 2,000 miles. This 5,000-mile total meant that the Brazil Railway Company controlled roughly one-half of all Brazilian railroad mileage at the time.[4]

With offices in Portland (Maine), London, Paris, New York, and

Rio de Janeiro, the company counted among its board of directors some of the most important names in railroad history. Included on the board were Sir William Van Horne, president of the Canadian Pacific Railway Company, and Minor C. Keith, vice-president of United Fruit and president of the Guatemalan Railway Company. Its approximately twenty holdings included the Sorocabana Railroad Company (São Paulo), the Paraná Railway Company, the Cia. [Compagnie] Auxiliare des Chemins [de] Fer au Brésiliens (Rio Grande do Sul), and the famous Madeira-Mamoré Railway Company. The company also held sole port concessions in Belém, Rio Grande do Sul, and Rio de Janeiro. With the purchase of the southern concession and the later leasing of existing lines in Rio Grande do Sul, the company created a monopoly on all lines south of the state of São Paulo.[5] The government concession that Farquhar purchased was originally granted to João Teixeira Soares on 9 November 1889. Teixeira Soares, who in 1895 completed an impressive line through the mountains between Curitiba (Paraná) and the port of Paranaguá, received the concession to build a railroad between Itararé, São Paulo, and Santa Maria, Rio Grande do Sul. In addition to this north-south line, the concession obliged Teixeira Soares to also build an ambitious east-west trunk line between the famous falls of Iguaçu and the port town of São Francisco, Santa Catarina.[6] Teixeira Soares's Compagnie de Chemins de Fer Sud-Ouest Brésiliens began construction in 1890. One year later he sold the concession rights to the Companhia Industrial dos Estados do Brasil, which in turn sold it to the Companhia São Paulo–Rio Grande in 1895.[7]

Percival Farquhar purchased the rights to a very extensive concession indeed. As modified by Consolidation Decree 397, the concession was to last for ninety years. Due to previous transfers and construction, Farquhar was now obliged to complete the line between Itararé and the Santa Catarina–Rio Grande do Sul border, in addition to the trunk line between the Atlantic Ocean and Iguaçu Falls.[8]

Under the terms of the concession, the federal government agreed to pay a guaranteed interest of 6 percent gold, calculated on the capital invested in the project. To control this expenditure, the Brazilian government required the Brazil Railway Company to deposit its funds in the London branch of the Société Générale pour Favoriser le Développement du Commerce et l'Industrie en France. To withdraw funds, the company first had to receive permission from the Brazilian government official in London. The capital guarantee was "not to exceed 30 *contos* gold, per kilometer for the total length of the railway" and was payable for thirty years. For its part the

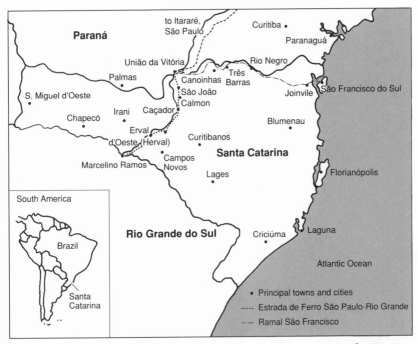

Figure 2   The Brazil Railway Company in the Contestado Region (Estrada de Ferro São Paulo–Rio Grande)

concession obligated the Brazil Railway Company to finish construction of the line by 17 December 1910.[9]

Sweetest among the concession's incentives was a massive land grant of a 30-kilometer strip along the entire length of the line (fig. 2). The Brazil Railway Company inherited this land grant when it purchased the concession. One company official described the area included in the grant as an "exceedingly rich, fertile and well watered [land], the climate of which is not disagreeable to the white race." Company figures showed the grant to contain 2,248,020 hectares in the states of Santa Catarina and Paraná. In Paraná alone the government ceded 1,700,268 hectares to the company. Crucial to development plans, the company planned to sell these lands to colonists, who would then use the railroad to ship their agricultural products.[10]

When Percival Farquhar acquired the rights to the railroad line, it had been completed to the town of União da Vitória, Paraná (see figure 2).[11] It was now the Brazil Railway Company's duty (via its subsidiary the Estrada de Ferro São Paulo–Rio Grande) to construct the roughly 200 remaining miles of the 550-mile line. In addition, the entire east-west trunk line required action, since the previous companies did nothing on this project.

The Brazil Railway Company launched construction of the União da Vitória–Marcelino Ramos stretch in 1907. The company's entrance brought "more animation and desire in all sectors" and meant that "a new rhythm [was] now imposed on various fronts." From União da Vitória an army of 1,000 track workers moved south toward São João, Santa Catarina. Soon, a tent city sprawled over the countryside to house them. The company filled large warehouses, first simply expanded canvas tents, with lengths of rail, wooden ties, and tools of every shape and size. Enormous steam-powered shovels and road graders gobbled up the earth to what must have been the amazement of local residents. Company efforts culminated with the inauguration of this 51-kilometer stretch on 30 April 1908. One year later, the company completed a second 50-kilometer stretch, naming the new station after President Penna, who attended the inaugural ceremonies.[12]

Beginning in April 1909, the company intensified its efforts to finish the line by the December 1910 deadline. Quickly the number of workers mushroomed from 1,000 to over 5,000. From the President Penna station the work moved southward to Erval d'Oeste (Herval). Labor gangs strained to construct this stretch, completing it in April 1910. This 164-kilometer section, completed in one year, more than tripled the construction average from the preceding two years. Perhap the early years of construction did not greatly alter life in the region. Now, however, the great push changed everything. For the first time passengers rode the train into Santa Catarina. São João station received 798 passengers in the second half of 1910.[13]

Pressed for time, the company now began to construct temporary wooden bridges along the length of the line. This measure pushed construction at a breakneck pace south towards the Uruguay River and the Rio Grande do Sul border. The contract, however, called for the completion of the track to the town of Marcelino Ramos, Rio Grande do Sul. To accomplish this, workers struggled to complete a large wooden bridge across the Uruguay River, which they accomplished on December 16. On 17 December 1910, Brazil Railway officials, local and regional officials, and the elite of the Contestado society boarded the gayly decorated Brazil Railway train in União da Vitória. Hours later they crossed the shaky bridge into Marcelino Ramos, and history had been made.[14]

In addition to this main line, in 1907 the company initiated construction on the east-west trunk line to run between São Francisco, Santa Catarina, and Iguaçu Falls. Company and government officials dreamed of the benefits the line would bring. Thousands of settlers would arrive, and agricultural production would skyrocket. At last, someone would exploit the region's enormous forest reserves and export the wild *erva mate* tea. Plans called for the track to climb 600 meters in 75 kilometers before intersecting with the company's main line at União da Vitória. From there the line would continue across Paraná to Iguaçu Falls. This latter portion was never constructed, however, due to the financial troubles of the company. Hence the São Francisco line covered only the 286 miles between that port town and União da Vitória.[15]

Construction of the São Francisco line paled in comparison with the União da Vitória–Marcelino Ramos line. Instead of the thousands of laborers on the main road, this branch never employed more than 500 track workers. In the first three years the company completed only 95 kilometers of track, compared to an average of 50, and then more than 100 kilometers per year on the main line. The inauguration of the Hansa station took place on 8 June 1910, and three years later work was finished on the stretch between Hansa and Três Barras. Lumber, *erva mate*, and other goods could now reach the port of São Francisco by rail. In addition to the shipping of goods, some 76,000 passengers rode the line in 1914, although this figure is misleading, since most passengers rode only the short stretch between the towns of São Francisco and Hansa.[16]

Track construction of the branch line stalled after reaching Três Barras in 1913. The financial troubles of the company, rebel attacks against the line during the Contestado Rebellion, and a series of floods all contributed to this stoppage. In addition, the railroad administration blamed a shortage of workers. Given these problems, the inauguration of the 286-mile São Francisco branch of the railroad, which now composed only one-half of the original concession, did not take place until 1917.[17]

Percival Farquhar's dream of creating a railroad empire in southern Brazil, one that would rival British successes in Argentina, never came true completely. Farquhar's strengths were acquisition and expansion, and his constant successes in these areas deprived the company of capital needed for the maintenance of existing lines. This contradiction did not create problems before 1912, when Farquhar regularly received large loans from European banks. In 1912, however, the Balkan War produced economic chaos, causing credit to dry up in Europe. Unable now to meet the obligations of his large acquisition and start-up costs, Farquhar filed for bankruptcy in 1913.[18]

In 1914 the court of Maine appointed W. Cameron Forbes, former governor of the Philippines, receiver of the company. Forbes hammered out a reorganization plan with creditor banks, allowing the Brazil Railway Company to continue operating in Brazil until 1940. Farquhar remained in charge of various operations within the country. In 1930 Farquhar supported Júlio Prestes in the presidential election, fearing that Getúlio Vargas would break up the Brazil Railway trust if he came to power. Farquhar's fears proved correct, and Vargas nationalized all of the company's holdings via Decree Law 2436 in 1940.[19]

As noted, the efforts and strategy of the Brazil Railway Company did not stop with construction of railroad lines. Inherent in the company's overall strategy was the development of surrounding lands, which would then produce higher transportation revenues for the railroad. The railroad began operation with an eager eye toward the forest reserves of Paraná and Santa Catarina as an important revenue source. The government of Santa Catarina agreed with the viability of this strategy, noting that "our extensive forests of the coastal mountains . . . and above all the enormous pine reserves of the Central Plateau, will, as soon as railroad transportation to the coast is offered, insure the success of any capital invested in its exploitation . . . producing yet another source of prosperity for the State."[20]

Armed with capital equal to US $100,000, in 1907 the Brazil Railway Company created the subsidiary Southern Brazil Lumber and Colonization Company to acquire forest properties in the Três Barras, Paraná, area. It was no accident that the branch railroad line crossed these lands. In the grand scheme, the lumber company would profit from the sale of lumber and the railroad from its transportation.[21]

Farquhar approached the purchase of timber lands with great zeal and a large bankroll. The latter became a necessity as local landowners, sniffing the possibilities of large profits, demanded high prices for their holdings. This led Farquhar to complain later that "many Brazilians are so constituted that, if my Southern Brazil Lumber and Colonization Company offered a reasonable price, they felt their land must be worth twice that and obstinately held out."[22] Nevertheless, the company paid the high prices, and in three years had purchased 227,000 hectares of forest lands.[23] For these holdings it paid roughly seven to ten times the going per hectare price, for a whopping total of US $1,141,429![24]

Having obtained large timber reserves, the Brazil Lumber Company now began constructing two sawmills. In 1910 the company erected and inaugurated a sawmill at Calmon, Santa Catarina. This small mill, located next to the railroad, was soon overshadowed by the giant sawmill at Três Barras. Operation of this latter mill, which became South America's largest, began with a week-long celebration in November 1911.[25]

Modernization and mechanization were the keys to the company's approach to the lumber business. It imported steam-powered cranes and saws. Both were the first of their kind in southern Brazil, allowing the mill to produce 200,000 board feet of lumber per day.[26] This extensive mechanization impressed the American Clayton Cooper, and his 1912 description of the mill gives a vivid impression of the company's presence in the area:

A visit made to . . . "The Southern Brazil Lumber and Colonization Co." at Tres [sic] Barras, Paraná, is clear in my mind. This company, under the control of the Brazil Railway Company, is conducted by American lumbermen who have utilized modern machinery of the latest type. . . . One of the great self-propelling log-rolling machines in use has the capacity of bringing in from distant parts of the forest 150 logs daily. . . . To watch these great trees crashing . . . breaking down the smaller forestry . . . and being finally deposited without the aid of manual strength on long flat cars . . . is a fascinating experience. The big steam loaders bring in the timbers by means of heavy wire cables . . . and no obstacle great or small questions seriously the progress of the pine monsters when the throttles of these forest engines are opened.[27]

To staff its lumber operations, the company hired Polish immigrants living in nearby immigrant colonies. In 1912, 400 men worked at Três Barras, and that number increased to 655 by 1915.[28] Interestingly enough, the state of Paraná objected to this hiring of Polish immigrants. State officials complained that they could no longer find immigrants to work in state construction projects, given the higher salaries paid by the Brazil Lumber Company.[29] The higher salaries did not hide, however, the dangers and demands of the job. Workers put in ten-hour days, and many suffered serious work-related injuries.[30] In 1919 the workers went on strike in protest over bad working conditions.[31]

Due to the financial problems of the Brazil Railway Company, the Três Barras mill shut down between August 1914 and June 1915. Business improved after the reopening, due mainly to a series of large lumber deals in Argentina. In 1916 the company showed a profit of US $166,500.[32] It continued to operate until 1940, when the Brazilian government nationalized the Brazil Railway Company. Today a large military base occupies former company lands around Três Barras.

Colonization in
the Contestado Region

Years of immigration promotion by federal, state, and local authorities explain the presence of Poles available to work for the Brazil Lumber Company. As documented by historians such as Emília Viotti da Costa, Thomas Holloway, and Warren Dean, the closing of the slave trade in the mid-nineteenth century forced the expanding coffee planters of São Paulo to look for alternative sources of plantation labor.[33] Planters sought to attract immigrant labor to Brazil under conditions that would tie them to the coffee plantations. To satisfy these needs the federal government, along with various state governments, began to subsidize the passage of immigrant families to Brazil. In addition, authorities established immigrant houses where families stayed until they found work on a coffee plantation.[34]

To tie immigrant families to the plantations, the Brazilian authorities now worked to block the cheap acquisition of land. In a brilliant essay, Viotti da Costa demonstrates well how the 1850 Land Law resulted from the planters' need to limit immigrant access to land.[35] By *selling* public lands instead of allowing claims by occupation, the law placed landownership out of the reach of the penniless recent immigrants. But Viotti da Costa is quick to explain that colonization could mean different and indeed contradictory things in Brazil.[36] Thus, in frontier and noncoffee areas colonization promised to populate and develop lands held in "waste" by Indians and subsistence peasants. In contrast to the coffee areas, immigrants in these areas would be given access to cheap land through government-sponsored immigration colonies. It was in this spirit that the government of Paraná began a colonization drive in the 1880s and 1890s.

In the mid-1800s the government of Paraná proudly announced its desire to colonize various areas of the state. Surely European immigrants would trade in their small, infertile plots for vast stretches of the southern countryside. After all, southern Brazil was not like the north, where winter freezes occurred annually, and snow fell occasionally. With immigrants within its colonies, Paraná would become an agricultural powerhouse, a breadbasket of the south, providing cheap foodstuffs for the growing cities to the north.[37] By 1908 the state, now part of the Republic, was crowing about its bright future, boldly claiming in English that

this *Eldorado* offers magnificent scope for large Syndicates, Capitalists; great or small who wish to obtain a good return for there [sic] outlay, to the people of all nations who wish to emigrate, the government offers great

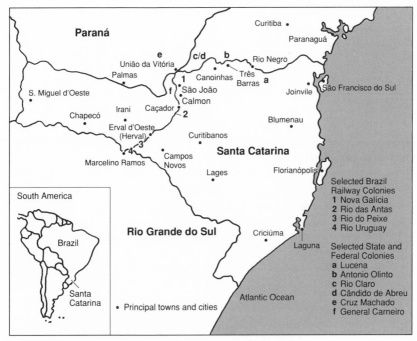

Figure 3 Colonization in the Contestado Region

advantages, and a sure future, and happy homes to the badly paid agricultural-
ist of Europe, or to the unemployed of great cities, who are willing to make
their way in a new Country.

The laws are just, the constitution is liberal, and education and religion
are free in this FREE STATE OF PARANA.[38]

Perhaps as important as economic development, immigration also
promised to "whiten" the local population. Officials wanted Europeans in southern Brazil and not the native peasant population of
caboclos, with its combined black, Indian, and white heritage. Thus,
according to one governor, "In addition to its [economic] relevance,
the importance of immigration increases when one considers it as an
ethnic factor of the first order, destined to purify the national organ-
ism of the vices of its origin and its contact with slavery."[39]

To colonize Paraná the government offered cheap lands in immigrant colonies. Colonists purchased one or more 25-hectare plots.
Given that the colonies comprised the most fertile lands in the
region, colonists could acquire an area large enough to be viable for a
family. A variety of payment plans were established, with the immigrants purchasing land in a series of yearly installments. Once on the

land, colonists helped pay off their debts by working on state construction projects.[40]

Government-sponsored colonization reached the southern boundary of the state in the early 1890s. This area included the valleys along the Peixe, Iguaçu, and Negro rivers, the contested border area between Paraná and Santa Catarina.[41] It was also the zone in which the Brazil Railway Company would operate some fifteen years later. By 1895 over fifteen colonies operated in the area. Some were private developments, but most were government sponsored.

In 1891 government surveyors reached a hilly area some 30 kilometers south of the Negro River. There, long green valleys met hillsides thick with pine and *erva mate* trees. Lots were marked off to be sold to Poles and Germans arriving in Paranaguá. They named the location "Lucena." Given the fertility of these lands the colony soon prospered, and in 1895 the government created more lots out of the surrounding public lands.[42] Lucena continued to grow into the 1900s. The government granted 139 new titles in 1908 and 276 new titles in 1909. All told, these new titles included nearly 10,800 hectares of colony land.[43] In 1909 the government announced that all of the colony's lots were occupied, forcing colonists to purchase private lands surrounding the colony. With this expansion the colony grew to 6,320 residents in 1910, an increase of 235 people in one year.[44] In 1912 the government still mentioned the "great search for land" at Lucena.[45] The result was a bustling colony, one in which "wheat, rye, flax and oats now [grew] where giant pine trees once stood."[46]

To the northwest of Lucena the state of Paraná founded the Rio Claro colony, also in 1891. Located on the northern bank of the Iguaçu River, it occupied public lands next to what were to become the Marechal Mallet and Dorizon railroad stations. Populated by Poles, in 1904 it was referred to as "one of the biggest [colonies] in the state."[47]

In 1906 the colony contained nearly 2,500 occupied and unoccupied lots, for a total area of over 50,000 hectares.[48] By this time the railroad operated in the area, and the colonists quickly took advantage of its presence. In 1908 one official claimed that the Marechal Mallet station was now the most important point of the colony, a place where colonists sold their products and bought necessary items.[49] Blessed with this access to the railroad the colony continued to grow, with the area of occupied lots increasing by 9,000 hectares between 1908 and 1909. A grasshopper plague caused extensive damage in 1909, but by 1912 the cultivated area devoted to corn and oats reached an all-time high. In that year 2,500 families lived in the colony.[50]

In addition to these large colonies, the state also sponsored several small settlements in what was to become the rebellion area. Thirty kilometers north of Lucena, along the Negro River, the government established the Antonio Olinto (Antonio Olyntho) colony in 1895. In 1907 the colony covered 1,476 hectares, and in 1910 contained over 2,000 Polish and Ukrainian residents. These were the immigrants that worked for Brazil Lumber at Três Barras. To the west, near the town of União da Vitória, three colonies operated. In 1908 the largest of these, the General Carneiro colony, housed 880 mostly Polish immigrants.[51]

Judged by these examples, the 1905–12 era signaled the rapid expansion of colonization in the Contestado area. Romário Martins, the noted historian of Paraná, agrees, claiming that "it was in the 1907–14 period that the greatest colonization movement [in southern Paraná] took place." According to Martins, 31,244 immigrants officially entered Paraná during this period.[52] The state of Paraná, however, was not the only entity promoting the colonization of the Contestado region.

In 1909 a federal official explained, "Due to the increasing numbers of immigrants who are entering [Paraná], the government acquired, last October, the Rio Claro property of Colonel Zacharias de Paula Xavier, with an area of 18,000 hectares, which is now being prepared as a new immigrant colony."[53] This new site, designated the Cândido de Abreu colony, was located just north of the present-day Santa Catarina border. It occupied lands adjacent to the Rio Claro colony, which at that time held 1,800 Polish families. Two leagues distant from the railroad station Paulo Frontin, the Candido de Abreu development contained "fertile, well irrigated lands."[54]

In that same year the federal government created a second colony out of public lands ceded by the state of Paraná. Located in the Contestado zone, the government opened the Cruz Machado colony in December 1910. As with other colonies, the Cruz Machado settlement grew up on the banks of the Iguaçu River, in the União da Vitória *município*. At the time of its official inauguration Cruz Machado was already an active place, containing 73,000 hectares of fertile land and 3,837 residents.[55]

To understand the incredible impact of publicly sponsored colonization, one must remember its timing. Colonization began around 1890, reaching its zenith in the 1905–14 period. The process involved massive numbers of immigrants and acreage. The colonies mentioned occupied nearly 200,000 hectares and contained some 25,000 residents. Yet this list was by no means all-inclusive. Colonization was not the exclusive domain of public officials, for it was during this same period that the Brazil Railway Company began to colonize its lands in the Contestado zone. As it did so, it added to the growing amount of once-public lands now in the hands of European immigrants.

In late 1908 a Brazil Railway official handed the following announcement to the editor of a small southern newspaper:

Dear Sir:

> I ask you to inform colonists and other interested persons that the Companhia da Estrada de Ferro São Paulo–Rio Grande [EFSPRG] is now dividing into lots lands of the highest quality, excellent for the planting of corn and other crops, whose area should include roughly 700 lots, along the railroad, 20 kilometers from this city [Campos Novos, Santa Catarina] and close to a [railroad] station. . . . Each 10 *alqueire* plot costs 250$000 . . . to be paid, over the course of eight years, either in cash or with labor. . . . Those who desire land under such conditions should pay the first installment of 80$000.

> F. Bacellar
> Chief of Colonization[56]

Colonization of Brazil Railway lands was under way, and local newspapers heralded the program. The *O Trabalho* newspaper of Curitibanos, Santa Catarina, quickly claimed that 2,000 European colonists were on their way to settle along the railroad line.[57] All trumpeted the quality of colony lands. One local resident claimed that "along the powerful river [the Peixe] are extremely fertile lands, proper for the cultivation of any and all vegetables."[58] A Brazil Railway employee later wrote that the land along "the Rio do Peixe on the São Paulo–Rio Grande is of very good quality for agricultural purposes and upon it diversified crops can be raised."[59]

The creation of immigrant colonies formed a key part of company development plans. Given the terms of the original railroad concession, Brazil Railway now owned vast land reserves along the Itararé–Marcelino Ramos line. The trick was to develop these lands and to promote agricultural production, thereby creating a demand for the transportation services of the railroad. Thus a company official argued that "colonists should be attracted, as they carry a threefold value to the company. They pay for certain of the lands; they add to the value of adjoining lands and make it more saleable, and they bring business to the railroads and ports."[60] Another official believed it good enough for the company to just break even on the development of colonies, for the "ultimate profit is in the transportation of the colonists' freight and property."[61]

The Brazil Railway Company hoped to attract Polish immigrants to the colonies. It also sought Italian immigrants working on coffee plantations in São Paulo, because "their desire to become property owners was well known."[62] To entice prospective colonists, the company offered to finance land purchases and to provide seeds, tools, and technical information. These latter items were to be paid for out of the colonists' harvests. The completion of the Itararé–Marcelino Ramos line guaranteed an easy access to markets. Finally, the federal government promised to pay the transportation of immigrants to the colonies.[63] In 1908 the railroad began surveying the lands included in the 1889 concession. Here we are speaking of lands adjacent to the railroad, lands located in the Peixe River valley. Lands west of the river were in Paraná, and lands to the east belonged to Santa Catarina. According to company officials, the railroad controlled 500,000 hectares along the line. By 1912 they claimed to have surveyed 300,000 hectares of the total.[64]

Under the terms of the grant, the railroad concession should have formed an unbroken string of holdings along the Peixe River. It did not do so because of existing *fazendas* in the area. Eventually the company received lands elsewhere in reimbursement for the area occupied by these claims.[65] Available records indicate the company occupied a total of 137,478 hectares along the Peixe River. As shown in table 1, seven separate concessions formed the grant. It was upon these lands, and others in Santa Catarina, that company colonization began in 1908.

In a flurry of activity the Brazil Railway Company established numerous immigrant colonies before the outbreak of the Contestado Rebellion. The Rio das Antas colony, established out of the 21,000-hectare Rio Prêto concession, contained 186 residents in 1915. To the north, the Nova Galícia colony, on the Lageado Liso and Legru concessions, contained 810 residents in 1910. To the south, near the border with Rio Grande do Sul, the company established the Rio do Peixe (93 residents in 1915) and Rio Uruguay (120 residents in 1915) colonies. Despite its large land concession and seemingly unlimited capital supply, the Brazil Railway Company was unable to succeed with its Peixe Valley colonies. By 1918, for example, Nova Galícia's population had fallen to 669. Rio das Antas's population dropped from 186 in 1915 to a meager 14 in 1918. Company officials blamed their problems on World War I, which shut off European emigration to Brazil. They also blamed state taxes, which created tariff walls and discouraged farmers from selling their crops to buyers in other states. It also seems that company statements as to the quality of the soil had been too optimistic; recently cleared forest lands lost their fertility after a few harvests. Finally, constant attacks against colonists during

Table 1   Brazil Railway Lands in the Peixe River Valley

Concession	Size (in hectares)
Legru	10,566
Lageado Liso	1,770
Rio Prêto	20,928
Rio 15 de Novembro	30,600
Lageado de Leãozinho	40,399
Rio do Peixe	3,025
Rio Uruguay	30,190
Total	137,478

Source: Various "Medições de terras" documents of the Secretaria de Obras Públicas e Colonização de Paraná, Arquivo Pública de Paraná, Curitiba.

the Contestado Rebellion caused many immigrants to flee the area. After the rebellion, the financial troubles of the Brazil Railway Company prevented further investment in the colonization program.[66]

The entrance of the Brazil Railway Company into the Contestado region was fast and furious. Thousands of workers invaded the area to construct the railroad. Teams of surveyors fanned out to demarcate newly acquired lands. Settlers arrived to cultivate these lands, something their brothers and sisters were doing in the state-sponsored immigrant colonies. For its part, the Brazil Lumber Company was busy buying the best woodlands in the region—causing land prices to skyrocket in its wake. Many long-time residents now found their access to land blocked, while local elites entered into land and labor deals with the capitalist enterprise. These events did not take place gradually over the course of many years. Instead, the Contestado region underwent an almost total transformation in less than a decade.

It is the task of the following chapters to describe this transformation in detail. Who were the winners and losers? What role did local landowners play in the process? How did local peasants react in the face of threats to their subsistence? Answers to these questions provide a detailed feel for the crisis engendered by the entrance of capitalism into the Contestado. With this knowledge we can then understand why a rebellion erupted in the southern *sertão* and why it did so in a millenarian fashion.

4

The Deadly Triumvirate

State Power, the Brazil

Railway Company,

and Local Landowners

in the Contestado

In 1908, in the Lajes municipality of Santa Catarina, dona Esperança Alves sought to purchase some 300 hectares of public land from the state of Santa Catarina. Dona Esperança claimed that "at present the land serves no useful purpose." District land agent Carlos Schmidt seconded this claim, adding that the lands were "of no use to the State." He went on to note that Dona Esperança was a wealthy woman, meaning that she could easily purchase the concession in one payment. No mention of squatters appears in the agent's report. The government approved the sale on 8 February 1909.

Judging from the documents, this concession proceeded without any controversy. A telegram from agent Schmidt to Florianópolis soon betrayed this sense of normality. In it he complained that "having initiated the survey of Esperança Alves' lands was violently impeded [STOP] Elias Lourenço Rodrigues threatened death if work continued [STOP] Forced to retire, wait government response." Something about the proposed sale, which was handled as a routine and uncontested transaction, upset Rodrigues, not to mention many others. The problem was that the village of Arraial de Canoas occupied the land granted to Esperança Dias Alves![1]

In April 1909, Lajes municipal superintendent Belisário Ramos sent an angry telegram of protest to the governor of Santa Catarina. In it he traced the history of Arraial de Canoas, placing its founding some 150 years earlier. He pointed to a document that ordered the construction of a church for the village. He also noted an 1847 provincial order halting a land sale in the area precisely because of the existence of Canoas village. At the current time the lands in question contained many residents, all descendants of the area's first settlers. In 1909 the town contained "two chapels, a public school, and the district police headquarters." In the face of the evidence the governor canceled the concession to Alves, turning the land over to the Lajes municipal council.[2]

The Canoas controversy illustrates the tenuous access Contestado residents maintained to their lands at the turn of the century. Land agent Carlos Schmidt ignored the unavoidable presence of residents on these public lands. No doubt dona Esperança's ability to purchase an area of state-owned lands in just one payment pleased government officials in Florianópolis. Perhaps Alves paid Schmidt to overlook the presence of residents on the property. If Schmidt ignored the existence of an entire village on public lands, how many other agents failed to note the multitude of squatter families on public lands involved in state sales?

The entrance of the railroad into the Contestado set in motion a process that would soon challenge the access thousands of Contestado subsistence peasants and *agregados* maintained to their land. Indeed, the development of the Contestado—the building of the railroad and the establishment of immigrant colonies—created a deadly triumvirate that would eventually expel thousands of local residents. As one part of this triumvirate, the state governments of Santa Catarina and Paraná threatened peasant access to land in two ways. First, as we have seen, they dedicated huge tracts of land to the establishment of immigrant colonies. Second, as land values rose these governments began to sell their vast reserves of public-owned land.

As a second member of the triumvirate, the railroad expelled countless locals in its struggle to establish control over the hundreds of thousands of acres it obtained from the federal government. In addition, its subsidiary, the Brazil Lumber Company, did likewise in its quest for the best forest hectarage in the region. Finally, a few powerful Contestado landowners joined the "march for progress" and began buying and selling large tracts of land, eventually expelling local *posseiros* and even their own *agregados*.

The actions of this triumvirate produced a regional land tenure revolution. For the first time the subsistence-oriented tenure pattern came under attack. It no longer made sense for *patrões* to grant *agregados* usufruct rights to hundreds of hectares to insure their own claims to holdings. As we shall see, then, the revolution in land tenure could not have happened without the crumbling of the patron-client relations that *agregados* and *posseiros* once relied upon to protect their possessions.

Brazil: Commercialization and
the Privatization of Land

To understand the land tenure transformation in the Contestado we must first review various land tenure issues at the national level. For centuries land in Brazil served as much as a status symbol as it did a means of production. Legal title to land could be obtained only through a royal grant known as a *sesmaria*. According to Emília Viotti da Costa, "The king's decision to concede the favor was based on his evaluation of the applicant, which involved considering his social status, personal qualities, and service to the Crown."[3] Thus, she argues, "although profit was the mainspring of the economy, control over men and land was as important in defining a landowner's social status as in securing capital accumulation."[4]

One should not think, however, that only *sesmaria* recipients occupied land in colonial Brazil. Virgin land was plentiful in that era, and thus, "Land could be acquired by squatting as well as by royal grant."[5] One also found *agregados* living in the countryside, working a piece of the planter's land in return for performing various services for the owner. These "free" groups were of course joined in the countryside by plantation slaves.

The conception of land as a guarantee of one's social status, a concept never challenged by colonial sugar and mining production, began to change in the early independence period. At that time the Industrial Revolution led England to concentrate on industrial production and to turn to agricultural imports to feed its population. A revolution in shipping facilitated this strategy, allowing freighters to carry more weight and travel longer distances.[6] With the resulting expansion of the international market acting as a catalyst for such a change, Brazilian landowners intensified their tropical agricultural production for sale in Europe. Land now gained increasing value as a means of production. Through it fortunes could be acquired by international sales of agricultural goods. As explained by Viotti da Costa, "The ownership of land always conferred social prestige, at first because it implied the Crown's recognition of the grantee's merits, then because it implied economic power. In the first case, then, economic power derived from social prestige while in the second case the reverse was true."[7]

The international demand for tropical agricultural goods produced the explosive growth of Brazilian coffee production in the second half of the nineteenth century. By 1901 Brazil grew three-fourths of the world's total supply. During this era then, "the center of the Brazilian economy moved south and southwest," with the impetus "the 'march' of coffee, as planters found it cheaper to break new ground than to recycle the plantation soils whose yields were dropping."[8] Such a rush for land would soon outstrip the ability of colonial laws to regulate landownership in Brazil.

Changes in the productive sphere in Brazil led to the passage of the *Lei de Terras* (Land Law) of 1850. With its passage, gone were the days where one obtained land through a royal grant. Legal title to land was now available only by purchase. According to the law, *sesmaria* recipients now had to legitimate their titles with a land survey and the payment of a land tax. "Squatters" could also receive title if they could prove that they actually cultivated the land in question. No one could claim more land than the largest *sesmaria* grant in the area. Revenues were to be used to pay for colonization and further land surveys.[9]

In her cogently argued work on the 1850 Land Law, Viotti da Costa notes that the new economic view of land did not become dominant in all of Brazil at once. Coffee planters in Rio de Janeiro and São Paulo led the way by rapidly expanding production to meet the growing European demand for their product. "The extent and rapidity of this transition depended on the degree to which a society was permeated by capitalist values."[10] Whereas such values became important in central Brazil in the early nineteenth century, developments in the Contestado region took on a much slower pace.

The increasing value of land, which prompted the passage of the national 1850 Land Law, did not produce similar action in Santa Catarina and Paraná until the end of the nineteenth century. By that time European colonization had entered into full swing (see chapter 3), especially along the Iguaçu and Negro rivers separating Paraná and Santa Catarina. It was also during that time that João Teixeira Soares received the governmental concession to build a north-south railroad through the interiors of these two states. Even though the line was not completed until 1910, as early as 1897 land agents noted the importance the railroad would have for interior production and commerce.[11] The trend towards a conception of land as an economic good now permeated the region. Some people began to view undefined, untitled holdings as obstacles to the rational use of the land. Santa Catarina and Paraná officials were quite willing to promote this "rationalization" process, for they held visions of state coffers overflowing with land legitimation and purchase revenues.

Paraná, Santa Catarina, and
the Sale of Public Lands

In September 1895 the government of Santa Catarina passed a law designed to rationalize the registration and use of land in that state. The law required *sesmaria* holders to revalidate their titles. Squatters could now gain legal title by proving *morada habitual*, that is, "customary residence," implying permanent continuous cultivation of the area in question before 1895. They then had to pay for the state survey of their claim and ultimately to purchase it for a minimum per hectare price. The land could be bought at once or over time, with payments made over a six-year period. Such *morada habitual* claims could not exceed 1,089 hectares for crop lands and 4,356 hectares for grazing lands. Failure to file a *morada habitual* petition would eventually result in the loss of a *posseiro*'s claim to the holding.[12]

A third section of the law called for the sale of *terras devolutas*. Literally meaning "unoccupied lands," this term referred to public lands, once the property of the national government, which had been turned over to the states via article 64 of the Brazilian Republican Constitution (1891). At this time the goverment fixed the sale price of these lands at 1.5 *milreis* per hectare. To prevent illegal actions by land-hungry *fazendeiros* and *posseiros*, the government warned that "we will be obligated to move, with a complete loss of any improvements, all persons who occupy terras devolutas, chop down or burn any trees, plant any crops . . . or practice any other act of possession."[13]

The entire *morada habitual* and *terras devolutas* process acted against the interests of the smallest, most isolated *posseiros*. To gain title by *morada habitual*, one had to file a claim at a district land office. This would be virtually impossible for an illiterate, isolated *posseiro*, especially if he lived some 50 to 100 kilometers from the nearest land agent. Then, even if a *posseiro* succeeded in filing a claim, he still had to pay a minimum purchase price and pay for a government survey of the land. Failure to meet any of these requirements meant that the *posseiro* lost all legal claim to the holding.

The smallest *posseiros* also lost in the sale of public lands. To make such a purchase, one had to post a thirty-day public notice of intent to buy a certain piece of property. If no one lodged a protest within that period, the sale could proceed. How likely was the small *posseiro*, who lived far from the town square, to know of the posting of a proposed sale that might affect his holding? How many even knew of the *terras devolutas* law? To add to the *posseiro*'s woes, the district land agent was most often an acquaintance of the area's large landowners. All of these factors threatened the small *posseiro's* access to land.

A review of the Santa Catarina public land concession figures from 1902 to 1913 demonstrates the magnitude of changes in land tenure during that period. Although figures are only partial for some years, and nonexistent for others, they nevertheless present a solid base upon which to estimate total concession hectarage. They also allow us to estimate the number of Contestado residents affected by the concessions. Here the term "concession" refers to *morada habitual* and *terras devolutas* sales and not to the legitimation of existing titles. Concession numbers from the present-day Paraná portion of the Contestado are not included, thus the figures represent only the three Santa Catarina Contestado municipalities: Lajes, Campos Novos, and Curitibanos.

As shown in table 2, a conservative estimate places total Santa Catarina public land concessions from 1902 to 1913 at nearly 255,000 hectares. Verified figures from the years 1909 and 1910 show that roughly 60 percent of all Santa Catarina concessions for those two years occurred in the Contestado zone. Using this percentage for the other years, this means that the state of Santa Catarina sold some 153,000 hectares of public land in the Contestado between 1902 and 1913. In addition, between 1909 and 1911 the railroad received title to 137,478 once federally owned hectares along the Peixe River, all of which, hence, were also in the Contestado zone. Between 1902 and 1913 then, more than 290,000 hectares of public lands were privatized in the Contestado.[14]

Comparisons of the total area of the Santa Catarina portion of the Contestado zone, its population, and the area included in public land concessions illustrate the revolution in land tenure that shook the region. With an area of some 1.85 million hectares, and a 1907 population of 46,000, the Contestado comprised one-fourth of the total area of Santa Catarina and roughly one-fifth of the state's rural population. In spite of its area and size, however, this region experienced well over 60 percent of the state's total land privatization before the rebellion!

One-fifth of Santa Catarina's rural population bore the brunt of the state's revolution in land tenure. If the Contestado's population spread evenly over its total area of 1.85 million hectares, then roughly 15 percent, or nearly 7,000 people, were affected by the transformation in land tenure. This is the absolute minimum estimate, however, and one that assumes that all of the region's 1.85 million hectares were inhabitable. This was probably not the case. Much more likely, the Contestado population concentrated in the conces-

Table 2   Santa Catarina Public Land Concessions, 1902–13

Year	Hectares Verified	Hectares Estimated	Concessions Verified	Concessions Estimated
1902		20,060	590	
1903		14,076		414*
1904		17,000		500
1905		17,000		500
1906	23,817		699	
1907		17,000		500
1908		17,000		500
1909	31,076		603	
1910	50,167			
1911		14,858	437	
1912		12,444	366	
1913		24,276	714	
Total Hectares		254,774		

*Estimate based on a reported 207 concessions for the first semester of 1903. Given the verified concession numbers from 1902, 1906, 1909, 1911, 1912, and 1913, I arrived at a conservative 500 concessions per year estimate. Given verified hectare/concession figures for 1906, 1909, 1917, 1919, 1920, and 1923, I arrived at a conservative 34 hectares per concession estimate. These, then, are the figures used to estimate complete concession numbers for the years 1902–13. Sources listed in note 14.

sion areas, which, as in the case of the railroad lands along the Peixe River, represented the region's most fertile areas. In this case it is entirely possible that land privatization affected as much as 30 percent of the Contestado's population. The revolution in land tenure, then, touched the lives of as many as 15,000 Contestado residents.[15]

Figures on public land sales present a general picture of the changes in land tenure that shook the Contestado region during the late nineteenth and early twentieth centuries. They do not, however, give us a detailed description of how the land sale process worked to deprive residents of their access to land. They cannot convey the anarchy and violence that the sale of public lands produced in the Contestado.

The secondary literature on the Contestado Rebellion also fails to give a detailed account of the land question. In his excellent work *Os errantes do novo século*, Duglas Teixeira Monteiro spends but one full page on the sale of *terras devolutas*.[16] In another book on the

Contestado, Maurício Vinhas de Queiroz acknowledges that many squatters lost their land during this era. His argument, however, relies on undocumented general assertions. He writes that during the late 1800s unoccupied public land became scarce as more and more ex-*agregados* established their own ranches. With the transfer of public lands to the states, many *posseiros* fell victim to *fazendeiro* land grabs. Thus, "expulsions became more frequent . . . and squatters were left with nowhere to go, or were forced to accept work conditions that under other circumstances they would never have accepted."[17] These undocumented assertions, unfortunately, end the author's discussion of the subject.

One must turn to various state and federal documents to obtain information on how people lost their access to land in the Contestado. Most helpful are the *terras devolutas* records kept by the government of Santa Catarina. In the Contestado, however, not only the sale of public lands but also the legitimation of existing titles produced conflict and loss of land. Newspaper accounts and state land agent reports illustrate this aspect of the changes in land tenure patterns.

The process of rising land values due to commercial development, in combination with government efforts to rationalize landholding and sell public lands, created an explosive and chaotic situation. State officials complained bitterly and continually about two things: illegal *fazendeiro* land claims and the occupation of public lands by poor squatters. Related to the first complaint, we must remember that *fazenda* boundaries were never clearly marked. Many documents refer to boulders, trees, and creeks as boundary markers. When faced with the legitimation of their titles, *fazendeiros* rushed to extend their claims to cover as wide an area as possible. This land grabbing threatened state interests, for *fazendeiros* claimed public lands as their own, lands that the state sought to sell for its own revenue purposes.

The comments of land agents on this activity show a sense of despair on the part of government officials. One government circular complained of "the state of anarchy of state-owned lands" and ordered that no private land surveys be conducted without the presence of a government official.[18]

In another statement the government spoke "of those [*fazendeiros*] occupying large areas who wish to escape compliance with the law of 1895."[19] Owners were cultivating everything in sight so as to claim that these lands had always comprised a portion of their holding. Thus, *fazendeiros* were continually "extending the area devoted to crops in order to create the appearance of habitual cultivation for title legitimization purposes."[20]

In 1907 the Santa Catarina public lands director estimated that as many as 500,000 hectares were illegally claimed as private holdings. *Fazendeiros* were making a mockery of the whole process, because a lack of funding prevented government enforcement of the law. As an example of this, the land director spoke of the Fazenda da Entrada near Curitibanos. There the government discovered that the Fagundes family illegally claimed 20,149 hectares. These were 20,000 hectares that the government could be selling as public land. But to complicate matters even further, landowners were selling these illegally claimed lands to other parties.[21]

Newspapers of the era regularly reported conflicts over the legitimation of landholdings. Unfortunately, these accounts do not mention incidences where *posseiros* lost land due to *fazendeiro* land grabs. This should not surprise us, given the position of these poor squatters and the pervasive elitism of the newspapers. They do illustrate, however, the kinds of tensions aroused by title disputes between large landowners.

One particularly well-reported case involved Generoso Domingues de Oliveira, Caetano de Oliveira, and their dispute over the Fazenda Bom Retiro in the Lajes municipality. In May 1909 Generoso requested the government survey of Bom Retiro so that he could legitimate his title to lands there. Four months later, Caetano disputed Generoso's claim, arguing that the latter was illegally occupying public lands. In response, Generoso charged Caetano with illegally occupying lands that he (Generoso) had earlier purchased from the state.

As tensions heightened at Bom Retiro, each ordered their cowboys to confiscate the other's cattle that grazed on the disputed land. Accusations continued for years, and in 1914 one João Martins de Moraes entered into the fray, accusing Generoso of illegally occupying lands he had earlier purchased from the state. By 1918 the area had still not been surveyed![22]

Perhaps it was disputes like this one—a case erupting due to an attempted state land survey—that led the editors of one regional newspaper to condemn the meddling of state officials in land disputes. Local officials could handle these cases, they argued, and such meddling only made "the process more complicated by superfluous expenditures and the establishment of a dual jurisdiction that [could] only plunge the situation into anarchy."[23]

Land officials from Paraná and Santa Catarina also complained of squatters on public lands. In 1900 a government surveyor from Paraná noted that in the Peixe River valley "one finds many squatters" and that "their numbers continue to grow each day."[24] In 1904 a Santa Catarina official lodged a similar complaint: "Even though the law guarantees them the first chance to purchase the land they occupy, the majority are so poor that not even with small payments extended over many years will they be able to afford the concession."[25]

Had squatters been able to afford the purchase of land concessions, this might have satisfied revenue-hungry state officials. Their inability to do so produced a standard comment: the existence of these people on public lands hindered the development of the area. Typical was this complaint:

Squatters, seeking to live by hunting and only the most rudimentary forms of crop production, are invading the best lands . . . beautiful stretches of virgin forest . . . at a loss to the State, while it would be better to reserve [these lands] for an intelligent and systematic colonization effort.[26]

Most disturbing to officials were the "hundreds of families" squatting on lands next to the railroad line.[27] To deal with them, Paraná officials went so far as to develop a plan whereby squatters could lease plots in another part of the state. But the people there wanted no part of this scheme, causing one official to speak quite candidly of the "just resentments on the part of our countrymen of the *sertão*, that, not without reason, often associate the ease with which foreigners receive state concessions of vast land holdings, and the stinginess they themselves face when dealing with the State."[28]

Public land sale documents best illustrate the damages squatters suffered from sales of *terras devolutas* in the Contestado. Here it is important to remember three key components of the 1895 Santa Catarina Land Law. First, *posseiros* could legitimate their untitled claims only if they could prove *morada habitual*, that is, a record of continual cultivation of a plot. Second, even with a *morada habitual* claim, the *posseiro* was still forced to purchase the claim. Third, any party could purchase unoccupied public lands by announcing an intent to purchase and posting it in a public place.

The records show that some poor *posseiros* did manage to gain legal title via a *morada habitual* claim. In 1905 Cecilho José Anphiloquio received a *morada habitual* concession of 30 hectares in the Lajes municipality. Six years later, in the same municipality, Aureo João Cabral received a 30-hectare concession to be paid for over the course of five years. More common, however, were cases like that of Delfino Telles Cordeiro, who in 1913 filed a *morada habitual* claim in the Canoinhas municipality. In 1916 a government official noted that Cordeiro died in a rebel attack during the Contestado uprising. Because his widow now had no money to pay for the concession, the official rejected the application.[29] The Cordeiros had lost their legal access to land.

Much more prevalent in the Santa Catarina documents are examples of large *terras devolutas* puchases not made with a *morada habitual* claim. The Santa Catarina records illustrate the often shady nature of these large transactions. Consider the case of a 1911 *terras devolutas* purchase of 1,500 hectares by Frederico and Mathias Graneman. The men wished to expand their cattle operation onto lands adjacent to the *fazenda* they already owned. In his report the district land agent approved the sale but did not mention whether or not *posseiros* already lived on the land. The state director of public lands, however, argued against the sale to the Granemans, given that they already owned a large *fazenda*. Despite this objection Governor Vidal Ramos granted the concession.

Several items stand out in this transaction. It was a large request, covering 1,500 hectares. Just three months elapsed between the initial request and final concession (June 1911–September 1911), compared to an average waiting period of over a year for most *terras devolutas* sales. The state sold the land for only 0.75 *reis* per square meter, a remarkably low price considering that sales to the poorest *posseiros* usually went for 1.5 *reis* per square meter. The timing and location of the sale are equally revealing. Located in the São Sebastião district of Curitibanos municipality, the land was near the railroad line, with the concession granted only a few months after the completion of the railroad. It was here, in São Sebastião, that the Contestado Rebellion erupted just one year later.[30]

This example hints at the collusion of large landowners and government officials in the sale of public lands (of course, many large landowners were government officials). Such cooperation was likely to occur because each side had something to gain from the deal. Large sales promised much revenue for the state, not to mention possible bribes to officials during the concession process. *Fazendeiros* received cheap access to titled land at a time when and in an area where the clear ownership of land was becoming increasingly important. The Graneman case is not an isolated example. Many *fazendeiros* expanded their landholdings through *terras devolutas* concessions, displacing, with government acquiescence, squatters already living on those lands.

Two cases from Canoinhas highlight *fazendeiro* land grabs, the loss of land by *posseiros*, and the ways in which landowners violated the 1895 Land Law with impunity. In the first case, in 1915 Theodore Grein, Jr. sought 250 hectares of public land with a *morada habitual* claim. Grein, a self-described large landowner, argued that he had cultivated the land for years, and that he had built several structures on the land. In 1916 the district land agent reported (a) that Grein did not cultivate the lands in question, and (b) that another family in fact occupied and cultivated the holding. The agent felt that this unnamed family should be given preference in any purchase application.

In 1918 the state land director ordered the district agent to encourage the anonymous family to file a *morada habitual* claim. If they filed it did little good. Grein received the title to the 250 hectares in August 1923. That is, he received the land in spite of having lied to the authorities, in spite of the fact that he never occupied the land, and in spite of the presence of another family on the land.[31]

In a second Canoinhas case, João Vicente Ferreira sought to purchase 360 hectares of *terras devolutas* for "industrial purposes" (*fins industriais*) in 1915. As in the Grein example, the district land agent discovered that several other people occupied and cultivated this land. Again, the agent felt that those already on the land should be allowed to press for a *morada habitual* concession. The agent's action proved irrelevant, since Ferreira eventually gained the legal title to the 360 hectares.[32]

As shown by these examples, even when agents in the field argued for squatters' rights, this in no way insured that these people gained title to the land. At any point on the bureaucratic line an official could ignore squatters' rights to first claim based on *morada habitual*. But again, we must remember that most land conflicts never made it to the bureaucratic level. A land law based on the ability of a squatter to come to the town square, read a sale notice, and protest said sale was not designed to protect their rights. In actual practice, force probably decided the outcome of contested local claims, and the official land sale documents do not tell us how many squatters the landowners simply killed or expelled in their drive for a *terras devolutas* concession.

As part of the *terras devolutas* sale process, the establishment of government-sponsored immigrant colonies reinforced the land tenure transformation in the Contestado. As described in detail in chapter 3, colonization involved thousands of hectares of fertile land and thousands of immigrants. Between 1890 and 1914 some 25,000 colonists moved onto nearly 200,000 hectares. The federal government did not hesitate to purchase large areas of land to attend to the needs of the ever-increasing numbers of immigrants. For example, in 1909 it acquired 18,000 hectares from *coronel* Zacharias Paula de Xavier to create the Candido de Abreu colony near União da Vitória. In the deal *coronel* Zacharias pocketed nearly US $55,000.[33]

A colonization effort of this magnitude placed severe pressures on land tenure patterns in the Contestado and led to conflicts between *posseiros* and colonists. The *posseiros* usually lost in these conflicts. In one *relatório* (government report), a Paraná official commented with satisfaction that at the Rio Claro colony, "The controversy has ended between colonists and a neighboring *posseiro*, who claimed control of a section of land in the western portion of the colony. Once it was verified that the *posseiro* had no legal right to the land, titles were issued to the colonists."[34] At the Lucena colony a Paraná official urged land-hungry colonists to expand their holdings "in order to increase crop production and accommodate the colony's excess population." After all, the official continued, "The process of land accumulation is simple."[35]

Not only *posseiros* but also Indians suffered from the wave of immigration into the Contestado. For many years Indians under the rule of cacique Paulino Arak Xo lived on *terras devolutas* between the Peixe, Jucaré, and Baile rivers, in what is today the state of Santa Catarina. In 1913 the government of Paraná (which at that time controlled these lands) ordered the Indians to move. The reason: the lands were "granted to the Immigration Service for use in European colonization."[36] And in a more oblique reference to expulsion, one commentator on the Antonio Olinto colony proclaimed that due to the efforts of Polish immigrants, "The savage forest which was once home only to Indians is today the site of fertile croplands . . . where a sense of progress and vitality reigns."[37]

Plans for an immigrant colony that never materialized provide a final example of the threats *posseiros* faced from the colonization aspect of the movement in public lands. In 1907 the municipal council of Campos Novos voted to create such a colony on municipal lands along the Peixe River. Wishing to take advantage of the railroad entrance into the area, they set aside 300 hectares near the future site of the Uruguay railroad station. Lots of 20 and 50 hectares would be sold, payable in annual installments of 20 *milreis*.[38]

People already lived on the fertile lands now designated for the colony. But with economic development and a hefty profit on the horizon, the council had no plan to protect the holdings of these *posseiros*. Article 9 of the municipal immigrant colony law clearly stated: "No one can occupy government lands until after having requested and obtained legal title, under the penalty of a 100$000 [one hundred *milreis*] fine and loss of any improvements on the land." In fact, the council planned on expelling the *posseiros* from their land. Article 10 warned: "Those now living on lands designated for the new colony must [if they wish to stay] request a lot in a different area of the colony, and vacate the land they now occupy. [*Posseiros*] will be given until the end of harvest to obey this order." To stay in the area, *posseiros* would have to begin the 20-*milreis* payments. Even if they decided to purchase a lot, the municipality would still force them to move somewhere else within the colony. And finally, the rest were given only until the completion of the next harvest to leave the land.[39]

It appears that the Campos Novos municipal council never opened the proposed colony. Nevertheless, the proposal shows that the expulsion of *posseiros* was the likely outcome of any colonization process in the Contestado. Lands along the Peixe River and the railroad track were now too valuable to be left to subsistence-level *posseiros*.

As economic development entered into high gear in the Contestado, once-unimportant stretches of *terras devolutas* now took on a newfound significance. The dramatic impact of this change brought tears to the eyes of one elderly Contestado resident in 1984. While standing on the sight of an old rebel redoubt, João Paes de Farias remembered that at one time "all lands were public" and thus it was easy to be a squatter. Today, he noted sadly, "All lands are privately owned."[40]

The Brazil Railway Company
and the Acquisition of Company Lands

At the same time that the Paraná and Santa Catarina governments began selling *terras devolutas*, the Brazil Railway Company, through its subsidiaries the Estrada de Ferro São Paulo–Rio Grande (EFSPRG) and the Southern Brazil Lumber Company, began to survey, occupy, and improve the vast holdings it now controlled in the Contestado. The company claimed ownership of over 500,000 hectares through the EFSPRG concession. By 1915 they had surveyed some 300,000 hectares of this total.[41] Such a large grant promised to create conflict on several levels in the region.

The completion of the railroad through the Contestado placed the governments of Paraná and Santa Catarina in a difficult position. At this time the Brazil Railway Company wished to begin the colonization of its lands, but found its efforts blocked by *fazendeiros* holding recently legitimated titles to holdings within the concession area. It seems that for many years the two states ignored the terms of the 1889 concession and legitimated claims. The company demanded the return of lands alienated from the concession. The states now faced angry landowners on one side and the powerful Brazil Railway Company on the other.

In their defense both states claimed that they alienated lands before the precise boundaries of the concession were established. This was a weak position. Lawyers from both Santa Catarina and Paraná recognized the strength of the Brazil Railway legal position and urged their governors to find a compromise solution. After much tough talk both states offered to grant the company lands located in other areas. The Brazil Railway Company agreed, and took possession of thousands of hectares in western Paraná and Santa Catarina. This produced a situation where company lands along the railroad line in the Peixe River valley (approximately 25,000 hectares) mixed with private holdings.[42]

The checkerboard pattern of company and private holdings along the Peixe River insured a real estate boom in the area. Land sale notices filled local newspapers, all boasting legitimated titles and a close proximity to the Peixe River and the railroad line. In Campos Novos such notices crowded the pages of the town's two newspapers in 1909 and 1910. One notice spoke of "crop lands, with a legitimate title, covering an area of 300 hectares near the Peixe River in the *município.*" Another proclaimed: "FOR SALE. A plot of land located on the left bank of the Barra Verde River, near lands owned by the E.F. São Paulo–Rio Grande." In 1910 one landowner purchased an ad for a particularly well-placed holding: "For sale, scrub and cultivated lands, along with an excellent house, located near Rio Bonito, just six kilometers from the E.F.S. Paulo–Rio Grande." Two other ads that year offered a total of 2,300 hectares for sale along the EFSPRG line.[43]

As with the commotion created by public land sales, the survey and occupation of Brazil Railway lands led to confrontations between the company and private individuals. The state of Santa Catarina regularly ordered company officials to appear "armed with their documents" at state land surveys. The company itself ordered local *fazendeiros* to appear at the surveys of company holdings.[44]

Some landowners charged Brazil Railway with acting in a less than legal fashion in dealing with various land claims. Consider the case of the brothers Antonio and João Almeida of Campos Novos. In 1910 the brothers appeared in the town of Campos Novos to protest actions taken by Brazil Railway lawyer Marcelino Nogueira, Jr. According to the protest, Nogueira tricked dona Theodora Maria Francisca, the mother of the Almeida brothers, into signing 1,352 hectares over to the railroad. Dona Theodora had recently inherited these lands from her husband.

According to the Almeida brothers, Nogueira approached their mother and told her that a survey of her husband's claim revealed 2,704 hectares in excess of his legal title. Nogueira then allegedly threatened dona Theodora with legal action by the state against this claim. Such legal action could be avoided, he then supposedly said, if dona Theodora would sign over, via *coronel* Henrique Rupp, 1,352 hectares to the railroad. Faced with this threat she signed the land over to the company.

As part of their protest the Almeida brothers stated that their mother was eighty years old, illiterate, and nearly deaf. Given these conditions, she should not have been allowed to make a deal with the railroad. Besides, she did not have the legal authority to dispose of land that by law required the consent of future inheritors. In summary, the brothers argued that (a) they in no way recognized the rights of EFSPRG to the land, and (b) that it had not yet been proven that their father held 2,704 hectares of illegally claimed land. Indeed, they argued, it was the railroad administration that determined that this excess existed, but the company was "an interested party, and, therefore, suspect." The brothers further noted that EFSPRG's use of trickery proved that the company held no legal right to the land.[45]

This case, in which the final disposition is unfortunately unknown, illustrates the kinds of issues that arose as the railroad expanded and solidified its presence in the Contestado. The Almeida case, however, involved a family with sizable holdings *and* title to these lands. What of the squatters without such advantages? Secondary sources speak of these people only in passing. Monteiro simply mentions the "expulsion of local residents" by the company. Vinhas de Queiroz claims, without sources, that "1911 began with the first expulsions of the squatters that occupied the area given to the Estrada de Ferro São Paulo–Rio Grande."[46] Fortunately, our sources provide a more detailed account of the destiny of these people in the face of EFSPRG actions.

To the officers of the Brazil Railway Company, the year 1911 looked promising. In December 1910 the company completed the line between União da Vitória and Marcelino Ramos. Now was the time to develop company lands along the route and to populate the area with European immigrants—immigrants who would grow cash crops and ship the produce on the railroad. As part of this plan the company announced, in full-page ads:

Notice, it is expressly prohibited to invade or occupy lands belonging to the Companhia E. de Ferro–S. Paulo–Rio Grande, lands located on both sides of the Peixe River, and in other areas. These company lands have been, or are now being, surveyed by the company.

From this day forward the company prohibits any usage of this land, and warns those now occupying these lands that they will face legal action . . . making them responsible for all damages and losses. . . .

For information on the purchase of company lands, please contact F. E. Cole, company land agent.[47]

Percival Farquhar's project to develop the southern interior now called for the identification and expulsion of squatters on Brazil Railway lands.

Company survey records testify to the existence of small-scale squatters on lands along the railroad line. Small dots on company maps identified *"casas de posseiros"* (*posseiro* houses). The surveyor of the Lageado do Leãozinho Brazil Railway claim wrote: "One finds small plots planted with rice, sugar cane, and cotton." In an equally oblique reference, the surveyor noted that on the Rio Uruguay claim, "One finds small plots planted with cotton, rice, sugar cane, orange, and banana trees." These crops did not grow on their own in the wild but were grown by small *posseiros*. In one survey, at least, the surveyor spoke directly of these squatters, mentioning the "huts and small houses inhabited by 'nationals' [squatters] that have established themselves without any type of property title."[48]

The presence of squatters on company lands greatly concerned company officials, enough so that complaints of their existence frequently appear in the official documents. Rosângela Cavallazzi da Silva includes two such examples in her master's thesis on the Brazil Railway Company.[49] In the first, the railroad was selling land in the Campos Novos area to one Theodore Jean Leon Capelle. The company warned Capelle of squatters on the land and issued the following disclaimer: "It is the problem of the buyer any questions which arise due to squatters on the land to be sold. The seller cannot be held responsible for any conflicts which emerge. . . . However, the seller will lend its moral support to the buyer in this matter [of the squatters]."[50]

In a second case the EFSPRG leased the *erva mate* collection rights on company lands in western Santa Catarina to *coronel* Manoel dos Santos Marinho. The document makes it quickly apparent that the company granted the concession as much to rid the area of squatters as to generate *erva mate* revenue. Here we have direct evidence of the company's desire to expel squatters, for in the contract the company flatly demanded that "the leaseholder is obliged to expel squatters found on the involved lands, in order that within twelve months no more squatters will be found on said lands."[51]

How many squatters lost their access to land as the result of EFSPRG actions? A variety of contemporary observers have noted, some with displeasure, others not, the expulsion activities of the company. Private Demerval Peixoto of the federal forces fighting in the Contestado condemned the actions of the railroad in regards to squatters. In his words the abrupt expulsion of squatters by the company contributed to the outbreak of the rebellion. He condemned the colonization "of certain areas with foreign elements, which deprives current residents of their land rights." He then criticized the "incorrect manner in which certain colonization officials, like the one at Rio das Antas . . . [provoked] the exit of long time *posseiros.*"[52] Because of the expulsions, wrote Peixoto, people in the Contestado hated the railroad. Thus, "the railroad was for them a monster: it expelled them from their claims on once government-owned lands." For these people EFSPRG stood for "Estrada Feita Somente Para Roubar p'ro Governo" (Railroad Built Only to Steal for the Government).[53]

Still smarting from the loss of state lands to the Brazil Railway Company, the government of Paraná also complained of EFSPRG expulsions of *posseiros.* Ironically, this official anger probably did not result from a genuine concern for the squatters. It more likely emerged from the wish that the state itself controlled these lands so that it could be the one to profit from land sales. Nevertheless, officials noted the expulsions:

In regards to the use of lands granted to the Company . . . a question of grave importance for those involved in controversies . . . the Government should analyze the situation to better protect the rights of numerous citizens who, in good faith, have occupied parts of the lands in question. These people are now being threatened with expulsion by the Company, according to reports received by the [governor of Paraná].[54]

Benjamin Scoz, a lifetime resident of Lajes, Santa Catarina, and soldier in the Santa Catarina force that fought against the rebels, remembers the actions of the railroad. He recalls that both the company and the government of Santa Catarina kicked *posseiros* off lands they occupied along the Peixe River. Benjamin remembers it being one of the prime causes of the rebellion.[55] Even as late as 1919 railroad officials complained of squatters, promising to continue working with "the authorities with a view to surmounting these difficulties."[56]

In late 1910 the railroad surveyed the site known as Jangada. Located just west of União da Vitória, the 50,000-hectare holding formed, they argued, part of the company's land concession. It was a fertile stretch of land, one dotted with the *erva mate* trees so valued in the region's economy. According to officials, no titled residents occupied the lands in question, but rather "numerous grain bins and houses dot[ted] the land, belonging to individuals who live[d] there without legal titles."[57]

Gertrudes Umbelina de Oliveira, Antonio Silveiro de Oliveira, and Caetano Nunes de Rocha took offense at this last company statement. In a protest filed in 1911 they claimed to have lived on a portion of the lands in question for over fifty years. The name of the holding was Santo Antonio do Iraty and not, as the company claimed, Jangada. They accused the company of changing the name so as to claim it as *terras devolutas*. They presented documents proving that ancestors first registered their claim in 1856. Gertrudes, Antonio, and Caetano reregistered the claim in 1895, as ordered by the Paraná Land Law of 1893.

The company quickly condemned the Oliveira-Rocha claim. Brazil Railway lawyer Manoel Nogueira, Jr. called these people *posseiros criminosos* (illegal squatters) and argued that "the claimants proved only to be the second or third occupants of this particular stretch of public lands," and that they lived there "without a legitimate title." In a later attack the lawyer argued that the 1895 measurement violated the law, for it only allowed *morada habitual* claims for a maximum of 6,000 hectares. Rocha and the Oliveiras actually received, so the company claimed, 16,000 hectares. To answer this latter attack the protesters produced documents proving that they had received title to only 6,000 hectares. This evidence satisfied the courts, and the government of Paraná revoked the EFSPRG claim to Jangada in 1916.

The fact that the Oliveiras and Rocha won their claim makes this case the proverbial exception that proves the rule. The protestors were fortunate for two reasons. First, they occupied a sizable amount of land, some 6,000 hectares. Second, the lands were registered in 1856 and again in 1895. Nevertheless they had to go to court to protect their access to this land. The company played hard, first by denying the existence of titled residents on the land and then by falsely accusing the protestors of holding 16,000 hectares.

The Oliveira-Rocha case, along with the previously mentioned incident involving a Brazil Railway agent and the Almeida brothers, illustrates how even prosperous landowners found their interests threatened during this era of change. Clearly, a portion of the area's economic elite did not benefit from the regional transformation. As such, this fact helps explain why some landowners joined the millenarian movement in 1912, thereby executing an alliance with the peasantry in opposition to the railroad.

If landowners holding clear land titles came under attack, what then, became of peasant squatters? What became of those *posseiros* who, unlike Rocha and the Oliveiras, were unable to state their case in court? What happened to owners of middle-size holdings of 250 to 500 hectares who perhaps did press their claims but lost in the face of powerful maneuvering by company lawyers? It all added up to a massive loss of access to land, a loss pinpointed today by local residents as responsible, at least in part, for the outbreak of the rebellion.

Unfortunately for the *caboclos* of the Contestado, the activities of the railroad were not their only concern. To the east of the Peixe River another company began to gobble up the land of the *posseiros*, threatening to squeeze them into the Santa Catarina interior. Unlike the EFSPRG, the Southern Brazil Lumber Company had no concession from which to begin operation. The company instead purchased or leased timber lands around its huge sawmill at Três Barras, along the Santa Catarina–Paraná border. Even without the benefit of a large land concession the company soon built the largest sawmill in South America and became an important employer of recently arrived Polish immigrants.

The Brazil Lumber Company spent phenomenal sums, when compared to land prices from but a few years earlier, to purchase enormous stretches of the interior forest. Between 1909 and 1914 it purchased 228,000 hectares at a cost of US $1,141,429. This total comprised ten separate deals, the smallest for 2,173 hectares and the largest for 50,000 hectares.[58] The company also purchased the timber rights to other forest holdings. Usually these timber leases ran for sixteen years. In them the company received the right to open up roads to facilitate transportation and to build any storage facilities needed to extract the timber. The company promised not to disturb any *erva mate* trees. Prices paid for these leases varied between 4 and 5 *milreis* per hectare.[59]

The purchase of the Bom Retiro *fazenda* in 1909 exemplifies the activities of the Brazil Lumber Company in the Contestado. Located along the Iguaçu River between União da Vitória and Três Barras, the lands of the *fazenda* extended well to the south. It included large stretches of virgin pine forest, 6,729 hectares of *erva mate* trees, and fields planted in beans and corn. The *fazenda* also contained numerous shacks belonging to the many unnamed "residents."[60]

The Brazil Lumber Company purchased the 30,000-hectare *fazenda* from the Vallões family for 1 *milreis* per hectare, at a total cost of 30 *contos*. Shortly thereafter the state of Paraná survey discovered that the Vallões family claim included 23,591 hectares in excess of their legal title. This meant that these lands were legally *terras devolutas* owned by the state of Paraná. The company in turn bought this excess land from the state at a price of 5 *milreis* per hectare, for a total of nearly 118 *contos*. This was an excellent deal for Paraná, as the state received five times more per hectare for these *terras devolutas* than did the Vallões family for their land. All together the Brazil Lumber Company purchased 53,591 hectares for roughly US $49,000.

The Bom Retiro purchase suggests the disastrous effects Brazil Lumber activities entailed for the area's *posseiro* population. Given state land laws, the company purchased 23,591 hectares of land ruled to be *terras devolutas*. How many people lived on this land, which was obviously on the fringes of Vallões family control? No direct evidence speaks to what happened to these people. We do know that the state never opened these 23,591 hectares to claims by *posseiros* living there.

A better picture of the fate of these *posseiros* is available by piecing together various postrebellion *terras devolutas* documents from the area. By 1918, the lands bought by the company were now in Santa Catarina as part of the 1916 border accord with Paraná. At that time the rejection of a series of land grant petitions meant the expulsion of *posseiros* by the Brazil Lumber Company. Between 1916 and 1919 the government rejected sixteen *posseiro* applications for land titles due to Brazil Lumber holdings. The applicants claimed they had lived on the lands for many years. The government responded that these lands now belonged to the Brazil Lumber Company.

A typical case is that of Francisco Euzébio Ferreira, who requested title to 100 hectares via *morada habitual*. The local land agent informed the state that Francisco lived in a house on this land with his wife and children and that they grew a variety of crops. The state denied his request, however, due to Brazil Lumber's claims in the area. In a similar example, Agostinho Gonçalves requested title to 210 hectares he claimed to have occupied since the 1890s. As happened so many times, the state denied Agostinho's request because "the lands requested by the applicant [had been] sold to the Cia. Lumber."[61]

These sixteen failed title requests must represent, however, only a tiny fraction of the cases where *posseiros* lost their access to land due to Brazil Lumber purchases. Sixteen *posseiros* managed to file a claim for their lands, a process marked with obstacles for the isolated, illiterate peasant. In the Bom Retiro case alone, then, the purchase of thousands of hectares greatly challenged the ability of hundreds of *posseiros* to grow subsistence crops.

Taken together, the Brazil Railway Company, through its subsidiaries, the EFSPRG and the Southern Brazil Lumber Company, gained title to enormous stretches of land in the Contestado region. Possession of a title does not signify actual control over the land, nor does it necessarily signify the expulsion of those already there. But it has been shown here that the Brazil Railway Company did begin to expel unwanted intruders from their holdings as early as 1910. The company, however, did not operate alone in the region. Here, as the third member of the triumvirate, local large landowners quickly seized opportunities presented by the changes taking place in the Contestado. Indeed, like the Brazil Railway Company, and the state governments of Paraná and Santa Catarina, these local landowners bought and sold vast areas of land, further increasing the pressure on the area's subsistence peasantry.

How Large Landowners Operated

In 1912 the state of Paraná increased the sale price of its *terras devolutas*, noting that this price hike corresponded to the "increasing property values in the region." Three years earlier the newspaper *O Trabalho* commented on the benefits of a proposed railroad link between Blumenau and Curitibanos. Among these the paper claimed that "land valorization will be the first benefit brought by the railroad. There will be regions where this increase will surpass 200 percent of the current land values."[62]

The large landowners of the Contestado soon realized the benefits they could derive from the valorization of land, a trend produced by the entrance of the Brazil Railway Company, the selling of *terras devolutas*, and the creation of immigrant colonies. Many of them began purchasing and/or commandeering large stretches of land to sell to individuals or foreign corporations. The Brazil Railway Company soon noticed their actions. In one court case the railroad lawyer noted that because of the construction of the track, "local property owners found . . . a motive to increase the values of lands they had obtained illegally." Some landowners' actions created an added expense for the Brazil Railway Company, especially in regards to land purchases by the Brazil Lumber Company at Três Barras. The Contestado elite quickly learned to play the "land-as-commodity game," leading Brazil Railway owner Percival Farquhar to complain that "many Brazilians are so constituted that, if my Southern Brazil Lumber and Colonization Company offered a reasonable price they felt their land must be worth twice that and obstinately held out." Subsequent company administrators seconded this view and criticized Farquhar for his tendency to purchase a property no matter what the cost. This of course caused locals to hold out for higher offers and allowed many of them to become quite wealthy.[63]

The foregoing information demonstrates the need for a detailed account of the kinds of land transactions large landowners made in the Contestado. The activities of a few of the largest landowners illustrate the intense movement toward concentration and privatization of lands that took place during that era. Most important, uncovering the actions of these planters adds one more chapter to the story of the *posseiro*'s loss of land due to commercial developments in the Contestado. Land purchases and sales by local *coronéis* formed the final tine in the three-pronged assault against existing landholding patterns in the Contestado, an assault composed of public land sales, Brazil Railway concessions and purchases, and *coronel* land dealings.

Henrique Rupp, the large landowner and political boss of Campos Novos, made nearly US $10,000 worth of land purchases between 1895 and 1908 (see chapter 3). Roughly half of these purchases involved lands near the Peixe River. The combination of economic and political power placed Rupp in the perfect position to take advantage of the opportunities presented by the construction of the railroad. He then strengthened his position even more by joining the railroad administration as a regional inspector.

In 1908 Rupp began his most ambitious, and apparently most successful, Contestado development project. On his lands near the station at Erval d'Oeste he began the Colônia Rupp immigrant colony—obviously with an eye towards cashing in on the railroad's presence. Erval d'Oeste was a busy place, home to recently constructed hotels and stores. One reporter on a tour of the area in 1910 noted that "we awoke before daybreak to the sounds of hammering . . . on *coronel* Rupp's property."[64] Upon Rupp's death in 1915 his family took over the administration of the colony, which involved selling 25-hectare plots. All together some 5,000 hectares were sold at the colony for nearly US $30,000.[65]

That Rupp used his railroad connection to promote his land dealings is demonstrated by a suit against him in 1910. In that year Ernesto, Beck, and Company filed suit against Rupp over a dispute concerning three land purchases. Few details remain, but it seems the company sought payment for these lands, which they claimed to have sold to Rupp. It warned that Rupp planned in turn to sell these lands to the railroad and asked the court to force Rupp to pay his debt before proceeding with the EFSPRG sale.[66] The court ruled against Rupp and ordered him to pay Ernesto, Beck, and Company 20.918 *contos*, or roughly US $7,000. Given the size of the payment, Rupp's holding must have been in excess of 2,000 hectares.

It is quite possible that Rupp also used his power as head of the Campos Novos municipal government to influence land deals. At least the local opposition newspaper *O Libertador* (Rupp's news-paper was *A Vanguarda*) implied as much in its 24 September 1910 edition. The paper complained that Rupp, as municipal superinten-dent, purchased a tract of land for 5 *contos*. But "today, after the great increase in land prices due to the railroad, these lands won't sell even for 3:500$000 [3.5 *contos*] because no one is willing to pay such a high price."[67] If this charge is true, it seems that Rupp misrepresented the price of this land, withdrew 5 *contos* from the municipal treasury, and then pocketed the difference between this amount and the real purchase price. Such actions would have increased his cash reserves at the crucial time that he was busy buying up land along the Peixe River.

Henrique Rupp's main political rival in Campos Novos was Au-gusto Carlos Stephanes. Stephanes owned *O Libertador*, the news-paper that constantly attacked Rupp. Trained as a lawyer, Stephanes represented Ernesto, Beck, and Company in its 1910 suit against Rupp. Like Rupp, Stephanes served at various times on the Campos Novos municipal council. It comes as no surprise that Stephanes was one of the area's largest landowners, and that he himself made a considerable fortune from a flurry of land speculation in the Peixe River valley.

Between 1899 and 1908 Stephanes purchased and sold a variety of properties in the Campos Novos area. Perhaps these deals served as a "dress rehearsal" to prepare him for the very large deals that were to come. With the construction of the railroad Stephanes realized the profits to be made from land speculation. In search of such profits he turned his sights on the area known as Rio Bonito, a fertile stretch of land on the banks of the Peixe River. Given the patterns of purchases and sales, it is evident that Stephanes wished to follow the Brazil Railway Company strategy and colonize these lands now next to the railroad.

To encourage Rio Bonito residents to sell, Stephanes offered 10 *milreis* per hectare for these lands. Judging from various documents, this was roughly two to three times the going rate for land. Some people, then, were apparently willing to sell out without violent eviction. It is doubtful, however, that Stephanes bothered with such offers in dealing with subsistence squatters. The timing of these deals is difficult to pinpoint, given the delays that regularly occurred during the registration process. It seems that Stephanes concluded many, if not most, of his deals before or during the Contestado Rebellion.[68]

The records in Campos Novos show that Stephanes made at least four land purchases at Rio Bonito before or during the Contestado

Rebellion. Three of these transactions totaled 3,810 hectares, at a cost of roughly US $12,000. The fourth transaction appears without size or price information. Each purchase involved a different seller, but Stephanes paid 10 *milreis* per hectare in each case. He now owned some of the most sought-after land in the valley, for in addition to its fertility, it bordered the railroad line.[69]

Once in control of the land, Stephanes implemented a private colonization scheme. He began selling 100- and 200-hectare properties to Italian immigrants living in the state of Rio Grande do Sul. Whereas he purchased the land for 10 *milreis* per hectare, he now sold it for 20 *milreis* per hectare. He completed ten such sales covering an area of 1,200 hectares. Stephanes then seized the opportunity to make a final, substantial profit from his Rio Bonito dealings. As registered in August 1919, Stephanes sold 3,289 hectares to the Pôrto Alegre, Rio Grande do Sul, colonization firm of Piccoli and Canduro. Stephanes received 35 *milreis* per hectare, for a total of 115 *contos*.[70]

The most interesting aspect of this sale is that it included the rights to exploit adjacent railroad-owned lands. This is very important for it proves that Stephanes maintained, as did so many *coronéis* in the area, some kind of amiable relationship with the railroad. It also emphasizes just how well Stephanes selected his purchases. He gained access to fertile land in the valley and to land bordered on one side by the railroad track and on another by company lands. He then made five final sales at Rio Bonito, involving an additional 744 hectares. One of these sales went for a whopping 50 *milreis* per hectare.[71]

In the space of a few years Stephanes sold 5,233 of the most valuable hectares in all of southern Brazil. Stephanes took advantage of his connections as a large landowner and municipal official to conduct several real estate deals at a time when the construction of the railroad caused a burst of land fever in the area. He received 160 *contos* for his efforts, or approximately US $30,000. This means that Stephanes pocketed a profit of some US $20,000 from his Rio Bonito dealings. Along with rival Henrique Rupp, he mastered the transition from large, interior landowner to budding capitalist. These men did not act alone, however, for elsewhere in the Contestado others also manipulated large amounts of land and money, changing the face of land tenure in the region.

To the north of Campos Novos, Arthur de Paula e Souza busied himself with a real estate scheme reminiscent of that of Stephanes. In União da Vitória, Paula e Souza served that city as mayor and chief of police. He owned a *grande casa commercial* (large retail store) there, and his steamer *Vitória* transported people and goods on the Iguaçu

River. When in town he stayed in his large brick house valued at US $1,000.[72]

Coronel Arthur de Paula e Souza owned one *fazenda,* São Zacharias, to the south of União da Vitória, and another to the east. He filed to legitimate his title to São Zacharias in 1901. According to the claim, São Zacharias covered 15,189 hectares. Some 50 kilometers south of União, both the Jangada River and the road to Palmas passed through the property. Paula e Souza's *camaradas* grew corn, beans, and mandioca on the property. Cattle grazed on various patches of pasture land. While not directly bordering the proposed railroad line, Paula e Souza's land was, nevertheless, within a few kilometers of the future line.

Coronel Paula e Souza's title legitimation at São Zacharias exemplifies the land tenure issues important during the years before the rebellion. The São Zacharias title covered 15,189 hectares. A subsequent official survey by the state of Paraná found that the *coronel* illegally claimed another 9,189 hectares. This does not mean that he occupied or cultivated these additional hectares, but that at some time he included them within the very vague borders of the *fazenda.* Nevertheless, the state of Paraná sold this additional area to Paula e Souza as *terras devolutas.*[73]

The state of Paraná benefited from this sale, for it now had an additional 15 *contos* (nearly US $4,500) in its coffers. Paula e Souza benefited, for he purchased 9,189 hectares at a bargain price. Knowing that state law allowed the purchase of lands claimed in excess of a title, it is quite possible that Paula e Souza expanded the borders of his claim just before the survey. This expansion probably placed him in conflict with whatever *posseiros* lived on these lands. Such details, however, did not likely concern him.

In addition to his São Zacharias holding, Paula e Souza pieced together a sizable holding known as Santa Leocádia. This property dominated the banks of the Iguaçu River east of União da Vitória. Pieced together by inheritance and purchase, the *fazenda* became the site of some of the bloodiest rebel attacks in the Contestado Rebellion.

Sometime in the 1890s Paula e Souza married Maria Cordeiro, daughter of one of the largest landowners in the upper Contestado region. When João Rodrigues Cordeiro died, he left a plot of land to daughter Maria and son-in-law Arthur. The couple wasted no time in building upon this 1897 inheritance. In that year they made four purchases at Santa Leocádia: three from fellow inheritors of the João Cordeiro estate, and one (the largest, for 5 *contos*) from nonfamily members Thomas and Zeferina Becker. The couple continued their accumulation in 1898 with six more purchases from Cordeiro estate beneficiaries. For their money they received very valuable properties, composed of croplands, pasturelands, and *erva mate* and forest holdings.[74]

Between 1905 and 1912 four more purchases completed the Paula e Souza acquisitions at Santa Leocádia, making him the dominant landowner in the area. To obtain these properties he spent some US $3,000. Municipal land records of these transactions do not include the area of each purchase, but Paula e Souza probably controlled some 5,000 hectares at Santa Leocádia by 1912, based on per hectare price information. To this day area residents still associate Paula e Souza with Santa Leocádia.[75]

Paula e Souza owned a significant amount of land even before the rapid commercialization of the regional economy. As land values rose, he quickly purchased more land. He then did what others, such as Henrique Rupp and Carlos Augusto Stephanes, were doing elsewhere in the region: he began to colonize his land. This was his chance to develop the area, to attract European immigrants, and to sell them land at prices far greater than he originally paid at Santa Leocádia.

Marked off into 25-hectare lots, Paula e Souza began to sell land to Polish immigrants. One newspaper article in 1912 mentioned the flourishing colony at Santa Leocádia, composed of Poles arriving from the nearby Rio Claro, Antonio Olinto, and Lucena colonies. Perhaps 11 August 1908 was a typical day in the establishment of the settlement. On that date Paula e Souza sold eight 25-hectare lots to men with names like Mirczak, Boliensky, and Kuldisky. While he probably purchased these lands for around 2 to 5 *milreis* per hectare, he sold the lots for 10 *milreis* per hectare.[76]

To the south, around Campos Novos, and to the north, around União da Vitória, longtime squatters faced expulsion in the face of *fazendeiro* land grabs. In a third area, around Três Barras and Rio Negro, similar events took place. There the activities of the Pacheco family provide the clearest picture of the stakes involved in the *fazendeiro* land grabs of the period. Perhaps more than any other family the Pachecos scored big by manipulating their control of lands desired by the Brazil Lumber Company.

Coronel João Pacheco, patriarch of the family, moved to the Rio Negro area in the 1890s. There he began to buy land at incredibly low prices. He purchased 2,344 hectares at Duas Barras for 250 *milreis*, a mere US $60. A deal for 2,997 hectares at Barra Grande was concluded for the same price. Pacheco's purchase of these lands so cheaply apparently aroused emnity, for an assassin's bullet killed the Pacheco patriarch in 1907. To his wife and twelve children he left 12,211 hectares of crop, pasture, and *erva mate* land.[77]

With the arrival of the Brazil Lumber Company the Pacheco brothers and sisters turned their inheritance into something much bigger. As landowners in the Três Barras area, it was surely they that Percival Farquhar accused of price gouging (see chapter 3), for the Pachecos received enormous sums from the sale of their properties. Leocádio Pacheco inherited 240 hectares from his father at Duas Barras. He then purchased 1,013 additional hectares there in 1908–9 and ultimately sold the entire holding to Brazil Lumber in 1910. The company purchased the holding for 15 *contos* (US $5,000), for an average price of 13 *milreis* per hectare. Leocádio profited 10 *milreis* per hectare, and his total profit thus came to nearly US $4,000.[78]

Pedro and Firmino Pacheco each inherited 480 hectares from their father in 1907. Like Leocádio, they added to these holdings. In 1907 they purchased 1,085 hectares at Canivete for 1 *milreis* per hectare. They then purchased an unknown quantity of land, "Canoinhas," for 2.5 *contos* (US $900) in 1910. Working together (as they always did), the two brothers then began to sell their lands to Brazil Lumber.

In 1910 they sold 420 hectares at the Canivete *fazenda* for 5 *contos*. In 1907 they paid 1 *milreis* per hectare for this land. In 1910 the Brazil Lumber Company paid them 12 *milreis* per hectare for the same land. They sold 2,500 hectares of the Bugre *fazenda* for some US $10,000 and leased another 600 hectares of prime timber holdings. At Corredeiro de Cipó, Brazil Lumber paid US $5,000 for 1,249 hectares. All told, Pedro and Firmino sold and/or leased 4,769 hectares to the Brazil Lumber Company in 1910. They received 50 *contos*, or nearly US $17,000.[79]

Pedro, Firmino, and Leocádio Pacheco were not the only family members who sold land to the Brazil Lumber Company. Indeed, the entire family did the same. As a family, they sold and leased over 16,000 hectares to the company, receiving some US $45,000 in return. These were lands inherited in 1907 and purchased between 1907 and 1910. No doubt the family understood that the Brazil Lumber Company would want the lands they were acquiring. Their business acumen allowed them to buy low (1 or 2 *milreis* per hectare) and sell high (12 *milreis* per hectare).

While the Pachecos benefited from their land sales, many others suffered from them. As noted, many *posseiros* lost their access to land as a result of Brazil Lumber activities. There is every reason to believe that Pacheco land deals in the area contributed to this process, and thus that many of these dispossessed *posseiros* were former Pacheco clients. But how did this expulsion process work? Whom did it involve? Fortunately a very telling example answers these questions.

In 1898 Aleixo Gonçalves took advantage of the Paraná law allowing *posseiros* to gain title through a *morada habitual* claim. In his *processo* he claimed to have resided on these lands since 1873, lands located south of the town of Três Barras, along the Jangada and Lageado rivers. On these lands he grew corn and beans, raised cattle, and harvested wild *erva mate*. The Paraná state surveyor verified that Gonçalves did indeed cultivate his 2,000-hectare claim, and the state granted title in April 1900.[80]

In January 1911, Pedro and Firmino Pacheco purchased pasture, forest, *erva mate,* and croplands at "Canoinhas-Pardos" for nearly US $800. Having sold so much of their land to Brazil Lumber, various family members now purchased lands at Canoinhas, since apparently this is where they decided to continue their farming operations. Here the conflict began, for these were precisely the lands to which Gonçalves held title since 1900. For their part the Pachecos argued that Gonçalves's claim was to the south of their purchase, and that he thus was a neighbor, not a claimant to the same holding. But a comparison of the maps included in the Gonçalves and Pacheco title applications proves that each claimed the same land.

As the conflict heated up, the Pachecos dropped their assertion that they and Gonçalves claimed different lands. Instead, it appears that they "persuaded" state officials to enter into the conflict on their side. In June 1911, the Paraná state surveyor claimed that Aleixo Gonçalves no longer lived in the area, and thus that he had no claim to the lands in question. A later anonymous entry further stated that "Aleixo Gonçalves . . . surveyed a portion of these lands many years ago," but that this survey was later declared void.[81]

Both of these assertions, that Gonçalves no longer lived in the area and that he held no title to the land in question, are false. As to the first, baptismal records document his presence in the area at this time. As to the second, the Paraná land records include title number 363, issued 23 April 1900 to Aleixo Gonçalves de Lima for the 2,000 hectares at "Invernada do Fundo." Nevertheless, with the power of the state on their side, the Pachecos won the dispute and received their title in March 1912.[82]

This example well illustrates that people lost their land in the wake of elite land grabs sponsored by the Brazil Lumber Company. The Pachecos, with the state on their side, gained control of the land in spite of a legal title to the contrary. This uncovers the complexities involved, for the Pachecos purchased the land in question from a third party. This third party held no legal right to sell this land. The Gonçalves case is especially interesting, since he held title to some 2,000 hectares and was a powerful man in his own right. As such it is another example of intraelite conflicts in the Contestado. It is also a special case, for Gonçalves went on to become one of the leaders of the Contestado Rebellion. Yet this example still speaks to the plight of the peasantry, for if the Pachecos succeeded in expelling a titled landowner, a figure of significant power and leadership talents in his own right, what chance did common *posseiros* have in the face of elite land grabs? No doubt many people suffered from the actions of the Brazil Lumber Company and local elites in the Três Barras area.

A final example of elite land activities in the Contestado brings us back to a case similar to that of *coronel* Henrique Rupp, a member of the regional elite who both dealt in land and worked for the Brazil Railway Company. Afonso Alves de Camargo, landowner and Brazil Railway lawyer, eventually became the governor of Paraná. Possibly taking advantage of his insider's knowledge, Camargo bought Contestado land cheaply and then sold it for an immense profit.

In the early 1900s Camargo set out to purchase the huge *fazenda* São Roque. This prime piece of property, located along the Peixe River, surrounded the town of Calmon. Did Camargo know at that time that EFSPRG would build a train station in Calmon? Did he know that the first Brazil Lumber Company sawmill would be in that same town?

Camargo purchased São Roque from the Carneiro and Araujo families. These families dominated the São João–Calmon area, owning the *fazendas* Capão Alto (10,118 hectares), Campo Alto (10, 881 hectares), Merim Doce (7, 441 hectares), Rio do Peixe (5,289 hectares), and Cruzeiro (5,012 hectares). Unfortunately, the documents do not detail the size of the purchases made by Camargo. It is known that in the late 1800s the São Roque *fazenda* covered an enormous twelve square leagues of territory.[83]

In 1914 a Paraná official charged Camargo with corruption in regards to his simultaneous positions as Brazil Railway lawyer and vice-governor of Paraná. In his own defense Camargo mentioned the purchase of São Roque but claimed to have bought it before joining the staff of the Brazil Railway Company. Shortly after buying the land "two important Americans" approached him at his *fazenda*. He claimed they did not want to buy the land; instead they came to offer Camargo the Brazil Railway job. Almost as an afterthought, Camargo mentioned that he "later sold this property [to the Brazil Railway Company] for a price lower than what the Company paid for other *fazendas* in the state." Camargo wished to downplay the São Roque sale, and it is true that he sold the land for 3 *milreis* per hectare at a time when the Pachecos sold their lands for 12 *milreis* per hectare. Nevertheless, the fact remains that Camargo sold 51,000 hectares for US $50,000. Both Camargo and the Brazil Lumber Company gained from this "sweetheart" deal.[84]

As a lawyer for Brazil Lumber, Camargo advised the company on its land deals in the Três Barras area. In his own words he was hired especially to deal with the Pacheco family. Camargo was accused of receiving kickbacks from public land deals between Brazil Lumber and the state of Paraná, which he denied. It is known, however, that he received a valuable contract to harvest *erva mate* on Brazil Lumber lands. Using images and rationales popular even today, Camargo concluded that he had acted in a patriotic manner in his dealings with Brazil Lumber. Yes, he supported the law prohibiting tax increases on lumber sales for fifteen years, for without this law the Brazil Lumber Company would not have come to Paraná. After all, "these men have brought their capital to develop this state, [thus] why not grant them certain protections? . . . I think they deserve even more protection."[85]

The Coming Crisis

The processes of Santa Catarina–Paraná public land sales and the entrance of international capital via the Brazil Railway Company caught the Contestado peasants between the jaws of an ever-tightening vise. The activities of local elites added further pressure, signaling the complete transformation of Contestado land tenure patterns in the space of fifteen years. Though one should not present too idyllic a picture here, in the late nineteenth century *posseiros* maintained access to land on the fringes of *fazenda*-controlled areas. *Agregados* also maintained a somewhat independent life-style, again on the fringes of planter properties, while enjoying some loose recourse to patron-client relations.

The entrance of capitalism and development schemes caused a land rush accelerated by public land sale policies. *Fazendeiro* interest in fringe areas grew as land values skyrocketed. Sales of large holdings to private companies resulted in the expulsion of *posseiros* from these lands. The establishment of state, Brazil Railway, and local immigrant colonies pushed *caboclo* residents off the land in favor of "whiter" European immigrants.

The *caboclos* of the Contestado resented these trends, but their voices of protest have largely been lost in the elite-dominated documentation. What has not been lost is the memory of the Contestado

Rebellion, and the knowledge that this rebellion occurred to a large extent because of peasant disgust with land expulsions. When Captain Matos Costa, a soldier sympathetic with the plight of the rebels, returned from a 1914 peace mission to a rebel redoubt, he reported that "the locals complain that Arthur de Paula e Souza and other bosses have stolen their lands, and that they now have no recourse to other public lands because these have been sold by the two states [Paraná and Santa Catarina]." In a similar vein, the rebel leader Elias de Moraes responded to a Matos Costa peace proposal by claiming that "we will only leave the redoubts after the deaths of Arthur de Paula [e Souza], Fabrício Vieira, Chiquinho de Albuquerque, Amazonas Marcondes, Affonso [sic] Camargo, Pedro Vieira, Pedro Ruiva, the brothers Miechniekowk [sic] of the Escada station, and others."[86]

Just before his death in a rebel attack against his *fazenda*, Arthur de Paula e Souza wrote a revealing letter to the editors of *O Diário da Tarde*. In it he emphatically denied any relationship between the rise of "fanaticism" in the area and land deals or *posseiro* expulsions. Paula e Souza, the man mentioned in both of the preceding quotes, claimed that all lands acquired at his Santa Leocádia *fazenda* had been former public lands. He acquired these lands fairly, under the rules of the law, without protest or question. Given that he played by the rules, how could anyone be upset over his land deals? Perhaps his fellow landowners did not protest these deals, but the *caboclos* did. Late in 1914 they killed Arthur de Paula e Souza.[87]

In addition to abrupt changes in land tenure, the events detailed in this chapter point to an extensive and complicated interaction of local elites with the forces of international capital (namely the Brazil Railway Company). Henrique Rupp, a powerful landowner, worked for the railroad, and there seems to have been some relationship between his personal land deals and company land activities. Much more obvious was the case of Afonso Camargo. He used his state of Paraná and Brazil Railway connections to sell vast stretches of Contestado land.

Not all Contestado landowners, however, reacted so enthusiastically to the railroad-initiated land boom. The Rochas and Oliveiras, as we have seen, almost lost their 6,000-hectare holding due to the machinations of Brazil Railway lawyers. The Almeida brothers fought a legal battle against company agents interested in seizing their family lands. Peasants, then, were not the only ones threatened with the loss of land.

In addition, the emerging economic boom ignited fierce intraelite competition. Politics and economics merged in the struggle between Henrique Rupp and Carlos Augusto Stephanes in Campos Novos.

They fought a war of words as the owners of the two municipal newspapers, and they fought one another in the courtroom over land deals involving the Brazil Railway Company. At the same time, both purchased more land to sell to colonists and both managed to maintain a positive association with Brazil Railway officials.

While there was no clear loser in the Rupp-Stephanes battle, the same cannot be said for the Aleixo Gonçalves–Pacheco family rivalry. A decades-long resident of the region, and an owner of clear title to a 2,000-hectare holding, Gonçalves was a *patrão* in his own right. Nevertheless, in 1911 he lost his land when the Pachecos scrambled to profit from Brazil Lumber Company land deals. Gonçalves would later fight back, however, as a leader of attacks against Pacheco properties during the millenarian rebellion.

Brazilians today, especially those from Paraná and Santa Catarina, rightly criticize the actions of the imperialist railroaders from the Brazil Railway Company. With its land grant, the company displaced thousands of people and left many with no choice other than to labor in the dangerous construction of the railroad. But as shown in this chapter, local elites also actively participated in the entrance of international capital into the Contestado. Indeed, one can argue that this support was crucial to the establishment of EFSPRG and the Brazil Lumber Company in the region.

But history is complex, and just as local elites aided the entrance of foreign capital, they also eventually hindered its success. For the Pachecos, their actions were obviously motivated by the desire to make as much money as possible from land sales to the Brazil Lumber Company. Their sales allowed Brazil Lumber to begin operation, and they welcomed the company's entrance. Indeed, even today Francisco Pacheco argues that Brazil Lumber brought progress to the region.[88] Ironically, however, the extraordinary prices Francisco's ancestors battled for and received helped drive the Brazil Railway Company into bankruptcy. Their actions cleared, yet then muddled, the path available to international capital.

A massive transformation in land tenure patterns was the fundamental change caused by the entrance of international capital into the Contestado region. But the issue of local elite participation points to further issues requiring exploration if we are to understand the origins and history of the Contestado Rebellion fully. These other ramifications included the growth of commerce, the dramatic increase in and creation of new forms of violence, and changes in patron-client relations. Together they point to the emergence of a crisis in the Contestado—a crisis of material, social, and spiritual proportions.

5

Progress and Anarchy

The newspaper *A Vanguarda* captured the mood in a 1908 article entitled "Estrada de Ferro São Paulo–Rio Grande." It was time to break with the past and create a new style of life in the Contestado. *A Vanguarda* urged its readers to accept and promote the changes begun by the railroad. The railroad "obliges us to break with our outdated patriarchal values . . . we should end this malaise, which, if justifiable when the shadow [of the railroad] was not upon us, will soon place us in the uncertain position of adopting a new life-style, *a new labor system* [emphasis added]." For *A Vanguarda* the changes on the horizon meant that "the pastures so poorly used by cattle ranchers would now be employed in the cultivation of wheat . . . which is more profitable than the cattle industry. Let's finish with the old routines, which see cattle as our only salvation, and realize that it is upon agriculture that our future wealth depends."[1]

Three points stand out in this article. First, it encouraged the end of old patriarchal values. Second, residents were encouraged to adopt a new labor system. Third, the article called for a shift from cattle ranching to crop production. Together these spell the transformation to capitalism, a transformation whereby *patrões* would no longer retain *agregados*, but would, following the lead of the railroad, hire wage laborers to tend to their crops. In 1910 *A Vanguarda* returned to the subject and noted the changes that had taken place in the region. The banks of the Peixe River had been transformed, and thus, "where in the recent past one saw but a few peasants living in primitive huts, . . . today . . . the panorama has changed, with houses everywhere, and locomotives proving the power of human activity, of capital, picks, shovels, and dynamite."[2]

In 1911 or 1912 Bemvindo Pacheco proudly posed for a photograph in front of the massive Brazil Lumber sawmill at Três Barras, Paraná.

Bemvindo, a local landowner and member of the powerful Pacheco family, did not, however, pose alone. Instead, the photograph captured Pacheco surrounded by his *turma*, that is, the labor gang he organized to work at the mill. Just years earlier Bemvindo had concentrated on cattle ranching and *erva mate* production, employing in the process several *agregados* and *camaradas*. Suddenly, however, he sold hundreds of hectares of forest land to Brazil Lumber, took advantage of his *patrão* status, and ordered his *agregados* to work at the mill.[3]

This chapter details the myriad socioeconomic changes that occurred in the Contestado during the first fifteen years of this century. Earlier we saw how the entrance of international capital transformed land tenure patterns in the Contestado. Now we turn to other changes that also touched the lives of the local population. As noted in *A Vanguarda*, picks, gunpowder, and dynamite did change the face of the Contestado. With these came thousands of workers to construct the railroad. On one hand, then, this entrance produced the commercialization of the region, indeed an economic boom in which thousands rushed to the area to take advantage of the railroad's presence. A population boom thus accompanied the spurt of commercialization, with Contestado *municípios* quickly doubling in size. In addition, these processes unleashed new levels and types of violence, as thousands of track workers, most of them from outside the region, fought among themselves, with the railroad security force, and with the local population. Indeed, hordes of workers sometimes invaded towns, looting stores and killing those who attempted to stop them.

On the other hand, the entrance of international capital transformed the role of the *patrão* in the Contestado. Once marginally involved in the commercial economy, the railroad's seemingly insatiable demand for labor allowed *patrões* to exploit the situation as labor brokers. Providing and organizing workers for track construction, they became indispensable to the railroad's plans, and hence key agents in the entrance of capitalism into this backwater area. Their increased importance, however, eventually pitted them against the railroad itself, and the railroad's attempts to break the control of the *patrões* produced further conflict and violence in the Contestado.

Together, this combination of pressures led to much suffering for the nonelite population of the Contestado. We have already seen how peasants lost their land as a result of railroad, state, and landlord land grabs, but peasants found themselves under attack in other ways as well. The destruction of the forest by Brazil Lumber deprived peasants of their access to *erva mate*. The *fazendeiro* rush to enclose holdings in response to climbing land values closed off common pastures, streams, and forests to *posseiros* and *agregados*. Further threats to peasant subsistence, new developments in the patron-client relationship, increased violence, and new forms of violence all worked to create a climate of chaos and uncertainty in the Contest-ado.

Commercialization and Population Growth

The construction of the railroad brought boom times to the Contest-ado interior. The commercialization of the Campos Novos and Curitibanos municipalities progressed daily as construction contin-ued between 1908 and 1910. In 1909 the Campos Novos newspaper *O Libertador* reported that "the increase in businesses has been aston-ishing, with the principal stores tripling their inventory." Such expansion had thus made some businesses "surprisingly profitable."[4]

New towns grew up around the railroad stations. To the west of Campos Novos the town of Erval d'Oeste arose next to the Limeira station. It was at Erval d'Oeste that *coronel* Rupp founded his immigrant colony. In 1910 numerous Campos Novos residents, perhaps following Rupp's lead, transferred their businesses to Erval d'Oeste. What was cattle pasture two years earlier was now a settle-ment boasting fourteen businesses. Included were two hotels, a billard-beer hall, a general store, a photography studio, and a slaughterhouse.[5] In the Curitibanos municipality railroad activities caused a similar boom, especially in the São Sebastião area crossed by the new line. There, according to municipal superintendent *coronel* Albuquerque, the railroad's entrance benefited all area businesses. Here too the railroad encouraged the creation of new settlements. On this subject Albuquerque reported that "at kilometer 128 of the railroad . . . a small village is emerging, one that promises to soon become a prosperous town."[6]

This period of unquestioning praise of the railroad by the locals, however, was about to end. Although once quite taken with the commercialization of the land around the railroad, *A Vanguarda* soon began complaining of Erval d'Oeste's growth. It pointed out the negative side of commercialization and worried about the movement of businesses to Erval d'Oeste. Campos Novos was becoming a ghost town. Many businesses had relocated to the banks of the Peixe River. Prices were lower in Erval d'Oeste than Campos Novos because of the proximity of the railroad. Not only were there fewer businesses, but also fewer customers for those businesses that remained. What could be done? The only hope was to open a road between Erval d'Oeste and Campos Novos. According to *A Vanguarda*, this was a life-and-death matter for Campos Novos, and it urged the governor to take immediate action.[7]

Some Contestado residents thus realized the boom-and-bust nature of the progress promised by the railroad. They realized that both winners and losers would emerge from the transformation of the interior. This process of boom and bust, with its winners and losers, occurred all along the railroad line. As early as 1908 Paraná officials were noting the positive and negative effects of the railroad in conjunction with its activities near União da Vitória. In that year a report on area colonies clearly captured this double-sided aspect of the process: "Today, the most important point of these colonies [Rio Claro and Euprosina] is the Mallet railroad station, where all the colonists go to sell their products and buy necessary goods . . . producing a trend quite prejudicial to older commercial establishments."[8]

Population figures for Contestado municipalities illustrate the scope of the boom that shook the area between 1900 and 1915. The Curitibanos municipality grew slowly from 5,240 residents in 1890 to 6,296 in 1902, and then soared to 11,000 in 1914. Campos Novos experienced a similar jump, growing from 4,681 residents in 1890 to 15,000 in 1914. União da Vitória also experienced slow growth between 1890 and 1900, only to see its population explode thereafter. In 1890 that municipality contained 2,533 residents. Ten years later, the population had increased by only 180 people. But between 1900 and 1906 the population jumped from 2,713 to 6,000. In 1920 the municipality contained 10,527 people. This jump is especially telling given that it occurred in spite of the creation of new municipalities from within the borders of União da Vitória between 1900 and 1910.[9]

Along with a mushrooming population, the commercialization of the interior meant increasing revenues for area municipalities. In 1904 Campos Novos's revenue amounted to 10 *contos*. In 1905 and 1907 this figure dropped to 9 *contos*. The year 1908 brought but a small increase in revenue, up to 11 *contos*. What happened next exemplifies the transformation of the area from a dusty backwater to a booming development zone. Between 1908 and 1912 Campos Novos municipal revenue *doubled* from 11 to 22 *contos*, a particularly dramatic increase considering the stagnation between 1904 and 1908. Revenue sources included industrial taxes and various urban taxes. Not surprisingly, land taxes constituted the largest source. In 1912 the leasing of municipal lands, along with taxes on land sales, produced over half the year's revenue.[10]

The rapid commercialization of the area and the dramatic increase in population and revenue graphically illustrate the changes taking place in the Contestado between 1900 and 1915. Towns blossomed overnight and populations doubled in five years. For the residents, however, the most graphic reminder of these changes rested elsewhere. It was their daily confrontation with an exponential rise in violence that emphasized that their homeland was in turmoil.

Violence on the Rise

This rise in violence seized the towns, the countryside, and the railroad zone. In 1910 the Santa Catarina state security force stationed six soldiers in Curitibanos and seven in Campos Novos. By contrast, the municipalities of Blumenau and Joinvile each contained only two soldiers. Yet Blumenau contained 60,000 residents and Joinvile 40,000, while Curitibanos and Campos Novos each contained less than 15,000 residents. Clearly the state based the size of the security force on the level of violence and unrest in a municipality and not on population.[11]

These additional security forces in the Contestado did not prevent unrest in the area. The government of Santa Catarina recognized this failure, and in 1911 it authorized the municipalities to create civil guard positions. Each municipality was to have at least four such guards, with the state and the municipalities splitting the cost of their salaries. Such a force was needed, the state admitted, because the current security force was "insufficient to provide aid to local police in those areas where it is most needed." The civil guards would help "maintain the order and respect for life and property, for which they will be most directly responsible."[12]

Much of the civil guard's work promised to be in the countryside, since the struggle for land produced many violent confrontations. On one level, *fazendeiros* and the railroad battled *posseiros* for control of ever-greater areas of land. On another, elites battled each other for control of this same land. These latter disputes emerged directly from the selling of public land by Santa Catarina and Paraná, lands now increasing in value due to Brazil Railway activities.

Confrontations between elites resembled action in the frontier West of the United States, with armed men threatening government officials and each other. On a hot summer day in 1900, a Santa Catarina land official wished to begin his survey of Valencio Maciel dos Santos's Fazenda do Serrado in the Curitibanos municipality. Suddenly he noticed a group of ten or so men approaching on horseback. As they neared he realized, as he later put it, "that they were armed to the teeth." It was the Cardoso brothers, there to stop the survey of lands that they claimed belonged to them. The tactic worked, at least for the several hours it took for the agent to round up enough armed men of his own to continue his survey.[13]

Eleven years later, in the Lajes municipality, agent Carlos Schmidt began surveying lands included in a *morada habitual* claim by the Nascimento family. During his survey of these lands, Bernardino Voz approached Schmidt, followed by nine heavily armed men. Voz "explained" that these lands belonged to him and not to the Nascimentos. Fearing for his life, Schmidt gathered his equipment and left. Apparently the intimidation worked, for Voz eventually received title to the land in question.[14]

This incident was not Schmidt's first during his career as a government land agent. In the Canoas case, mentioned in the previous chapter, one resident threatened to kill Schmidt if he continued with that survey. The surveying of *fazendas*, indeed the whole *terras devolutas* sale program, created much unrest and violence in the Contestado. As one Santa Catarina official lamented, the entire process produced "numerous fights . . . [and] . . . daily homicides."[15]

This type of intraelite violence had long been present in the Contestado. As shown in previous chapters, *patrões* regularly gathered their clients in defense of their interests against other *patrões*. Now, however, the rise in land values caused such violence to increase. Soon it became important to establish specific property boundaries, instead of the vague claims of a previous era. In addition, such considerations now placed *fazendeiros* in increasing conflict with state authorities. Intraelite violence may have been well known in the region, but it now carried a new sense of urgency.

Contestado residents soon discovered that violence was also on the rise in the towns. In November 1909 Police Commissioner Cândido Alves Marinho of Campos Novos warned residents of the illegality of discharging firearms in town. His was a futile plea, written in response to three days of pandemonium during which 1,500 shots were fired in the vicinity of Campos Novos town. During these three days it had been impossible to walk the streets, "because people were shooting at the town, hitting several houses."[16]

Most Contestado officials quickly blamed the railroad for this wave of "urban" violence. When the Brazil Railway Company began its construction push on the União da Vitória–Marcelino Ramos line in 1908, it faced an immediate shortage of labor.[17] Most of the area's residents led a subsistence-level existence. The company thus contracted with various local *coronéis* for labor gangs composed of *agregados* and *camaradas*. This was still insufficient to satisfy the company's labor needs. For that reason it turned to contracting workers from Rio de Janeiro and the Northeast. These workers became a prime source of the turmoil and violence that plagued the Contestado.

By the end of 1906 the railroad employed 1,200 track workers on the União line, paying them a wage of 4 *milreis* per day.[18] Construction on the line proceeded slowly between 1906 and 1908. In November 1908 the company hired Achilles Stengel as chief of construction, and work soon reached a feverish pitch. It was Stengel who ordered the company to contract laborers from outside the area. Hire they did, and within two months 3,800 more men joined the workforce. By the end of 1909 as many as 8,000 men worked on the line.[19]

The Contestado towns soon felt the presence of the EFSPRG track workers. Newspapers began complaining of the startling numbers of unsolved murders and robberies. In 1909 the *Região Serrana* spoke of the "five or six thousand men that live the law of the gun." It then charged that the railroad made no effort to police the workers and noted that "given its labor needs, the railroad turns a deaf ear to all complaints." By 1911 a Paraná official spoke of the "growth in crime in this region . . . which has passed all reasonable limits" and then blamed the railroad for this violence.[20]

Construction workers could terrorize and paralyze entire populations. Such was the case in Curitibanos when the *turma* of labor contractor Raphael Batista shot up the town. The horde rode through Curitibanos breaking into buildings, and it destroyed a wooden bridge on the outskirts of town. Even more violent was a 1912 Christmas Eve "riot" in Canoinhas. Forty workers from the "Rayual Brazil" (Brazil Railway) rode into town during the Christmas celebration, broke into buildings, roamed the streets, and killed a local policeman when he attempted to intervene. Only hours later did a group of armed citizens succeed in arresting the workers.[21]

Blood frequently stained the banks of the Peixe River during railroad construction. One old-timer remembers many murders and robberies committed along the line, and added that bodies were frequently found in the river. In 1910 a Campos Novos newspaper graphically wrote of the dozens of bodies found in the river, "some without arms and legs, and others with their stomachs ripped open!" Perhaps a 1914 estimate by a Florianópolis newspaper was not too far off the mark when it suggested that nearly 1,000 workers died during the construction of the União da Vitória–Marcelino Ramos line.[22]

Even more Contestado residents now began to realize the negative consequences of the railroad's entrance into the region. Slowly, area newspapers retreated from their banner headlines proclaiming the railroad as the salvation of the region. Perhaps the railroad did indeed mean progress, but it also meant unrest, death, and destruction. By late 1910 Contestado newspapers began attacking the railroad administration for *instigating* much of the violence in the Contestado.

Perhaps the newspapers complained because the violence was essentially new to the region. Thus the term "urban" violence accurately describes the unrest caused by 8,000 railroad workers, many of them drawn from the ranks of Brazil's urban poor. These were marginal people in the sense that marginality is the kind of deviance that can threaten "the workings of a whole society." For as Patricia Aufderheide explains, marginal behavior is that "outside the bounds of established networks of social relations."[23] Construction workers, even those in *turmas* managed by local *patrões*, were hence "freer" to commit new, random acts of violence than local clients tied to *patrões* by kinship and co-godparent relations. This new, "uncontrolled" violence clearly worried many Contestado residents.

Nevertheless, for the elites of the Contestado, violence among the lower classes was quite different from the violence that threatened their own economic interests and authority. In November 1910, *A Vanguarda* lashed out against the railroad administration. It accused Achilles Stengel of ordering the company's private security force to attack local businessmen. According to the newspaper, Stengel recently ordered all businesses at Erval d'Oeste to close by 10:00 P.M. When a few businessmen resisted this order the security force invaded "businesses, insulting and threatening [the owners], shouting that in these parts Dr. Achilles is the sole authority." *A Vanguarda* appealed to the governor of Santa Catarina to reestablish the rule of law and to protect locals from the company police force.[24]

A Vanguarda later reported that such complaints failed to reduce company-led violence in the Contestado. In mid-December 1910 the newspaper printed a scathing attack against the authoritarian and brutal activities of the railroad and Stengel. This was not, the paper assured its readers, a personal attack against Stengel; it represented, rather, the fulfilling of the newspaper's duty to report the facts. This caveat was important, for the owner of *A Vanguarda, coronel* Henrique Rupp, worked for Stengel and the railroad! That the journal printed such an attack thus illustrates the level to which company-led violence produced tensions between EFSPRG and local elites.

In its 15 December 1910 edition, *A Vanguarda* complained that Stengel pursued his plans without respect for the rights of property. According to the article, Stengel ordered the houses of his opponents burned to the ground, forcing them to leave the area under the threat of death. For these reasons, *A Vanguarda* most disliked the private security force, a force composed of "bandits, vagabonds, criminals, and outlaws." Thus, "terrorized by the security force, and in fear of their lives, the poor tavern owners and peasants abandon their land, flee the area, and judge themselves lucky to have escaped with their lives." Instead of protecting the population from the numerous crimes along the Peixe River, the railroad's private police force terrorized local residents. Concluding with what was destined to be an ironic statement, *A Vanguarda* complained of the passivity of the local population in the face of this company violence![25]

Like the violent acts committed by track workers, violence on the part of the railroad administration was of a new sort in the Contestado. Here was an extralocal threat to the interests of some local bosses. Clearly the railroad administration wished to establish their authority in the region, which meant challenging local *patrões*. Such a strategy was bound to increase the level of violence in the Contestado. To concentrate solely on the reactions of local elites to the entrance of the railroad, however, would ignore the history of that group most directly threatened by the transformation of the Contestado region: those in the subsistence sector.

Threats to Peasant Subsistence

In 1912, at the Brazil Lumber complex in Três Barras, Paraná, Clayton Cooper, an American visitor, watched as the huge steam-powered cranes ripped towering pine trees from the earth. "To watch these great trees crashing through the jungle," he noted, "breaking down the smaller forestry that chances to rise in the path, . . . is a fascinating experience."[26] Notice that Cooper mentioned the "breaking down of smaller forestry" in the operation. This is important, for *erva mate* trees comprised a significant portion of this "smaller forestry."

The produce of this smaller forestry, of the *erva mate* trees, formed an important part of the Contestado economy. Several *fazendeiros* purchased government concessions to harvest the wild tea on public lands. These *coronéis* then organized *turmas* to do the actual harvesting. On the other end of the spectrum, the smallest subsistence-level peasants also collected *erva mate*. For them the consumption of the tea formed an important part of their diet. In addition, many peasants traded their *erva mate* for goods at local general stores.[27]

According to Benjamin Scoz, a longtime Contestado resident who fought with the Santa Catarina state force in the rebellion, many

posseiros depended on the collection of *erva mate* for their liveli-
hood. They collected the *erva mate* on public lands and on the fringes
of large private holdings. The initiation of Brazil Lumber activities,
however, destroyed whole stands of *erva mate* trees, depriving *posseiros* of their living. This destruction was in addition to the increased competition from *coronéis*, armed with their *erva mate*
concessions for public lands. The increasing numbers of European
immigrants also harvesting wild *erva mate* further threatened local
access to the crop. Scoz thus remembers the suffering of those
caboclos in the years preceding the rebellion. Many wandered about
looking for food, while some found employment in the construction
of the railroad and at the Brazil Lumber sawmill.[28]

The destruction of *erva mate* trees formed part of the larger issue
of the loss of land by Contestado peasants. Two trends exacerbated
the problems of land loss by these subsistence peasants. The first was
the enclosure of large sections of the interior. This was followed
by the enforcement of trespassing laws. These trends worked to seal
off the region from the once-pervasive subsistence life-style.

Enclosure received its biggest boost from the railroad. On his visit
to Brazil Railway properties in São Paulo, Paraná, and Santa Catarina,
Fredrick Molitor discussed the company's enclosure policy and noted
the fence work in progress on company lands. As he left the area in
1915 he proudly claimed the completion of fencing along the entire
União da Vitória–Marcelino Ramos line. As for local landholders,
reports of their enclosures began appearing in area newspapers as
early as 1909. Near Lajes, for example, two stories appeared in the
winter of 1909 telling of *fazendeiros "fechando campos"* (fencing
their lands).[29]

This movement toward enclosure, toward the end of the open
range, received official sanction in both the Lajes and Curitibanos
municipalities in 1912. In Lajes, Law 312 of that year made it illegal
to graze cattle on cultivated lands. The law established a 30-*milreis*
fine to be paid to the owner of the cultivated land. In Curitibanos an
October law signed by *coronel* Albuquerque ordered livestock
owners to keep their cattle on their own property "to keep them from
wandering onto neighboring claims."[30]

The enclosure movement resulted from the emerging land boom
in the Contestado region. The rush to buy public lands and legitimate
titles led large landowners to clearly demarcate their property boundaries. The advent of colonization and the railroad turned land into a
valuable commodity, one well worth protecting. The two 1909
newspaper articles mentioned both dealt with this type of private
enclosure. One article reported a land dispute in which one Bernar-

dino Xavier da Silva began building fences to avoid further title problems with his neighbor. In the other, Francisco Nunes de Vargas complained that his neighbor was constructing fences on lands owned by Vargas.

The enclosure movement emerged from land disputes between large landholders, but nevertheless it most directly affected area peasants. Trespassing notices warned against planting crops and grazing cattle on lands posted "no trespassing."[31] Given that they were printed in newspapers, it would seem these notices were only directed toward landowners. Nevertheless, it is hard to imagine that such restrictions did not also apply to squatters. For that matter, *agregados* of one *fazendeiro*, occupying lands vaguely claimed by another *fazendeiro*, probably also found themselves without land if the opposing landholder succeeded in fencing his claim.

Two examples demonstrate how the enclosure movement involved not only *fazendeiros* but also squatters and *agregados*. In 1910 Domingos Bottini placed a no-trespassing notice in a Campos Novos newspaper. The notice did not warn against grazing cattle or planting crops on his property. Rather, it warned that the footpath crossing his land was for private use only. Those caught on the path would be forced to face the consequences. The reference to a footpath leads one to believe that Bottini aimed this notice not at other *fazendeiros*, but at *posseiros* and possibly *agregados* not associated with his holding.[32] After all, these latter groups used such paths for a variety of reasons, such as to fetch water from a local creek or to reach their *patrão's* house.

In a similar vein, the 1912 Lajes act outlawing cattle grazing on cultivated lands also applied to subsistence-level peasants. The provisions of the law placed the responsibility for such grazing with the owner of the cattle. Significantly, the law also noted that in case the owner was unable to pay the fine, responsibility then shifted to that person's legitimate representative. This use of the term "legitimate representative" refers, no doubt, to the *patrão*. In that case this provision dealt with *agregados*, for who else would have cattle, be unable to pay a fine, but yet have a "legitimate representative"?[33]

The land boom of the early 1900s forced many subsistence-level peasants off their lands in the Contestado. For those who managed to maintain access to land, the enclosure movement threatened to limit even this tenuous access. *Posseiros* who once crossed someone else's land to reach their own plot, or to draw water from a creek, now found their way blocked. For years the *agregados* of one *fazendeiro* maintained some independence by grazing a few head of their cattle on land perhaps technically belonging to someone else. Now, however, this someone else, another *fazendeiro*, began building fences to mark boundaries, thus curtailing the *agregado*'s access to pasture and hence independence.

Threats to subsistence did not only affect isolated peasants uninvolved in vertical social relationships. Changes in the Contestado soon challenged the foundations of the patron-client relationship. For this reason we must now turn our attention to this fundamental component of the regional society.

Coronelismo

Changes in patron-client relations occurred as local elites assumed roles as labor brokers. According to Eric Wolf, brokers are "groups of people, who mediate between community-oriented groups in communities and nation-oriented groups which operate through national institutions."[34] This mediating function, Wolf adds, can be both political and economic. Sydel Silverman restricts the concept to those intermediaries who deal with "critical" issues linking town, region, and nation and who constitute the exclusive link between the local and extralocal.[35]

In the Contestado, and indeed in Brazil as a whole, political brokers emerged with the declaration of the Brazilian Republic in 1889. At that time suffrage was expanded in Brazil, with income restrictions dropped in favor of allowing all literate male citizens to vote. Moreover, the decentralization of the political process plus the destruction of the imperial two-party system meant that national leaders now relied more heavily on local leaders, that is, the large landowners.[36] Those running for state or national office depended on these *coronéis* to deliver the interior vote. In return, the *coronéis* received the support of regional or national elites, public funds with which, say, to undertake infrastructure development in their area, and free reign to "consolidate their domination in the municipality."[37]

A certain amount of reciprocity insured the cooperation of local bosses and regional and national elites. Likewise this limited reciprocity operated between *coronéis* and the new local electorate. Many times bosses secured votes with gifts of clothes or promises of municipal improvements. As Maria Isaura Pereira de Queiroz notes, however, many a *coronel* threatened violence to force people to vote.[38] In addition to wielding weapons of reciprocity and violence, *coronéis* also controlled the entire voting process. On the municipal level the council president, usually the local political boss/*coronel*, named all electoral board members for all districts. This power of appointment then gave a *coronel* total control over elections, since electoral boards counted the votes![39]

Coronelismo, that is, the political side of brokerage, functioned in the Contestado as it did in Brazil as a whole. As such it produced interesting results in regional elections. An example is the January 1909 election in the municipality of Curitibanos for Santa Catarina state senators and representatives. At that time, *coronel* Albuquerque, the area's dominant political boss, served as the president of the Curitibanos municipal council and hence controlled the election process.

The vote was to elect one state senator and three representatives. For senator, Dr. Felippe Schmidt, the candidate supported by *coronel* Albuquerque, received 996 votes in the municipality. His opponent, Raulino Adolpho Horn, received just two! In the race for the three state representatives, *coronel* Vidal Ramos, Dr. Henrique Almeida, and Dr. Celso Bayma also each received 996 votes. *Coronel* Elyseu Guilherme da Silva, however, received just six. Afterward, *coronel* Albuquerque congratulated himself on running such a clean election and condemned the opposition for resorting to every sort of illegal method to win the contest.[40]

Coronelismo as a political phenomenon was pervasive in the Contestado, and as such it is crucial to our understanding of the Contestado region. It was on an economic level, however, that the assumption of brokerage functions by *patrões* led to a crisis in patron-client relations. Assumption is the key word, for before the twentieth century labor brokerage was not present in the Contestado. During that era most *fazendeiros* controlled enough hands to work their cattle and grow a few crops. Sometimes they did contract a few additional workers to help harvest a corn or bean crop. These workers were paid a small wage and were drawn from the population of small landholders in the area. It seems the *fazendeiro* directly contracted these people.[41] Certainly no large labor gangs moved about harvesting crops on Contestado *fazendas* as had happened elsewhere in Brazil after abolition.[42]

Labor contracting of a sort began in the Contestado at the turn of the century. It arose in response to the expanding *erva mate* trade. In Canoinhas, Bonifácio José dos Santos, who later joined the rebels, started in the business on a small scale. With but a few men he began harvesting *erva mate* and planting a few crops. Within a few years he had contracted more workers, amassed a sizable fortune, and become a regional power figure.[43]

The king of *erva mate*, however, and one of the Contestado's most powerful *coronéis*, was Manoel Fabrício Vieira. Based in União da

Vitória, Vieira purchased the *erva mate* harvest rights to large areas of public land in Paraná and Santa Catarina. He concluded his first contract in 1906 in Santa Catarina. In return for collection rights to the entire Campos Novos municipality, Vieira promised to harvest at least 40,000 *arrobas* per year, for which the government would pay 200 *milreis* per 15 kilos. In 1908 he then concluded a similar deal with the state of Paraná for lands west of União da Vitória.[44]

Bonifácio José dos Santos probably never managed more than one labor gang in the harvesting of *erva mate*. Manoel Fabrício Vieira's operation, however, developed much further. At least this is the impression given by a 1910 *O Trabalho* story on the town of União da Vitória. The article praised Vieira as one of the region's leading citizens. It noted that the *coronel* derived an ever-expanding portion of his income from the harvesting of *erva mate*. By 1910 Vieira "employed various labor gangs in the harvesting of *erva mate*."[45]

Given the status of the *erva mate* industry in the Contestado, the use of harvest *turmas* apparently functioned well within the norm of the patron-client relationship as it existed at that time. Bonifácio José dos Santos probably oversaw his one harvest *turma* just as other *patrões* oversaw the ranching activities of their *agregados* and *camaradas*. Manoel Fabrício Vieira's situation was somewhat different. He indeed employed several *turmas*, which made personal supervision difficult. Here the initiation of labor contracting and *erva mate* harvesting began to modify the face-to-face patron-client relationship.

Even Vieira, however, was far from a labor broker in the classic sense of the term. The concept of a labor broker, as employed by Wolf and Silverman, implies mediation between a local elite and an extralocal entity. Vieira, however, gathered the labor and employed it himself. He was a patron working his clients. He was not a mediator providing labor to an extralocal contractor.

The development of a true labor brokerage network, with access to labor gained through bonds established in the patron-client relationship, did not develop in the Contestado until the entrance of the railroad. Here the word "develop" fails to express the speed with which such a network emerged with the entrance of international capital into the area. After 1908, labor brokerage exploded on the scene. It was a question of timing. Construction on the União da Vitória–Marcelino Ramos line began in 1906. This, however, was a halfhearted, underfunded effort. Not until 1908, with the hiring of Achilles Stengel, did a real construction effort begin. By that time the railroad administration faced a 1910 contract deadline. The Brazil

Railway Company thus threw all its weight behind completion of the line, and labor became a crucial commodity.

At this time various government agencies reported the standard railroad administration complaint: a lack of workers threatened the success of the venture. On the main line (União da Vitória–Marcelino Ramos), the company complained of a lack of workers for the upkeep of the line. On the São Francisco artery, "between kilometers 336 and 409, where the track crosses swamps and marshes" the company "delayed construction because of the difficulty in finding laborers to work under such poor conditions."[46]

This shortage of labor should come as no surprise. Several obstacles blocked the assumption of a classic wage regime, as has happened elsewhere in the world at different times. For example, Marx detailed the transition to capitalism in Europe and the obstacles faced by manufacturing firms in hiring workers, such as partial peasant retention of the means of production.[47] For the Contestado, the simple lack of an adequate population hindered the ability of the railroad to hire construction workers. In addition, many able-bodied residents still maintained tenuous access to land, in spite of the trends that threatened to end that control. Such an access was no doubt enough to discourage them from freely seeking wage labor on the railroad.

To solve the labor problem, the railroad administration looked to migrant and immigrant labor. As noted, by 1909 some 8,000 men worked on the track construction. Many workers, if not the majority, came from the ranks of the urban poor of Recife, Salvador, and Rio de Janeiro. The company "recruited" these people, writes Duglas Teixeira Monteiro, "more or less by force."[48] As for the use of immigrant labor, Ruy Wachowicz argues that the company recruited workers directly from Poland and Russia. This promised to be an economical solution for the company, since the federal government would pay for the transportation of these immigrants under the colonization regulations in vigor at that time. Wachowicz, however, does not include information on how many Europeans actually arrived on the job in this manner.[49]

To recruit and manage construction labor the company worked through local elites, who now became labor contractors. In fact, the Contestado reality forced such a structure upon the railroad administration. The railroad needed help simply to control 8,000 workers. In addition, access to local labor, given the patron-client nature of the society, would require the cooperation of local elites. At this point further details are difficult to provide, given the lack of information in both the Contestado Rebellion secondary literature and the literature on railroad building in Brazil as a whole.[50] Fortunately, the Wachowicz article and a few other sources provide at least a glimpse into the workings of the labor contracting system.

Several local elites in the Contestado organized *turmas*. Pedro Ruiva was one such elite member. A landowner from the Canoinhas area, Ruiva commanded two *turmas* along the line near Caçador. Raphael Batista, whose men invaded Curitibanos, was another contractor, as was Guiseppe Lyro Santi, who later died in a conflict with *coronel* Manoel Fabrício Vieira. Vieira himself also managed *turmas* employed in the construction of the line.[51]

Local *patrões* contracted with the company to supply the labor for a particular portion of the line. Apparently the migrant workers from the Northeast and Rio de Janeiro worked under these local elites, although the exact mechanism by which these groups established contact is unknown. Upon completion of a section the railroad paymaster paid the *patrão*, who was then to pay his workers. According to Wachowicz, the administration favored the contract system, for instead of dealing directly with a large number of laborers, it dealt instead "with a smaller number of labor contractors, who were in daily contact with the workers."[52]

It seems that local *agregados, camaradas*, and displaced *posseiros* also labored in the construction of the line. The secondary literature on the Contestado implies this, but never directly approaches the subject. Nevertheless, the land and labor activities of the Contestado *patrões* point toward this conclusion. Before and during construction many *patrões* sold large areas of land to persons interested in the colonization of the area. If they found no other access to land, *agregados* and *posseiros* displaced by these sales quite probably resorted to the rigors of railroad construction work. What became of those people displaced, for example, by *coronel* Henrique Rupp's development of the Erval d'Oeste colony? With these land and labor activities taking place as they did before and during the railroad construction, no doubt at least some displaced locals found employment with the railroad. One can assume that a similar process occurred with those displaced by Arthur de Paula e Souza's colonization of his Santa Leocádia *fazenda*.[53]

Displaced peasants sought work on the railroad as a last resort to ward off starvation. They were now "free" to do so in the Marxist sense of the word. On the other hand, *patrões* directly involved in labor contracting likely forced their current clientele into the brutal life of lifting rails and swinging spike hammers. Consider, for example, the hypothetical case of an *agregado* of Manoel Fabrício Vieira. Before the entrance of the railroad this *agregado* probably worked a few days a month directly for Vieira. The rest of the time he, along with his family, cared for his own cattle and tended the subsistence crops he grew. But now that Vieira worked as an *empreiteiro* (labor contractor), this same *agregado* probably faced, against his will, hard labor on the line for twelve to sixteen hours a day, seven days a week.

Sometimes a complex situation developed involving peasants recently torn from their means of subsistence and forced into *turmas* by their *patrão*. Here we return to the case of the clientele of Bemvindo Pacheco near Três Barras, Paraná. Bemvindo, we will remember, was the *patrão* who made several land sales to the Brazil Lumber Company beginning in 1910. As Brazil Lumber took possession of these properties it expelled many of the now ex-Pacheco clientele living there. As the colossal sawmill opened at Três Barras, perhaps some of these displaced people began working in the industry.

In addition to this "free search" of employment by displaced people, it appears Bemvindo Pacheco also forced some of his current clients (those maintaining an access to land) to work at the sawmill. Again, remember the photograph of Bemvindo standing with his *turma* in front of the Três Barras mill. Faced with the opportunity to act as a labor broker with Brazil Lumber, Pacheco took advantage of his *patrão* status to order his *agregados* to the mill. "Order" is the key word, for it is unlikely that *agregados* willingly gave up their semi-independent life-style for the brutal life of industrial labor.

The significance of this emerging conflict between patrons and clients will be analyzed in detail in the next chapter. Now, however, let us examine the conflicts that developed between the Brazil Railway administration and local elites in their role as labor brokers. Two examples illustrate this conflict, which shockingly came to light with the robbery and murder of the EFSPRG paymaster near Erval d'Oeste in October 1909. The first example involves a *patrão* implicated in the robbery but later exonerated. The second involves those actually arrested in the case and an examination of the implications of the crime itself.

Coronel Maximino de Moraes owned the Fazenda Andrade in the São Sebastião district of Curitibanos, the very district crossed by the EFSPRG line. Described as a wealthy landowner, he was also an important official in the Curitibanos Republican party. As an elections board member in the São Sebastião district he participated in various state and national elections.[54]

Two years after the paymaster robbery, the newspaper *O Trabalho* printed an important letter recently sent by Achilles Stengel, chief of railroad construction, to *coronel* Moraes. In the letter Stengel admitted that "there were those who, wishing to speculate and distract my attention from the true authors of the crime, wished to involve your name in this assault." Stengel was now proud to report that an investigation into the matter had cleared the *coronel*'s name. This absolution clearly pleased Moraes, for it was he who asked *O Trabalho* to reprint the letter.[55]

The Stengel letter is important, for it reveals the tension that existed between the two men. Stengel noted: "We have always respected one another, in spite of the fact that in terms of material service we have not always been in complete agreement. This is natural, given that you have felt cheated, while I have tried to defend my interests, without, of course, threatening your own." From this we can see that the conflict emerged over railroad issues. Moraes, a large landowner near the line, was perhaps involved in a land dispute with the company. Stengel's letter, however, refers to service, implying that Moraes provided construction labor for the road. Perhaps, then, the conflict emerged over issues of labor contracting. The conflict was quite serious, prompting Stengel to end his letter by noting the potentially explosive nature of the situation while also praising Moraes's character: "It is much easier, and more satisfactory, to conclude a just agreement. This is something that would be impossible by violent means, the use of which would go against the good and honorable qualities you possess."[56]

The same conflict between labor brokers and railroad administrators produced the train robbery itself. On October 24, 1909, Zeca Vacariano and a force of twenty men pulled off their daring daylight assault. An EFSPRG train carrying the company payroll left União da Vitória headed south for Erval d'Oeste. Suddenly Vacariano and his men rushed out on horseback as the train approached the tunnel at kilometer 208. Forcing the train to stop, the men killed three security guards, mortally wounded the paymaster, and stole the 381 *contos* guarded in the vault. As they left Vacariano swore that he would one day kill Achilles Stengel.[57]

The train robbery caused quite a sensation in the area. The railroad security force began a manhunt but never managed to capture Vacariano. Soon reports arose that several local *patrões* helped Vacariano plan the assault and then protected him thereafter. *Coronel* Manoel Fabrício Vieira's name was most often mentioned as a coconspirator. The subsequent arrest of Vieira's brother-in-law strengthened the case against the well-known *coronel*. In addition, another man arrested for participation in the assault testified that Vacariano planned the entire affair at the house of João Pinheiro. Pinheiro, it turns out, was "the foreman of workers employed by Manoel Fabrício Vieira." Vieira, however, was never arrested.[58]

Zeca Vacariano (referred to as *coronel* Vacariano in *O Libertador*) commanded two labor gangs on the EFSPRG. His assault of the pay train, and his threat to kill Achilles Stengel, laid bare the level of conflict between local elites and the railroad administration. In explanation of this conflict, Maurício Vinhas de Queiroz developed an argument that has become standard in the secondary literature. He writes that the railroad paid such a low rate for contract labor that Zeca Vacariano could not pay his men. The robbery took place, Vinhas de Queiroz concludes, because Vacariano sought money with which to pay his workers.[59]

Perhaps a different set of issues led Vacariano to strike out against Stengel and the railroad. In its account of the robbery *O Libertador* noted that Vacariano and other *empreiteiros* "had contracted with the company, but had not paid their workers." The newspaper then reported that given the lack of payment, "Dr. Achilles secured their salaries, and paid them directly to the workers." Vacariano, with help from other *coronéis*, the newspaper concluded, robbed the paymaster to gain revenge for Stengel's interference in the patron-client relationship.[60]

Did Stengel pay the contract laborers out of a sense of decency and responsibility to his workers? This seems unlikely given that he regularly failed to pay his own charges on time, delaying payments for two to three months.[61] Rather, the reasons for Stengel's action lay elsewhere. Wachowicz argues that the railroad relied on *empreiteiros* to recruit and organize thousands of migrant workers. To this we can add that *empreiteiros* were also vital in providing access to local labor. Once EFSPRG gained access to the needed labor, however, and once this labor was organized, did *empreiteiros* become an unnecessary burden to the railroad administration? Construction was to end in 1910. The railroad, therefore, did not need to guarantee its access to labor for years to come. Once sufficient manual labor was employed by 1909, perhaps the railroad calculated that it could insure its presence until the end of construction.

The existence of the company's private security force no doubt influenced the administration's calculations. This dreaded force, feared by elites and nonelites alike, was in full operation in 1909.[62] They roamed the construction zone committing all types of atrocities against the workers, ruthlessly enforcing Stengel's personal law.[63] Once the labor had been delivered, the company calculated that this force could terrorize the workforce into staying with the construction.

Local *patrões* had done their job well, so well in fact that the company no longer needed their services. They had delivered enough labor, the company assumed, to finish construction. Stengel did not directly pay those construction workers out of any sense of altruism.

He did so to bypass the *patrões* and to break their control over labor, and hence their source of power. Vacariano's raid, as planned in conjunction with other *patrões*, was their reaction to the railroad's threat to their control.

This argument, that the railroad administration attempted to break the power of the *coronéis*, demands a reexamination of the Maximino de Moraes–Achilles Stengel conflict and an introduction of Maximino's brother, Elias de Moraes. Like his brother, Elias owned land near the railroad in the São Sebastião district of Curitibanos. He also actively participated in politics and served on the district electoral board. In a letter written to *O Trabalho* in early 1910, he praised the Republican party, party chief Lauro Müller, and Curitibanos political boss *coronel* Albuquerque.[64]

Nevertheless, Elias de Moraes, *fazendeiro* and political boss, joined the rebels when the Contestado Rebellion erupted full scale in 1912. It seems likely that Elias, like his brother, also quarreled with Stengel over land and labor issues, although this cannot be confirmed. What we do know is that in 1914 he praised the insurrection as a fight against the company that had dared to build a railroad in the area, and he urged the population to blow up railroad bridges and tracks.[65] Vacariano and his men assaulted an EFSPRG train and robbed the contents of its vault. Elias de Moraes made his fight against the existence of the railroad itself. Both were reacting to the threat the railroad posed to their positions as *patrões*.

According to Duglas Teixeira Monteiro, the entrance of the Brazil Railway Company forced local *patrões* to make an important decision. Either they cooperated with railroad officials, or they were left behind. The latter option might mean a life of isolation and limited authority. The cases of Maximino de Moraes and Zeca Vacariano, however, suggest that even those who cooperated with the railroad could see their power challenged by the actions of company officials.[66]

In an example taken from the central highlands of Peru, Florencia Mallon demonstrates that the use of labor brokers by the foreign Cerro de Pasco Mining Company carried within it the seeds of its own destruction. Beginning in 1902, the ever-increasing demands of this capitalist enterprise over a twenty-year span eventually stretched the precapitalist patron-client relationship to its breaking point. Faced with the expanding demand for labor, local elites relied increasingly on naked violence to force their charges into the mines. Peasant resistance, combined with Cerro de Pasco's desire for a skilled and steady labor force, spelled the end of labor contracting by local elites.[67]

A similar, but in many ways different, situation developed in the

Contestado with the entrance of the foreign-owned railroad. As with the entrance of Cerro de Pasco in Peru, the entrance of the railroad produced an immediate demand for large numbers of laborers. Given the socioeconomic position of local *patrões*, the railroad turned to them to recruit, organize, and deliver construction workers. As in Peru, the entrance of a foreign capitalist enterprise produced a violent situation, where thousands of workers fought among themselves and the local population, and where a private security force terrorized both groups. It also led to violence as *patrões* resisted company efforts to limit their control over the workers and hence their power.

In the Contestado, however, the challenges to the system of labor brokerage did not gradually increase over the course of twenty years. Instead, in the space of two years the railroad turned to *patrões* for labor and then sought to wrest control of that labor from these labor brokers. The Cerro de Pasco Company saw a continuing need for workers well into the future. The EFSPRG required labor for a short period, basically for less than the two years required to complete construction before the December 1910 deadline. That limited need, combined with the power of the private security force, compressed time and produced a quicker break with local elites in the Contestado case.[68]

The conflict between local elites and the railroad administration occurred on different levels. Campos Novos political boss Henrique Rupp criticized the railroad through his newspaper, *A Vanguarda*. This criticism is significant, for Rupp worked for EFSPRG. Such were the tensions created by the railroad's entrance that a local elite firmly allied with the company felt compelled to criticize its actions. Likewise, the working relationship between Maximino de Moraes and Achilles Stengel was less than harmonious, even though it did not lead to a violent clash.

This tension between local elites and the railroad did erupt into violence with *coronel* Vacariano's assault on the EFSPRG paymaster. The attack laid bare Stengel's efforts to bypass the *patrão* labor brokers once they had delivered sufficient labor. In this sense Elias de Moraes's war against the railroad represented the ultimate patron reaction against EFSPRG moves to limit their power base.

The Contestado was too small to allow both capitalists and local *patrões* to share control over labor. As the capitalists attempted to eclipse local elite rule, the latter resisted. This resistance was only partially successful. Vacariano's and Elias de Moraes's attacks certainly failed to drive the railroad out of the area. Nevertheless, the attacks demonstrated the enormous resources local *coronéis* still possessed. Vacariano and Vieira relied upon these resources to avoid arrest after the train robbery. Achilles Stengel was a powerful man, enough so to challenge the interests of the *coronéis*. Still, he did not possess enough power, however, to arrest a *coronel* like Vieira. The railroad was the stronger participant in the struggle, but that did not prevent the struggle from taking place.

The Crisis Intensifies

Virtually all the violence associated with the building of the railroad—the expulsion of *posseiros*, worker violence, and *patrão*-company conflicts—occurred within the 1906–10 period. The entrance of the railroad into the Contestado created anarchy. New towns emerged overnight as railroad construction pierced the Contestado zone. The movement of businesses to the railroad zone threatened to turn populations such as Curitibanos and Campos Novos into ghost towns. Such a threat caused some elites to draw back from their earlier glowing pronouncements on the railroad and the progress it meant for the area. They now viewed progress not necessarily as a savior, but more as a double-edged sword. It might have meant the development and commercialization of the region, but it also meant attacks by hordes of rough construction workers and, worse yet, the threat of violence by a private police force not beholden to local interests.

On another level, *agregados* and *posseiros* found their access to land increasingly narrowed by a variety of actors. The railroad expelled residents from company holdings. *Fazendeiros* began fencing their properties as the increasing value of land made clearly marked boundaries a necessity. They also declared off-limits footpaths and trails used by *agregados* and *posseiros*. Areas once considered public were now private. The once-accepted use of common paths now became trespassing.

Of all the transformations that gripped the Contestado, the most crucial were those directly involving patrons and clients. As we have seen, *patrões* entered into a new realm of economic importance by serving as labor contractors for the railroad. For a time, this made them key figures in the construction process. Once the labor was recruited and organized, however, the railroad administration acted to break this control. Some *patrões*, like Maximino de Moraes, nevertheless remained allied with the company. Perhaps Maximino, and others like him, grudgingly recognized the power of the railroad to topple them and thus remained content with whatever they could gain from an association with the enterprise. Others, such as Zeca

Vacariano and Elias de Moraes, correctly viewed the railroad as the ultimate threat to their power and as the harbinger of the end of an era. For them there could be no cooperation. When the railroad attacked, they fought back. Their actions laid bare the contradictions created by the use of a precapitalist patron-client relationship by an industrial enterprise.

What, however, became of the clients of these Contestado *patrões?* They, like all Contestado residents, witnessed the rise of violence in the area. Indeed, they felt the violence as the patrons forced them from their holdings and into railroad construction work. The rapid entrance of a capitalistic industrial enterprise compressed time in the Contestado, and clients soon faced an uncertain future. Holders of a once semi-independent life-style, they now faced the new demands of a wage labor construction regime, forced into the situation by their *patrão,* by their *compadre.* The figure once associated with their subsistence and protection now threatened their life-style and survival. The crisis between *patrões* and railroad administrators would soon be dwarfed by this emerging crisis between patrons and clients. It was this crisis that prepared the population for the preachings of an eccentric backlands prophet.

6

Millenarianism and
the Crisis of Subsistence

When the wandering prophet José Maria arrived in the Contestado
(see chapter 1), he continually expressed his pacific intentions. So too
did his followers when they regrouped one year later, after their
leader's death at Irani. As we know, however, the millenarian movement begun by José Maria evolved into a long and bloody rebellion.
Given the actions of the Brazil Railway Company, the state governments of Paraná and Santa Catarina, and local Contestado landowners, we can now understand why a violent rebellion erupted in
the region. The subsistence peasantry, joined by a few landowners,
fought back against public and private land grabs and against what
they correctly perceived as a threat to their life-style. But why a
millenarian movement? Why a movement that preached the need for
a moral regeneration of society, the need to establish holy cities, and
the need for a restoration of the monarchy?

Answering these questions requires detective work on the part of
the historian. What follows is an analysis of the ideology and structure of the millenarian rebellion, for examining what the rebels said
and did illustrates their hopes and fears, and indeed their goals as
believers in a millenarian call. Such an analysis leads to a further
examination of the Contestado patron-client relationship and the
crisis produced within it by capitalist transformation. It was the
emergence of this crisis, one of material and spiritual proportions,
that prepared the Contestado population for the special preachings
and promises of the millenarian call.

The Movement Begins

In 1911, when the army deserter José Maria began his travels across
the Contestado, he first gained fame as an herbal *curandeiro* (healer),

a man so powerful that he brought a dead boy back to life. Soon he began preaching to his newfound followers the need to abandon the evil republican form of government. In its place he urged the restoration of the Brazilian monarchy as the holiest form of government here on earth.[1]

José Maria's followers readily adopted this view of the monarchy as God's law. The captured millenarian rebel Pedro Ferreira Amaro told his interrogators that "the monarchy comes from heaven." Maurílio Gomez, another rebel prisoner, spoke of José Maria's desire for "the return of the monarchy, which is God's law," as opposed "to the republic, which is the law of the devil." Finally, two years after the death of José Maria, one rebel leader reminded Brazilian officials that "God created the rule of kings on earth," and that "it is the return of this rule that we desire."[2]

In conjunction with his call for the restoration of the Brazilian monarchy,[3] José Maria began nightly readings from *A história do Imperador Carlos Magno e os doze Pares de França* (*The History of Charlemagne and the Twelve Peers of France*).[4] His followers gathered around the campfire, and José Maria dramatically recounted the heroic exploits of the Holy Roman Emperor and his fearless twelve "lieutenants." Involved in a holy war, Charlemagne and his men risked their lives in the fight against the infidel Moors. At least one regional newspaper blamed the subsequent rebellion on these readings, which, the journalist claimed, "fanned the passions of the ignorant peasants."[5]

As with most millenarian movements, the *fanáticos* of the Contestado continually defined and redefined the structure and ideology of their movement. Unlike other examples, however, this movement's leader, José Maria, died just months after first gathering a following. At this point the Contestado landowner Euzébio Ferreira dos Santos, one of the earliest and most devout of José Maria's flock, assumed, after a year of inactivity, leadership of the revised movement. He immediately called for the creation of a *cidade santa* (holy city) at Taquaraçu, the scene of José Maria's first activities in the Contestado. But it was not Euzébio who made this decision. Instead, José Maria himself had ordered the move in a vision experienced by Euzébio's son Manoel.[6]

With the creation of this holy settlement, people would live among *a irmanidade*, that is, among the brotherhood of those who had removed themselves from the unchaste world. This settlement at Taquaraçu, and others like it, would emerge as the new centers of the world, thus replacing the now pernicious cities of Curitibanos, Lajes, and even Florianópolis. Within the holy cities, believers would escape the catastrophes soon to befall the outside world. As one ex-rebel put it, he moved to such a holy settlement because "there much holiness resided" and thus "those that went would live, while those that did not would die."[7]

Included in, and indeed essential to, the founding of the holy city of Taquaraçu was the belief in the resurrection of José Maria. According to legend, José Maria predicted his own death at the battle of Irani. At that time he promised, however, to return one year later, this time with the holy army of St. Sebastian.[8] It was in Manoel's vision, then, that José Maria picked Taquaraçu as the location of his return. On his way to Taquaraçu in December 1913, Euzébio Ferreira dos Santos pleaded with neighbors to join him, employing the claim that José Maria had returned from the dead, and that he was waiting at the new holy settlement.[9]

At this point the belief in immortality expanded to cover all those who joined the movement. Once hostilities began, the rebels believed that if shot they would go to heaven and then return to fight again. (This belief in resurrection thus conveniently dealt with the fact that army bullets killed rebel soldiers!) One ex-soldier remembers hearing the rebels shout "me mata peludo—e depois eu te pago" ("kill me now 'hairy one,' [the rebel nickname for soldiers] and I'll pay you back when I return").[10] In 1985 one rebel veteran recalled this belief in resurrection. At that time he joked that all the resurrected rebels must now be living in the United States, for none of them had returned to the Contestado![11]

As people joined the movement and moved to Taquaraçu, a sense of guilt emerged among believers, a sense that the problems that gripped the Contestado were punishment from God. Along these lines, one rebel prisoner spoke of the monarchy as the only thing capable of helping the lives of sinners. Under questioning he claimed that "our families require the protection of religion to be content; the monarchy is the only law that can help the lives of sinners [emphasis added], and that is what José Maria wanted for the happiness of his people."[12] One rebel survivor evoked similar feelings in a 1985 interview. Rosa Paes de Farias, daughter of rebel leader Chico Ventura, spoke of the "War of St. Sebastian," that is, the Contestado Rebellion. She described the war as a castigo, or punishment, and remembered that Euzébio preached as such, saying he had heard this from José Maria.[13]

A prayer found on the body of a dead rebel graphically evoked images of sin, guilt, and punishment. In it God threatens hunger, pain, and suffering for those who do not follow his orders. In fact, because of sins already committed, God threatens to withdraw divine protection: "I will send kings to battle each other, armies to fight one another, and sons to fight fathers and mothers." It is only "thanks to my Paternal love that you have been saved thus far," because otherwise "you would have already been condemned for your injustices."[14]

To summarize, the movement began with the healing activities of an army deserter from the state of Paraná. Subsequently, it was José Maria himself who began preaching the evils of the Republic and the need to reestablish the monarchy as God's one true law on earth. But José Maria died in the battle of Irani, leaving it to devout followers to define the movement's character further. And define it they did, for after José Maria's death emerged the belief in resurrection and the imagery of sin and punishment. Most important, however, the need to build holy cities now entered into the rebels' plans. There the believers would worship God and escape the catastrophes soon to befall the general population.

It was in these holy settlements, Taquaraçu in particular, that the movement reached maturity, becoming progressively more radical in its "us versus them" mentality. Such a mentality guaranteed an eventual conflict with civil authorities, for beyond a certain point the millenarian believers would refuse to share the world with the forces of evil. And for their part, given the disaster at Canudos and the drive to consolidate Brazilian nationhood, civil authorities refused to share the country with a band of armed and dangerous religious fanatics.

Life in the Redoubts

Believers approached Taquaraçu with trunks on their backs and their children gathered at their sides. Carts loaded with personal belongings creaked along slowly behind ragged herds of goats and cattle. Upon arrival they all faced the first difference between the holy settlement and the outside world: those who had shared with those who had not.

The practice of communal sharing at Taquaraçu did not mean that residents turned over all their possessions to the community. It meant, rather, that all shared enough to keep the community clothed and fed. It meant, according to one ex-rebel, that "no one could sell something to another." Instead, "If I needed a dress it was given. Everything I needed was given."[15] The rebels rigorously enforced this ban on selling within the redoubts. Manoel Batista dos Santos remembers the execution of one man who refused to divide his salt with his neighbors. Another woman met a similar fate for refusing to share her supply of beef.[16]

This was a millenarian movement, and inside the holy settlements religion dominated all aspects of daily life. A wooden chapel was constructed in Taquaraçu and, indeed, in other rebel settlements.[17] In front of the chapel lay the *quadro santo* (sacred square), marked by a cross in each of the four corners. It was here that the daily *as formas* (the formations) took place.

Every morning at sunrise, village residents filed onto the square, beneath the shadow of the chapel. Standing literally in formation, they listened as leaders spoke of daily concerns such as food distribution and work details. Religious instruction followed. Then the procession would begin, with residents praying in front of, and then kissing, each of the crosses. At that point, as the ex-rebel Manoel Batista dos Santos so vividly described, all would lift their voices in a deafening cry of "Viva José Maria," a cry that rumbled through the surrounding hills and valleys. Rebels repeated this same procession at noon and sunset.[18]

The testimonies of rebel survivors paint a picture of life dominated by prayer and religious thought. David Riveira remembers the *pura reza* (constant praying) within the settlements. Likewise, Salvador Batista dos Santos recalled the importance of prayer and mentioned the nightly singing of prayers. Rosa Paes de Farias mentioned the great faith of the rebels and the importance of prayer in maintaining that faith. Rosa's brother João commented that rebel men always prayed to José Maria before entering into battle. Particularly devout was Chiquinho Alonso, the military advisor of the Caraguatá redoubt and mastermind of the successful September 1914 attacks against the towns of São João and Calmon.[19]

Within the holy settlements, a group of women known as "the virgins" occupied a special position of authority. Actually, it seems that José Maria first began using teenage girls, referred to as *as virgens*, as intermediaries between himself and the local population. According to Rosália Maria de Castro, who moved with her family to a redoubt at the age of twelve, girls became virgins because "they heard a voice telling them to do so." People believed that these virgins possessed special powers. Always dressed in white with ribbons in their hair, the virgins were, on a mundane level, in charge of food distribution within the camps.[20]

A fifteen-year-old girl named Maria Rosa exerted by far the greatest influence among the movement's virgins. Blessed with the ability to communicate with José Maria, she became the conduit between the departed leader and his followers. According to the historian Maurício Vinhas de Queiroz, what in fact took place was something quite different. He argues that a council of leaders, composed of Euzébio Ferreira dos Santos, Elias de Moraes, and others, would inform Maria Rosa of the orders of the day, which she would communicate to the settlement's population as if the orders were from José Maria.[21]

Survivors of the rebellion tell a different story. João Paes de Farias is sure that Maria Rosa spoke with José Maria, and it was she, and not Euzébio or Elias de Moraes, who gave the orders. At the time, a captured rebel soldier also swore that the chain of command ran from José Maria to Maria Rosa, and then to Euzébio and Elias de Moraes.[22] And here we should note that our informant Rosália Maria de Castro did not like Maria Rosa, because the latter never allowed her to leave camp.[23] It seems then, that Maria Rosa did exercise considerable authority over at least some of the members of the millenarian movement.

Within the redoubts a new and different type of morality reigned, one that clearly distinguished the movement from the practices of the outside world. Adultery was prohibited. So too was marriage between godfathers and godmothers, since the rebels considered this an incestuous union. Country dances, so popular in the Contestado region, did not occur within the redoubts nor did various types of games.[24]

In spite of the movement's strict morality, both Maria Isaura Pereira de Queiroz and Duglas Teixeira Monteiro argue that an upbeat and festive mood dominated life in the settlements. Festive life centered around weekly, and sometimes daily, religious celebrations, especially those held in honor of a patron saint.[25] One ex-rebel interviewed by Monteiro claimed that the holy settlements "attracted youth 'that loved noise and celebrations.'"[26] Another ex-rebel remembered guns shot into the air as the usual method of demonstrating one's joy during religious festivals.[27]

Weddings provided a chance for celebration within the redoubts. Rosália Maria de Castro attended several such weddings in which the ceremony was the same as in a regular church, except that now Elias de Moraes acted in place of a priest. The same was true, according to Rosália, for baptisms.[28] The rebels went so far as to record these weddings and baptisms in oversized ledgers.[29]

A new sense of morality and a pervasive religious fervor dominated life in the camps. Two events demonstrate just how important each was to the movement's self-definition. The first involves the eldest son of Chico Ventura (one of the movement's leaders), who seemed to have problems believing in the resurrection of José Maria and the whole *santa religião* (saintly religion). His wife, on the other hand, became especially devout in her observance of the religion. One day she wrapped herself in a white sheet and announced that she would soon join José Maria in heaven. This attitude infuriated Chico's son, and he beat her for this fanatical belief in the religion.

Upon hearing of this incident a group of rebels decided to punish Chico's son for his disbelief. They tied him to a tree and were contemplating how best to kill him for this heresy when another group of rebels arrived on the scene. This second group untied him, arguing that he was Chico Ventura's son and therefore undeserving of such treatment. They then rushed him away from the planned execution site.[30]

If disbelief was a punishable offense, so too was a breach of the movement's moral code. Manoel Ferreira dos Santos, son of Euzébio, assumed leadership of the holy city of Taquaraçu based on his ability to communicate with José Maria. One day, before the first army attack against Taquaraçu, Manoel spoke of a recent conversation with José Maria. In this vision, according to Manoel, José Maria had ordered him to sleep with two of the virgins. This outraged the community, as it violated the sanctity of the virgins. Leader or no leader, son of Euzébio or not, the community immediately expelled Manoel, and nothing more was heard from him.[31]

The near execution of the son of a leader for his disbelief, and the expulsion of the son of the movement's founder, attest to the development of the movement's ideology. The rebels now presided over an alternative vision of the world, one quite separate from the surrounding secular world. This alternative vision did not, however, call for a violent clash with the unchaste world, at least not in the beginning. To uncover the roots of the violent clash is our next task, for it will illuminate the further development of the millenarian ideology. Ultimately, such an understanding will help explain why a specifically millenarian movement emerged in the Contestado.

A Nonviolent Appeal
and a Violent Response

If the reports of army officers and ex-rebels can be believed, José Maria's appeal was a nonviolent one in the Contestado. According to army officer Demerval Peixoto, under José Maria the *fanáticos* "rejected violence and avoided conflict."[32] Here it is important to remember the incident in late 1912, when the *fazendeiro* and *coro-*

nel Francisco de Albuquerque ordered the Santa Catarina state police force to attack the *fanáticos*. Rather than stay and confront the force, José Maria and his followers abandoned camp and moved to Irani, Paraná. As they did so, José Maria reportedly remarked that he "very much wished to avoid violence."[33]

Once at Irani, the *fanáticos* continued to proclaim their non-violent intentions. As *coronel* Gualberto's force approached Irani, José Maria sent two emissaries to meet with the army commander. Even at this point, after hostile locals had forced him and his flock to abandon various camps, José Maria sought peace. The emissaries thus requested "time to disperse pacifically" and repeatedly stressed their nonviolent intentions.[34] Gualberto, as we now know, ignored these pleas, and both he and José Maria died in the ensuing battle.

This nonviolent spirit continued one year after José Maria's death, as the rebels built the holy city of Taquaraçu. Not even the failed December 1913 army attack against the settlement changed this spirit. As proof of this nonviolent attitude, one rebel survivor recalled the treatment extended to a captured soldier after the December attack. The infantryman, a teenage boy, suffered severe wounds in the battle. Rosa Paes de Farias and other women rebels dressed the boy's wounds and comforted him as he cried for his mother. Saddened by his subsequent death, they organized a religious service and buried him alongside other rebels. "We treated him very well," Rosa remembered. "But," she added ominously, "he was the last soldier we ever buried."[35]

As the army prepared for a second attack against Taquaraçu, the *fazendeiro* Rocha Tico went to negotiate peace with the rebels. On his return he reported that the *fanáticos* "sought to harm no one, but would fight back if attacked."[36] What followed was the Taquaraçu massacre, where army machine guns killed over 100 women, children, and elderly rebels. In reaction, the believers transformed their movement into a full-scale rebellion.

Rosa Paes de Farias remembers the outrage the massacre produced among the rebels. Their nonviolent attitude disappeared. The *fanáticos* declared war against the *peludos* (the hairy ones), their nickname for government soldiers. But they declared war not only against the army, Rosa stressed, but against an entire evil society as well. Earlier, Rosa and her friends organized a proper burial for the young soldier. Now the rebels combed the countryside in search of army graves. Once located, the rebels exhumed the bodies and left them hanging in trees as a warning to their enemies. The sight of their comrades' bodies terrified army soldiers, and tales of the practice are legendary in the Contestado.[37]

The account of the army chronicler Demerval Peixoto confirms the notion that the Taquaraçu massacre was a turning point in the Contestado Rebellion. In Peixoto's mind, the massacre ended any hopes of a peaceful settlement between rebels and the Brazilian authorities. The massacre at Taquaraçu, he noted, "exacerbated tensions, and led the rebels to seek a horrible vengeance." Far from destroying the movement, the soldier Herculano Teixeira d'Assumpção later wrote, the massacre instead strengthened the rebels' resolve.[38]

"We lived in Taquarassu practicing our religion[—]we didn't steal and we didn't kill." Thus begins a rebel note left in São João, Santa Catarina, in one of the few buildings that survived the rebel attack of September 5, 1914. The note goes on to condemn the massacre at Taquaraçu, where soldiers "killed women and children."[39] The massacre illustrates two important facets of the Contestado Rebellion. First, it provides yet another example of the development of the rebel ideology, most of which took place after the death of founder José Maria. Once nonviolent, the movement now moved into a violent confrontation with the evil society. This, we have shown, is not what the rebels wanted. Faced with repeated attacks, however, they moved to defend their beliefs.

On another level, the massacre, and the pre- and postmassacre ideology, demonstrates the faith of the rebels in the power of the millenarian vision. The world was filled with evil, and only by establishing holy cities could people escape this evil. Convinced that this was true and compelling, the rebels expected the justness of their call to appeal to the masses. It did appeal, as hundreds, then thousands, joined the movement. No force was necessary to convince people to join their movement. Indeed, the *fanáticos* sought to avoid violence with civil authorities. After all, they were right, and soon all would see the justness of their cause—and join them in the struggle.

Many blamed the large landowners, the *patrões*, for the changes and troubles—the loss of land, the sending of cattle hands to work on the railroad, the exponential increase in violence—that gripped the region. But again, given their faith in religion and in the power of the millenarian call, they felt that violence would not be needed to convince the *patrões* to change their ways. In fact, as Herculano Teixeira d'Assumpção noted at the time, their call was already challenging these *patrões* for the allegiance of their clients. Faced with the choice between loyalty to the movement or to the *patrão*, more and more peasants were now choosing the former.[40]

The Taquaraçu massacre led the rebels to abandon their nonviolent attitude. They believed that a society so evil as to ignore

God's law and kill women and children in the holy city must now be destroyed. The rebels had not lost faith in their cause, but they had given up hope that the evil outside world could be saved. In early August 1914, the rebel military commander Chico Alonso gave the order. Area residents had one month to move to any of the rebel redoubts in the Contestado, and thus the sinners were given one last chance for salvation. Those who did not would be considered the enemy and would be shot on sight. Hundreds more now joined the rebellion, ahead of the 1 September 1914 deadline.[41]

Who, however, was to guide the movement through its clash with the civil society? Who were the movement's leaders, and from what sectors of society did they come? Were all of them "bandits," as many at the time argued, motivated solely by their desires for political and economic gains? Were they political opportunists who exploited an illiterate, backward peasantry for personal gain? Or, were they true believers, ready to die for José Maria and the sacred religion?

In reality, we know that bandits, political opportunists, and true believers assumed leadership roles (or at least claimed such roles) in the Contestado Rebellion. By examining the timing of adhesions to the movement, however, we can pinpoint the relative positions of these leaders within the rebellion. Such an analysis shows that a small, committed core of leaders, devout in their belief in the millenarian visions of José Maria, founded and controlled the movement until those last days in the Santa Maria redoubt.

As José Maria began his travels through the Contestado, it was Euzébio Ferreira dos Santos who invited the mystic healer to celebrate mass in honor of St. Sebastian, the patron saint of the village of Perdizes Grandes. And who better to invite José Maria, for Euzébio had founded Perdizes Grandes at the turn of the century as a center for religious celebrations. Famous for his religious zeal, Euzébio oversaw the construction of the village's wooden chapel, which he dedicated to St. Sebastian. A landowner of some means, Euzébio annually donated a portion of his assets for the upkeep of the chapel.[42]

Thrilled by José Maria's appearance in the *sertão*, it was Euzébio who later cultivated the idea of the prophet's resurrection and led the movement's rebirth. It was he who spread the word that all should move to the holy city of Taquaraçu to await José Maria's return.

Once within Taquaraçu, Euzébio joined a small core of leaders, and there his fame as an ardent believer in the millenarian cause continued to grow. Later, the soldier Demerval Peixoto would refer to him as a "fervent believer in the resurrection of the Monge [José Maria]." Herculano Teixeira d'Assumpção meanwhile spoke of Euzébio as "an unconditional believer" in José Maria.[43] It was Euzébio's son Manoel who first ruled Taquaraçu because of his visions of José Maria. But the rebels recognized the father as one of their leaders throughout the rebellion, and he lived in all the major rebel redoubts from Taquaraçu to Santa Maria. Founder of the reborn movement, landowner and sponsor of the chapel at Perdizes Grandes, Euzébio Ferreira dos Santos was a true believer in the *santa religião*.

Along with Euzébio, Chico Ventura witnessed the rebirth of the movement. And like the former, Chico moved to Taquaraçu, where he served in a leadership capacity until his death at the hands of government soldiers in 1915. It was at Chico's house, in December 1913, that Euzébio and daughter Teodora wrapped themselves in sheets, emerged "fanaticized," and then ordered the move to Taquaraçu. Like Euzébio, Chico Ventura was a *fazendeiro* near Perdizes Grandes.

Chico Ventura's daughter, Rosa Paes de Farias, still remembers her father's strong faith in José Maria and the *santa religião*. Rosa's brother João thinks that their father originally moved to Taquaraçu against his will, pressured by Euzébio Ferreira dos Santos. But once in the redoubts, João stressed, his father's belief in the sacred religion became unconditional. Others agree with Chico Ventura's children. In his interview, rebel survivor David Riveira repeatedly mentioned Ventura's devotion. "He was a good man," David also remembered. Likewise, Rosália Maria de Castro remembered Ventura as "a very good and very religious man."[44]

A wealthy landowner and member of the Republican party of Santa Catarina completed the core of the rebel leadership. Elias de Moraes was described as "the well-known *fazendeiro* . . . rich, . . . with links beyond the interior wilderness." He joined the movement during the days of the Caraguatá redoubt. Once an elections official for the Curitibanos municipality, Moraes served as a major in the National Guard.[45]

The true nature of Moraes's commitment to the millenarian vision is unclear, although it was seemingly much more tenuous than those of Euzébio Ferreira dos Santos and Chico Ventura. We know that Elias's brother Maximino de Moraes was employed by, and had conflicts with, the Brazil Railway Company (see chapter 5). From that it can be concluded that Elias de Moraes might also have clashed with the railroad administration. Perhaps Moraes joined the rebellion for secular reasons, as a means of getting even with the railroad. A letter he wrote to a friend after joining the movement seems to confirm this. In the letter he condemned the *caminho de ferro* (railroad) and urged his friend to destroy various railroad bridges. For his part Moraes promised to destroy one major bridge and to attack station houses at São João, União da Vitória, and Rio Negro.[46]

If Moraes joined the rebellion for "secular" reasons, it nevertheless seems that he "got religion" once inside the redoubts. At least one rebel, anyway, spoke of Moraes as a very religious man.[47] He stayed with the rebellion until the bitter end, through the last year of starvation and disease. But regardless of the nature of Elias's beliefs, at least one member of his family became "fanaticized." This was dona Dúlcia, Elias's wife and *comadre* (baptismal godparent) with Euzébio Ferreira dos Santos. According to the historian Maurício Vinhas de Queiroz, dona Dúlcia visited Euzébio at Caraguatá, returned home, and forced her husband to move with her to the redoubt. In a more dramatic fashion, local historian Zélia de Andrade Lemos also mentions dona Dúlcia's belief in the *santa religião*. Dúlcia became so fanaticized, writes Lemos, that one day when Elias was out she "set out with her family [for Caraguatá] in such a rush that she forgot to release the goats from their milking stalls."[48] Faced with his wife's actions, Elias de Moraes also moved to the holy settlement.

Compare the biographies of these three leaders to that of Bonifácio Papudo (Bonifácio José dos Santos) of Canoinhas, Santa Catarina. A resident of the Contestado since the 1890s, Bonifácio participated in the Santa Catarina government-sponsored occupation of Canoinhas in the early 1900s. By that time he owned fertile land in the area and was the *patrão* to numerous peasants. He employed them in the harvesting of *erva mate*.[49]

A municipal officer in Canoinhas, Bonifácio Papudo lost power to a rival faction in 1914, that is, at the height of the Contestado Rebellion. The rebels, who now occupied a vast portion of the Contestado, counted thousands among their ranks. More rushed to join the movement each day. By this point, rebel military commander Chico Alonso was making plans for the final rebel offensive. Perhaps, Bonifácio no doubt thought, this rebellion just might succeed.

Sensing an opening, Bonifácio jumped at the chance to regain control of the Canoinhas municipality. On the morning of 15 July 1914, Papudo and another eighty men tied white ribbons to their hats, mounted their horses, and set out for Canoinhas. The plan was to invade the town and regain control of the government. The white ribbons were important, for Papudo claimed he had now joined the millenarian movement and was fighting for the glory of José Maria. The soldiers who repelled the attack later described how Papudo and his men cried out "Viva José Maria" and "Viva a Monarquia."[50]

Defeated in his politically inspired attack against Canoinhas, Papudo retreated into the forest, where he created his own redoubt. There he continued to express his devotion to the millenarian cause while carrying out a series of raids against local *fazendas* and another attack against Canoinhas. Papudo was no millenarian rebel, however, and when things got tough he did not turn to the millenarian vision for strength. Faced with persecution from federal forces, Papudo surrendered to General Fernando Setembrino de Carvalho in January 1915, just six short months after he joined the millenarian cause. The general recognized that Papudo was not a millenarian rebel and that he thus presented little threat to the army. So Setembrino de Carvalho granted Papudo an unconditional release.[51]

Along with Papudo, Antonio Tavares, Jr., participated in the July 1914 attack against Canoinhas. He too had lost his municipal post, and he too assumed the mantle of millenarian rebel in late 1914. From his redoubt west of Canoinhas, Tavares executed a series of successful raids against immigrant colonies in late 1914. Like Papudo, however, Tavares soon surrendered as the pressure from federal troops increased. At this point a letter Tavares wrote to General Setembrino de Carvalho laid bare his political motives. In it he admitted that he was fighting for political reasons, and here he added his desire to see the state of Santa Catarina win in its border dispute with Paraná. At this point he assured the general that "we haven't abandoned civilization."[52]

The actions of Tavares and Papudo differed dramatically from those of Euzébio Ferreira dos Santos, Chico Ventura, and Elias de Moraes. Politically motivated, Tavares and Papudo only assumed the veneer of millenarianism when it was convenient for them to do so. They were the last to join the rebellion (if one can call what they did joining the rebellion) and the first to surrender. Perhaps their small group of followers did indeed believe in the *santa religião*, although there is no evidence to prove this. What is known is that another political opportunist was quite shocked by the fanaticism of the residents of one rebel redoubt he joined. Thus, when Henrique Wolland surrendered to authorities, he complained of the habits of the rebels, a group he described as in constant prayer. Indeed, one gets the impression that he was quite glad to be free of the fanatics![53]

The existence of political rebels, the contrasts with the leadership core, and the development of the movement's ideology allow for several conclusions as to the nature of the millenarian rebellion. On one level, this was truly a religious movement. The core of the rebel leadership believed in the millenarian vision—apparently as strongly as did the majority of the rebel population. Prayer and religious ceremonies dominated life in the redoubts. The rebellion was not simply a political struggle in which a few leaders employed a millenarian scheme to trick an ignorant peasantry into fighting for their personal goals. Political leaders, such as Bonifácio Papudo and Antonio Tavares, joined the rebellion late and surrendered early. Meanwhile, Euzébio Ferreira dos Santos, Chico Ventura, and Elias de Moraes stayed from start to finish, through the heady times at Taquaraçu, where food was abundant, to the times of disease and hunger as the rebellion died.

The Contestado Rebellion was also not a straightforward class-based rebellion. It was not a political rebellion in which the peasantry rose up to destroy the landlord class. In the 1960s many Brazilians argued this point. For Noel Nascimento, the Contestado Rebellion was a peasant war masquerading as a millenarian movement ("O fanatismo religioso de que se reveste a luta componesa").[54] Religion was pretext for revolution, and the Contestado rebels fought for the "end of the feudal regime which ruled the isolated interior at that time."[55]

Nascimento, however, wrote at a time of mobilization in Brazil, a time when the peasant leagues of the Northeast became a viable threat to *fazendeiro* control. In the Contestado, however, the composition of the rebel population argues for a diferent interpretation. In this case, we know that contemporaries referred to the three key leaders of the rebellion as *fazendeiros*. Euzébio Ferreira dos Santos, Chico Ventura, and Elias de Moraes all owned significant amounts of land and cattle. Euzébio and Elias de Moraes maintained ties with the Republican party of Santa Catarina. All three maintained patron-client ties with numerous peasants.

To be sure, poor peasants formed the majority of the rebellious population in the Contestado. But according to rebel testimony, people from all stations in life joined the movement. Rosália Maria de Castro remembers rich people in the redoubt, although most were poor. Likewise, Maria de Jesus Pedroso, Rosa Paes de Farias, and João Paes de Farias remember the presence of rich people in the redoubts. Finally, there is the example of Cipriano Rodrigues de Moraes, who, as a small boy, joined the rebellion with his parents and brother. At that time his father, who owned 800 hectares of good land and 1,600 head of cattle, "became crazy, got religion," and moved to Taquaraçu.[56]

While not a revolutionary movement, the actions of the Contestado rebels nevertheless demonstrate a class-based agenda with class-specific demands. As mentioned, rebels expelled Manoel Ferreira dos Santos when he claimed José Maria had ordered him to sleep with the virgins. In other words, rebels expelled one of their leaders, himself the son of a *fazendeiro*. Clearly, this is an example of followers resisting manipulation by leaders.

Likewise, the proposed execution of the rebel military commander's son, after the son beat his wife for devotion to the *santa religião*, further illustrates rebel willingness to challenge leaders. Rebels also killed those who refused to share their possessions with the rest of the community. Finally, rebels eagerly attacked those *fazendeiros* who refused to join the movement.

The willingness of peasants to challenge their own leaders highlights the tension between the restorationist and utopian elements in most millenarian rebellions.[57] The Contestado case suggests that millenarian imagery is not inherently revolutionary in that the goal was the restoration of the unequal patron-client tie. Nevertheless, at times such a desire to restore can appear revolutionary if it challenges new social and class relations such as wage labor, absentee ownership, and the involvement of foreign capital. Such protest would then become, in the words of Patricia Pessar, "revolutionary, but in a reactionary form."[58]

And yet, a close reading of the Contestado Rebellion suggests that even the form was not so reactionary. Rebel peasants certainly did not seek a simple restoration of "traditional" relations. Instead their actions, such as the expulsion of a leader, set new standards for elite behavior that stood in stark contrast to an unspoken "moral economy" before the rebellion. Indeed, rebel actions sent notice that this was not to be a simple restoration of precapitalist relations.

Why, however, did a specifically millenarian movement emerge in the Contestado? What was it about the nature of the prerebellion society, the entrance of industrial capitalism, and the changes it engendered that led people to seek salvation, moral regeneration, and a return to the monarchy? To answer these questions we turn to a theoretical examination of millenarianism in order to better understand the material and spiritual disruptions created by capitalism, the ramifications of local *patrão* participation in capitalism's entrance, and hence the special appeal of the millenarian call in the Contestado.

Millenarianism in Theory and Practice

Clifford Geertz, in his classic collection of essays *The Interpretation of Cultures*, set forth the terms "ethos" and "world view" to place the role of religion in its cultural context. Ethos, we are told, is the "moral (and aesthetic) aspects of a given culture, the evaluative elements," while world view is "the cognitive, existential aspects [of a culture]."[59] Later, Geertz explains that ethos is "the approved style of life," while world view is "the assumed structure of reality."[60]

In a given society, ethos and world view should reinforce one another. That is, the way things ought to be (ethos) and the way things are perceived to be (world view) should be in agreement. There exists a reciprocal, or mutually reinforcing, relationship between ethos and world view. Returning to Geertz, we see that there should be "a meaningful relation between the values a people holds and the general order with which it [a people] finds itself." Indeed, "the ethos is made intellectually reasonable by being shown to represent a way of life implied by the actual state of affairs the world view describes." Meanwhile, "the world view is made emotionally acceptable by being presented as an image" of a way of life authenticated by the ethos of a society.[61]

But how do ethos and world view relate to religion in a society? Here Geertz argues that religious practice establishes, reinforces, and demonstrates the moral norms of the ethos. In other words, religious practice and religious symbols "sum up . . . the way one ought to behave." Religion, or religious practice, is thus the mediator between morality and reality, between ethos and world view. Religious belief demonstrates that everyday life is ordered along the moral concepts of the society. Conversely, religious belief demonstrates how the values of a society are found in everyday life. According to Geertz, we see that an essential role of religion is that it demonstrates "a meaningful relation between the values a people holds and the general order of existence within which it finds itself."[62]

Evidence from the Contestado, presented in chapter 2 and summarized here, confirms the importance of religion and religious ritual to patron-client relations. Interviews with rebel survivors and the descendants of powerful landowners demonstrate the universality of ritual kinship ties. Evidence of patron religiosity in the construction of chapels, and in the remark by a Pacheco grandson that he found his grandfather's religious zeal an embarrassment, suggest that *compadrío* involved much more than material exchanges.[63]

Patron religiosity and the importance of religious ritual are further demonstrated by patron saint celebrations. Anthropologists argue that the association of the landowner with the patron saint increased the prestige of the *patrão*, but the practice of offering a feast also reconfirmed, or even sanctified, the landowner's reciprocal obligation to his followers.[64] Euzébio Ferreira dos Santos, landowner and rebel leader, was well known for his sponsorship of the annual feast in honor of St. Sebastian. He even invited José Maria to the event in 1911. Other area landowners boasted of their sponsorship of saints' festivals and the construction of chapels for such celebrations.[65]

What happens, however, when economic change calls into question the ethos–world view system? What happens when a way of life, which is steeped in, and indeed sanctified by, religious symbols and practice is challenged by rapid change? The result is likely a crisis of spiritual as well as material dimensions: material, in that loss of land, or an abrupt change in labor patterns, is likely to accompany those developments powerful enough to call the ethos–world view system into question; spiritual, because those material changes challenge life as it should be and thus call into question a way of life sanctified by religious tradition.[66]

Historically, threats large enough to call into question the ethos–world view system in peasant societies have originated from two sources: colonialism and the expansion of capitalism. But how, exactly, have colonialism and capitalism affected peasant societies? Here the issue becomes whether or not pressures remain external to a society. In terms of an external-internal continuum, do external pressures negatively affect all members of a local society? If not, does this mean that some members of the local society, most likely local elites, are themselves participating in the expansion of capitalism or are aiding the forces of colonialism?

When colonialism or capitalism threatens *all* members of a society, *including* elites, then a unified response against that threat becomes more possible. This emphatically external threat does not call the society's ethos–world view into question. People do not question the validity of their own culture, and no crisis *internal* to the society develops. Instead, members of the local society wish to defend unified society, and their shared beliefs, against the external forces of change. At this point a secular movement, aimed precisely at defending both society and culture from external attack, adequately serves as the vehicle for this defense.[67]

The internal crisis of values—the crisis created by the divergence between a society's ethos and its world view—is more likely to emerge when local elites cooperate with the external forces of change. Colonial and capitalist administrators often seek out local elites to act as brokers, given elite control over land and labor. In return for providing such commodities, local elites gain new access to larger and different forms of power and resources. The conflict, however, emerges when local elites violate local norms in providing land and labor to outside groups. Now, elites no longer act the way they *ought* to. They no longer, in the words of Patricia Pessar, fulfill "duties that have been sacralized through religious meanings and institutions."[68] The external forces of change have now been internalized and threaten to tear the peasant society apart from within. The crisis is no longer of a material nature only, but of a spiritual nature as well. Such an internal crisis prevents a unified secular reaction against colonialism or capitalism, precisely because developments have shattered the unity of the society.

The key to understanding millenarian movements lies in an analysis of their appeal to those suffering from an internal crisis of values.[69] Millenarian imagery speaks of the moral misdeeds of a people. It calls for the moral regeneration of a society and advances the need for salvation. People are encouraged to build a new holy world to replace the current evil one.[70]

These ideas of salvation, the need for moral regeneration, and the building of holy cities must be especially appealing to those seeking a return to a time when a religiously informed "what ought to be" corresponded with the perceived reality. For if, as Patricia Pessar writes, elites have abandoned their duties sacralized by religious practice, we can thus understand the need for moral regeneration and salvation. And by establishing holy cities, where *all* would live, elites would be forced to abandon their ties with external actors. Millenarian movements promise to heal the suffering caused by a spiritual, as well as material, crisis. They promise to heal the special crisis that occurs when the actions of a local elite lead to the internalization of the external pressures of colonialism and capitalism.

Contestado Elites and the Crisis of Subsistence

In searching for the roots of the millenarian movement in the Contestado, we must examine the events and trends that challenged the ethos–world view system in the society. Here we turn to the entrance of capitalism—to the building of the railroad through the region, European colonization, and the mass privatization of public lands. In particular, we focus on the Contestado elite and their participation in the process that eventually threatened peasant subsistence and the entire co-godparenthood complex.

In the broadest sense, the transition to capitalism produced a land tenure revolution in the Contestado. The Brazil Railway Company received public land grants totaling over 135,000 hectares in the Peixe River valley alone. Its subsidiary, the Southern Brazil Lumber and Colonization Company, purchased some 227,000 hectares of forest lands in a three-year period. Together, the federal government of Brazil, in cooperation with the states of Paraná and Santa Catarina, turned nearly 200,000 hectares over to European immigrants in the Contestado between 1890 and 1914. During that same period the states of Paraná and Santa Catarina sold an additional 250,000 hectares of government-owned land (see chapters 3 and 4).

For their part, the elite in the Contestado seized upon the land rush created by the entrance of the railroad, and as such they furthered the region's land tenure revolution. We have seen how in 1908 *coronel* Henrique Rupp of Campos Novos created the Colônia Rupp colony on his land near the Erval d'Oeste railroad station. There he sold 5,000 hectares worth of 25-hectare plots. Augusto Carlos Stephanes, also of Campos Novos, sold nearly 5,000 hectares along the railroad line. Arthur de Paula e Souza divided his Santa Leocádia property into lots and began selling them to Polish immigrants also in 1908 (see chapter 4). *Patrões* were now expelling *agregados* and *posseiros* from the land.

In labor terms, planter cooperation proved crucial to the successful entrance of capitalism into the region. *Patrões* such as Pedro Ruiva, Manoel Fabrício Vieira, and Maximino de Moraes took advantage of the railroad's need for workers and began operating as labor brokers. This meant that they forced their own clients to work on the railroad, and they managed the thousands of urban poor from Rio de Janeiro and the Brazilian Northeast sent to work on the line (see chapter 5).

At this point we return to the photograph of a smiling Bemvindo Pacheco, taken in front of the huge Brazil Lumber Company sawmill at Três Barras. A large landowner and *patrão* to many *agregados*, he had, between 1910 and 1913, sold and/or rented more than 11,000 hectares to the Brazil Lumber Company. With Bemvindo in the photograph stands the crew he organized to work at the sawmill. No doubt *agregados* who once lived on the land Bemvindo sold to Brazil Lumber now found themselves working at the sawmill. Bemvindo Pacheco had become a labor contractor.[71]

The point made by the examples of Henrique Rupp, Manoel Fabrício Vieira, and most graphically by Bemvindo Pacheco is that the entrance of capitalism was not a faceless affair in the Contestado. Board members of the Brazil Railway Company and Brazilian government colonization officials did indeed make decisions that changed life for the Contestado subsistence peasantry. But in the Contestado it was Henrique Rupp, local landowner and godfather to his *agregados* and *camaradas*, who sold land to outsiders and thus deprived many of his clients of their access to land. Likewise, it was the local *patrão* Bemvindo Pacheco who sold lands worked by his *agregados* to the Brazil Lumber Company and then sent these men to work in the sawmill.

The entrance of capitalism into the Contestado threatened a way of life and, indeed, the possibility of peasant subsistence. Many *agregados* found their access to land blocked by land sales to European immigrants and foreign enterprises. Many were now forced to labor in railroad construction for twelve to sixteen hours a day, seven days a week. Once the inhabitants of shacks on isolated stretches of a *patrão's* holding, they now slept in cramped, fetid camps with thousands of others—camps located tens of kilometers from their family dwellings.

Gone was the time when the *patrão* worked cattle alongside his *agregados*. Gone also was an era when the nature of *agregado* labor obligations left them with space to raise their own crops and cattle. These *agregados* thus faced two related threats: first, a direct attack against subsistence, as when they were expelled from lands they had occupied for years; and second, those sent to work on the railroad faced a new, capitalist work regime, one involving an exponential rise in labor obligations when compared to their cattle-ranching duties. But worst of all, it was their *patrão*, the godfather of their children, who forced this change.[72]

The external pressures brought to bear on the Contestado had now been internalized. Cooperating with the capitalists, Contestado *patrões* broke with their moral obligations to guarantee peasant subsistence, an obligation mandated by the co-godparenthood tie. Thus, they threatened not only subsistence, but also an entire way of life built around a reciprocity (albeit of an unequal nature) born of mutual material needs and sanctified by the religious co-godparenthood institution.

At this point a crisis of material *and* spiritual proportions gripped the Contestado: material in that many peasants lost their land and were forced, for the first time, into a wage labor regime; and spiritual in that an internal crisis of values emerged as patrons broke a relationship mandated and sanctified by religious tradition.

Here we return to Clifford Geertz's ideas on religion, ethos, and world view. Using this terminology, we see that the ethos of the Contestado society, one of patron dominance *and* patron reciprocity, no longer corresponded with the reality of patron threats to *agregado* subsistence and way of life. This led to the questioning of the ethos–world view system. Indeed, it produced an internal crisis of values given that religious belief and practice (via co-godparenthood ties) had insured that "what ought to be" actually was.

Millenarianism As Solution

José Maria began his travels through the Contestado region precisely during this time of turmoil. He preached of the need for a moral regeneration of society and for a return to the monarchy. Such ideas struck a responsive chord among the many in the Contestado suffering from an internal crisis of self-doubt. The emergence of a millenarian movement in the Contestado is understandable, for as a religious movement it alone, as opposed to a political movement, addressed both the material and spiritual nature of the transformation now gripping the Contestado. It promised to heal these crises by ending the self-doubt and even the guilt of the "sinners." Patrons were to join the movement and thus resume their material and spiritual responsibilities vis-à-vis the peasantry. This re-creation of the reciprocal patron-client tie was not left to chance, however, and rebels enforced the ethic of sharing and threatened leaders who violated the movement's moral code. Finally, by declaring war against an evil enemy, the movement promised to destroy the sources of the external pressures that had brought a transformation to the Contestado region.

Earlier we saw how an imagery of self-blame and guilt pervaded the ideology of the millenarian movement. The changes gripping the Contestado, many felt, were a punishment from God. Rebels referred to themselves as sinners. Why, then, the emphasis on suffering as punishment? And punishment for what?

In her comparative article on Brazilian millenarianism, Patricia Pessar notes that Brazilian folk Catholicism attributes "disease, crop failure, and other misfortunes to divine punishment." Here Pessar defines folk Catholicism as "a cultural system consisting of an integrated set of beliefs, values, and institutions . . . with which people orient their actions." Such a folk type of Catholicism dominated the Contestado. The tendency of the peasantry to blame themselves for the current crisis was thus no doubt connected to the nature of folk Catholicism as practiced in the region.[73]

For in a sense peasants themselves participated in the very process producing the crisis. Male *agregados* went off to work on the railroad. There they faced squalid camps, dangerous working conditions, violence among workers, and the confiscation of their salaries by their *patrão*. Male *agregados* left their wives and children alone to manage subsistence crops and their few head of cattle. Quite possibly these family members also faced additional responsibilities in fulfillment of their husbands' or fathers' estate labor duties. As such, female heads of households especially felt the pressures of the transition to capitalism. As managers of the household economy, they faced the threat to subsistence and change of life-style caused by the absence of husbands. At this point they perhaps blamed their husbands for participating in this process. For these men had broken with their own expected roles and duties as patriarchs within their own families.

Small wonder, then, that women joined the millenarian movement with great enthusiasm and in large numbers. As a journalist for *A Folha do Comércio* noted, "The rebels believe in José Maria, and those that are informed say that it is the women who are most fanatical."[74] The soldier Teixeira d'Assumpção also noted this greater fanaticism of women, speaking of several who went alone to the redoubts because their husbands refused to join the movement.[75] These doubts about their own participation in the crisis, combined with the sanctity of the patron's position in the society, led the peasantry, then, to at least partially blame themselves for society's current ills.

Imagine, then, the power of a call for deliverance from the current crisis of self-doubt and blame. By establishing holy cities, people would change their lives and change the direction of the evil world. A moral regeneration would release them from their suffering and save them from their past sins—sins that were at least partially responsible for their current predicament. A moral regeneration of society was the first step toward healing the internal crisis of values in the Contestado.

By creating a new world the millenarian movement then promised to re-create the fit between ethos and world view. To do so it evoked elements of both the old and the new. On the one hand, the millenarian vision, with the force of God and religion on its side, promised to pull patrons back into a situation where patron actions corresponded with the norms of society. With tradition on the rebels' side, the millenarian call was at first a peaceful one. Participants believed in the power of this tradition to pull patrons "back into the fold" and thus re-create a society now called into question. On the other hand, things would be different in the holy cities. There, a forced communal sharing would insure that the principle of reciprocity was indeed followed in the material realm.

At this point the rebel demand for the return to the monarchy comes into focus, given the association of the monarchy with ideas concerning patron paternalism. Consider Patricia Pessar's cogent discussion of Brazilian messianic leaders and their practice of sharing donations with their followers. By doing this, she argues, such leaders acted as ideal patrons, thereby placing them in sharp contrast with local elites who at that moment were abandoning their clients. The

monarchy, according to Pessar, thus represented a time when paternalism regulated the patron-client relationship, for "who, after all,
best epitomized the meanings and values that morally united the
vulnerable peasant with the elite than the monarch?"[76]

Remember that José Maria gave nightly readings from *A história
de Carlos Magno* (*The History of Charlemagne*). Surely he dwelled
on the numerous passages that emphasized the Holy Roman Emperor's paternalism. Perhaps he read from this passage, which speaks
of the period in which Charlemagne "rested for a number of years in a
profound spiritual retreat, dealing only with issues related to the
well-being of his vassals, who loved him because of the care he took
to see that they were treated in a just fashion."[77]

Numerous *patrões* answered the call to join the millenarian
movement, and they did so *as the heads of immediate family
members and agregados*. João Paes de Farias remembers the day his
father, Chico Ventura, decided to join the movement. Of course
Ventura's wife, two sons, and daughter went with him. But so too did
the entire Ventura *clã* (clan). Such a clan, composed of *agregados,
camaradas*, and others, was no doubt fairly large given Ventura's
status as a *fazendeiro*. As with Ventura, the movement's leader,
Euzébio Ferreira dos Santos, himself a middle-level landowner, also
moved to Taquaraçu "with all his people" ("com toda o pessoal
dele").[78]

We have seen how the millenarian movement, by promising
salvation and a moral regeneration of society, offered hope to a people
suffering from an internal crisis of self-doubt and blame. We can now
see how it further promised to heal the crisis by re-creating the
reciprocal patron-client relationship within the borders of the holy
cities. That is, the ethos of planter dominance, mixed with planter
paternalism and subsistence guarantees, would once again corre-
spond with planter actions. Thus we can now understand why
virtually all *patrões* who joined the movement rose to leadership
positions.

Not all Contestado patrons heeded the call to join the millenarian
movement. Indeed, most landowners cast their lot with the federal
forces, going so far as to organize civilian battalions financed and
outfitted by the federal government. Also, the Brazil Railway Company continued to operate its railroad and lumber concerns in the
region. After establishing the holy cities and healing the wounds of
the internal crisis, the movement trained its sights on other targets. It
would now face the external threat posed by the railroad and unrepentant patrons in what would be the third and final portion of the rebel
strategy for victory and salvation.

In response to an army peace proposal, Elias de Moraes wrote: "We will leave the redoubts only after the deaths of Arthur de Paula [e Souza], [Manoel] Fabrício Vieira, Chiquinho de Albuquerque . . . and others, and only after the restoration of the lives of those women and children killed by the government forces at Taquara-ssu."[79] Moraes's letter, written in late 1914, mentions the Taquara-çu massacre, the event that produced a violent shift in the ideology of the movement. In the words of ex-rebel Rosa Paes de Farias, gone were the days when the millenarianists "welcomed everyone with open arms."[80] For, when faced with the pacific call to join the movement, many *fazendeiros*, including those named in the Moraes letter, had responded by attacking the believers. The Taquaraçu massacre was thus the last straw, the final proof that these *patrões* now fought with the side of evil. Because they ignored the mille-narian call to reassume their duties as good *patrões*, the rebels now sentenced them to death.

Following Chico Alonso's September 1914 deadline for joining the movement, the rebels began attacking the recalcitrant *fazendeiros*. They repeatedly attacked the Fazenda dos Pardos, whose owners, the Pacheco family, had sold lands to Brazil Lumber and sent their farmhands to labor at the sawmill. They attacked Zacharias de Paula Xavier, the seller of large land tracts to European immigrants, and forced him to abandon his *fazenda*. And as Moraes's letter shows, the rebels condemned to death Manoel Fabrício Vieira and Pedro Ruiva, two *patrões* heavily involved in labor contracting for the railroad.[81]

With steady resolve the rebels also pressed on with a series of attacks against *coronel* Arthur de Paula e Souza, the *patrão* so despised for his expulsion of *agregados* and *camaradas* from lands he had recently sold to Polish immigrants. In fact Paula e Souza recog-nized two ex-*camaradas* (as he called them) among the rebel pris-oners captured during a series of September 1914 attacks against his Santa Leocádia holding. Later that same month, the rebels succeeded in killing the now-hated *fazendeiro*.[82]

Finally, there is the case of Adeodato, the last leader of the rebellion. The son of an *agregado* on the *fazenda* of Manoel Dias, Adeodato was the godson of this *fazendeiro*. Sometime in 1915 Adeodato led an attack against the Dias *fazenda*. He and his men burned Dias's crops and house, and Adeodato killed the *fazendeiro*. That is, Adeodato killed his godfather!

According to the historical sociologist Duglas Teixeira Monteiro, Adeodato's murder of his godfather signified the final rebel rejection of cross-class *compadrío* in the Contestado. Rather, the rebels gave up hope, especially after the Taquaraçu massacre, that former *pa-trões* who had not already joined their cause would change their evil ways. These patrons had thus become the enemy, the external enemy, along with the railroad. As such, co-godparenthood ties or not, they were to be killed, as they had foregone their chance to join the movement and reassume their duties as good *patrões*. But this did not signal the end of cross-class *compadrío*. For if the rebels opposed these ties, why, then, did cross-class co-godparenthood ties remain strong, as Monteiro himself admits, in the redoubts? The rebels did not oppose interclass *compadrío*, but rather opposed those individual *patrões* who refused to recognize the duties entailed in such a relationship.[83]

If unrepentant *patrões* eventually became an external enemy, the firm they most associated with, the railroad, was from the beginning a target of rebel anger. Between 1912 and 1916 rebels destroyed bridges and tore down telegraph lines. They attacked those European immigrants settled on railroad lands. In their most successful attack, that of 5 September 1914, the rebels destroyed railroad stations at Calmon and São João, cut the track between those two points, and burned down the Brazil Lumber Company sawmill at Calmon. In their wake they left nearly 100 dead and several railroad cars in flames. Taken together, a Brazil Railway Company employee soon admitted, "the *fanático* trouble of the past two years caused the practical abandonment of the line."[84]

After promising to heal the internal crisis of values through salvation and the reestablishment of the reciprocal patron-client relationship, the millenarian movement now struck against the external sources of the crisis. By destroying the railroad, sawmills, immigrant colonies, and unrepentant *patrões*, the rebels would rid the region of the forces that caused a crisis in their society.

Here we can counter Linda Lewin's argument on strategy, made in reference to the bandit Antonio Silvino of the Brazilian Northeast. She argues that Silvino's attacks against railroads and telegraphs were not protests against modernization, but rather simple strategical moves aimed at slowing down his pursuers. Thus Lewin claims that "Silvino's assaults . . . should not be construed as 'primitive protest' against the state, but viewed as more pragmatically determined by his intelligent grasp of the tactics of his own survival."[85]

Did rebels attack the railroad for purely strategic reasons? At the time, army officer Demerval Peixoto clearly understood that such attacks made good tactical sense. He pointed out that destruction of railroad track made troop provisioning four times slower and more expensive.[86] But Peixoto also found a deeper meaning in the attacks, one that signified opposition to the changes created by the railroad's entrance. Because with its entrance "there was, certainly, the exploitation of many peaceable people who, upon seeing themselves deprived of the fruits of their lands overnight, preferred to oppose the progress which had brought them misery."[87] Rebel attacks made tactical sense, for they hindered the army's ability to fight the rebels. But such attacks also promised to deal with the pressures unleashed by the construction of the railroad—that is, the pressures that produced an internal crisis in the Contestado. The actions of the Contestado rebels demonstrated that attacks that made sense strategically could also make sense as an expression of protest as well. Strategy and protest are not, as in Lewin's article, mutually exclusive categories.

Discussions of strategy and protest, of ritual and meaning, and of leaders and followers help revise our understanding of the Contestado Rebellion. At the time of the war, many Brazilians saw it as simply an uprising of crazed peasants who blindly attacked all signs of civilization. We now know that the rebels were very selective in their attacks and, indeed, that these attacks illustrate the material and social tensions created by the entrance of the railroad. Landowners were asked to join the rebellion, and some did—a fact that negates the argument that Brazilian millenarian movements were simply class wars masquerading as religious uprisings. Nevertheless, a class-based agenda clearly appears in rebel actions against their own leaders.

The complex history of the Contestado demonstrates the advantages of shifting our focus to include followers and not just leaders. Such a focus uncovers not only rebel tactics and government responses, but also the meaning behind religious traditions and practices. It combines material, political, social, and cultural elements to explain the specific appeal of a millenarian vision to a people in crisis. As such this shift in focus explains not only why leaders established millenarian movements, but also why peasants joined them. Such a focus demonstrates the crucial role peasants played in shaping the history of the Brazilian Old Republic.

7

Conclusion:

The Power of the

Millenarian Call

In 1911 the sermons of José Maria reached a particularly receptive audience. They did so not because it was an ignorant audience, one easily fooled and fanaticized by mystical figures, but because the nature of the millenarian call very much addressed the specific concerns and fears of that population. We now understand why this was so, given the nature of socioeconomic relations in the pre-rebellion society, the nature of the entrance of capitalism, and how this entrance transformed the region.

The emergence of what has been termed here the internal crisis of values, the role the local elite played in the creation of such a crisis, and thus the special appeal of the millenarian movement can all be highlighted by a counterfactual example involving the Contestado *patrão* Zeca Vacariano. A local landowner, Vacariano led two labor gangs working on the construction of the railroad. In chapter 5 we saw how the railroad administrator Achilles Stengel planned to break with tradition, pay Vacariano's workers directly, and thus bypass the patron's control over his laborers. For at this point Stengel no doubt calculated that sufficient numbers of workers now worked on the line. In addition, construction would end in a year, and he presumably felt that the strong railroad security force could control the workers, the presence or absence of their *patrão* notwithstanding. This was his chance to break Vacariano's power and to rid himself of a now superfluous middleman. Faced with such an obvious challenge to his authority and to his source of economic power, Vacariano reacted violently. It was he, then, who led the famous assault on the Brazil Railway Company pay train in 1909. After killing the paymaster and security guards, Vacariano escaped with 381 *contos*, never to be heard from again.

The counterfactual quotient comes into play when we consider what would have happened if other *patrões* had joined Vacariano's raid against the railroad. The possibility of such action was admittedly remote given the particulars of the regional transformation. In addition to labor recruitment, many landowners benefited enormously from the rising land values spurred by railroad activities. And landowners expected further benefits as the railroad opened new markets. Nevertheless, what if the Brazil Railway Company had alienated landowners by attempting to seize all lands covered under the original railroad concession? Recognizing that the entrance of the railroad now threatened their authority and, indeed, their economic base, perhaps they too would have created a unified front, determined to destroy Stengel and the railroad.

We know that some local elites quarreled with the railroad over labor brokerage issues. For example, disagreements occurred between railroad administrator Stengel and the powerful *patrão* and labor broker Maximino de Moraes. Maximino's brother Elias de Moraes, himself a landowner and *patrão*, became one of the leaders of the millenarian rebellion. And it was this same Elias de Moraes who then encouraged old friends to attack the railroad and destroy key bridges.

Finally, there is the case of Manoel Fabrício Vieira. A powerful *patrão* and landowner, he had directed labor gangs in the harvesting of *erva mate* before the entrance of the railroad. At the time of the paymaster robbery, Vieira's men worked on track construction and cut and sold ties to the railroad. Most important, investigations into the robbery soon implicated Vieira himself. His brother-in-law was arrested in connection with the assault, and the robbery was allegedly planned at the house of Vieira's foreman. In addition, some felt that Vieira aided Vacariano's escape.

Manoel Fabrício Vieira thus emerges as a calculating man, ready and willing to aid any actions that would benefit his power as a member of the local elite. Such a view corresponds to statements made by Contestado residents who knew the *patrão*. Perhaps Vieira aided Vacariano because he too quarreled with Stengel over terms of materials and labor contracts. And based on the nature of Vacariano's success, perhaps Vieira himself toyed with the idea of some kind of action against the railroad.

Had local Contestado *patrões* been more united in their recognition that the railroad threatened their power, how would they have reacted? Violently, it seems, based on the actions of Zeca Vacariano and even those of the rebel leader Elias de Moraes. At this point they would have gathered their clients together, as they had done so often in the past, to create personal armies. That is, they would have pulled their men off railroad construction to use them now in a fight *against* the railroad and its powerful security force.

Such a response, led by area *patrões*, would have amounted to a political rebellion in the Contestado. By pulling their men off construction and using them in personal armies, patrons and clients would once again have been unified. Patrons would now have been acting in an acceptable fashion, thereby diminishing the threat of an internal crisis. In defense of a now unified society, a political rebellion would have likely emerged as the reaction to an external threat. Gone, then, would be the appeal of the millenarian movement's promise to heal internal splits, and thereby to re-create a society, for by opting to oppose the railroad the patrons would have opted in favor of their clients.

Here, however, we need not rely solely on a hypothetical example to explore the complexities of millenarian movements. The examination of another Latin American rebellion allows us to test the hypotheses raised for the Contestado further and explore the reasons why millenarian movements are likely to emerge. At this point a comparative digression is needed to present the case of a rebellion in Mexico that contained both nonmillenarian and millenarian phases. For by using the concepts of an external-internal continuum, and an internal crisis of values, we can clarify both the nature of the Caste War of Yucatán in particular and of millenarian movements in general.

A Comparative Digression:
The Caste War of Yucatán

In the summer of 1847 Maya Indians from the Yucatán Peninsula rose up in a violent rebellion against *ladino* residents and Mexican government officials. One year later the rebel Maya controlled four-fifths of the peninsula and threatened the key administrative and commercial city of Mérida. This was the Caste War of Yucatán, a rebellion that would end only after the beginning of this century.[1]

Like the Contestado Rebellion, the Caste War emerged in reaction to the commercialization of a backwater region. Unlike the former, however, the Caste War was not, in the early years at least, a millenarian rebellion. The explanation for this difference lies in the history of Spanish colonization, the nature of the local (Yucatán) Maya society, and the nature of the nineteenth-century commercialization of the region.

When the Spanish *conquistador* Francisco de Montejo invaded the

Yucatán Peninsula in 1527, he could not have imagined that it would take 170 years to establish Spanish control over the entire peninsula.[2] Fierce Maya resistance was one reason for this delay. The other was a lack of precious metals on the peninsula. Up through the eighteenth century the Spaniards held economic dominance only over the north-western third of the peninsula.

In the interior, a limited degree of socioeconomic differentiation afforded indigenous elites access to the best lands and to communal labor in return for elite guarantees of commoner subsistence. It also meant that elites led fights in the colonial courts against Spanish land grabs of communal holdings. Socioeconomic differentiation did *not* signify, however, that native elites adopted Spanish customs. Here the exclusion from membership in the Spanish bureaucracy insured that such acculturation did not happen.[3]

The Spanish liberalization of trade laws began to challenge the isolation of the interior Maya in the late eighteenth century. The challenge continued after Mexican independence in 1821, as *ladino hacendados* employed newly claimed powers of state to expand plantings of henequen and sugar for sale on the now open market. Faced with poor soil conditions in the Northwest, planters now turned to the isolated interior in search of the fertile soils their crops required.[4]

The combination of economic and legislative incentives turned the interior, once the weakest area of Spanish control, into the economic center of the peninsula. By 1844, *ladino*-owned sugar plantations in the interior region counted for 71 percent of the peninsula's total sugar production. In that same year the sugar production of two previously isolated interior departments, Tekax and Peto, nearly doubled the combined output of all other departments. To work the new plantations, *hacendados* trapped Indians from recently usurped lands into debt peonage contracts.[5]

Both *macehuales* (commoners) and Indian elites lost land to expanding *ladino* plantations. In addition, *ladino* debt peonage threatened native elite access to Indian labor, labor elites employed in cultivating private crops.[6] As a result, the interior Maya launched a unified attack against the *ladinos*.[7] This was the Caste War, a nonmillenarian rebellion that by May 1848 nearly drove all *ladinos* off the peninsula.

What began as a unified "secular" war, however, would soon become a millenarian rebellion. The Mexican army scored a string of victories in late 1848 and 1849. Internal divisions within the Maya, including the murder of two rebel leaders, weakened fighting capacity. Most important, the rank-and-file Maya troops refused to continue fighting, preferring instead to return home to plant the next year's corn crop.[8] Perhaps followers now questioned the action of their leaders and began to see the continuation of the war as a threat to their own subsistence. Whereas the threat to the Maya had once come from external sources, it now came from within their society.

It was during this period of internal turmoil that a wooden "Speaking Cross" appeared to redirect the Maya and their struggle. Employing millenarian imagery, the Speaking Cross blamed the current crisis on Indian disunity and the failure to worship God properly. It promised hope, however, by proclaiming that the Indians were God's children fighting God's war. Such promises of hope and victory reaffirmed the justness of the Maya war. In addition, by establishing a home base and limiting their field of military operations, the Cross promised to end the threat to subsistence posed by the orders of rebel military leaders. So directly did this call inspire those suffering from an internal crisis of doubt that the rebels continued their war against the *ladinos* for another fifty years![9]

In 1848 the interior Maya rose up in a unified rebellion against the external pressures caused by the expansion of sugar production. Four years later they heeded a millenarian call that now addressed the particular needs of a society laid to waste by internal division and military defeat. Such is the nature of the external-internal continuum that the Caste War of Yucatán contained both "secular" and millenarian phases over the course of this fifty-year-long rebellion.

The Theory Revisited

The analytical tools set forth in this book—an internal crisis of values and what is termed the external-internal continuum—aid our understanding of why specifically millenarian movements emerge among the peasantry. This framework, as the Contestado Rebellion and Caste War examples demonstrate, points on one level to the role of local elites and their relationship with the external forces of change. If they do not cooperate, or, better yet, if they are excluded from colonization or commercialization processes, then the solidarity of the local society will likely remain intact. Excluded from acting as land or labor brokers, elites are thus not likely to stretch established reciprocal ties to their breaking point. They will not use their authority as leaders to engage in activities that would question established social and cultural norms. At a certain point in such situations (as happened in the Caste War), external developments are thus likely to affect negatively all members of a local society. With their culture and shared society under external attack, locals will likely respond in a unified and nonmillenarian fashion.[10]

Compare this situation to the issues raised by local elite coopera- tion with the external forces of change. Attracted by the promise of new sources of power and wealth, such elites rely on established ties to provide land and/or labor for use in colonial or capitalist projects. In such a case external developments do *not* negatively affect all members of the local society. Local elites now profit, while nonelites lose their land and are pressed into new and different types of labor service. Threats to subsistence and an established way of life now come not only from external sources, but from internal ones as well.[11]

The point here is not that local elites and nonelites lived in utter harmony before the arrival of colonization and/or capitalism. As shown for the Contestado, local *patrões* exploited *agregado* labor and acted in violent ways toward the latter. Rather, the point is that the exploitative but reciprocal patron-client relationship, which guaranteed client subsistence in the Contestado, changed with local elite land sales, the assumption of brokerage duties, and the subse- quent expulsion of *posseiros* and *agregados*. Local elites now threat- ened *agregado* subsistence and even the limited form of patron-client reciprocity. External pressures produced an internal crisis.

As shown in chapter 6, the key to understanding the emergence of millenarian movements rests in understanding how and when the transformation of a society produces a spiritual *and* a material crisis. For the Contestado, we have seen how the entrance of the railroad, state-sponsored colonization, and local elite actions produced a ma- terial crisis for the nonelite of the region. As to the spiritual crisis, this internal crisis of values emerged when patrons abandoned duties sanctified by religious tradition and practice.

Returning to the ethos–world view concepts of Clifford Geertz and their application to millenarianism by Steve Stern, we see that in the Contestado "what ought to be" (ethos) no longer corresponded with "what actually was" (world view).[12] At one time the religious institu- tion of co-godparenthood sanctified planter dominance. It did so, however, at the cost of making patrons morally responsible for the subsistence of their godchildren/*agregados*. The expulsion of peas- ant squatters thus produced not only a material crisis of subsistence, but also a spiritual crisis, given the breakdown of norms sanctified by religious tradition and practice. The ethos of limited planter reciproc- ity and subsistence guarantees no longer corresponded to the reality of patron threats to *agregado* subsistence.

During the first phase of the Caste War, a unified local society rebelled against what was perceived as a common external threat. In the Contestado, the external threat of industrial capitalism produced an internal crisis of values. Given the breakdown of norms sanctioned by religious practice, people began questioning their own actions, and their own faith, in search of the answers to the current crisis. And here the accelerated pace of this transformation heightened the sense of crisis. In less than a decade, thousands lost their access to land, due as much to the actions of Contestado landowners as to the actions of railroad officials. Virtually overnight *agregados* faced explusion and/or a radically different work regime on the railroad. The speed of the transformation thus helped produce, and then intensify, the internal crisis in the Contestado.

With its vision of salvation, moral regeneration, and a return to an idealized past, the millenarian movement addresses the specific concerns of a society suffering from an internal crisis of values and self-doubt. Herein lies its special appeal, for it speaks to both the material *and* spiritual crises that colonization or the transition to capitalism can at times produce. Through salvation and moral regeneration the movement promises to heal the doubt and suffering caused by the breakdown of an ethos–world view system held together by religious practice. In its return to an idealized past, the millenarian vision then promises to re-create a society and to unify it around what were once accepted norms and obligations.

Having re-created a society once gripped by an internal crisis of values, the vision then calls for a unified attack against the forces of external change. On a material level, the vision promises to destroy the forces of evil that produced the crisis. In the Contestado, this meant killing unrepentant *patrões* and destroying the land-grabbing Brazil Railway Company. In the latter portion of the Caste War, it meant death to traitorous Indian *caciques* who dared to negotiate peace with the *ladinos*, the destruction of *ladino* plantations, and the defeat of the Mexican army.

The promise of an end to doubt and suffering and the promised destruction of the forces that produced such suffering is the combination of spiritual and material concerns that explains the special appeal of millenarian visions during certain crisis periods. On an analytical level, it is the idea of an external-internal continuum and the internal crisis of values framework that combine to give us a more sophisticated feel for why millenarian movements erupt among the peasantry. These tools force us to enter into the social milieu of those involved in a rebellion. The framework asks us to view events from the peasants' point of view, to ask not only why someone or some group began and led a millenarian rebellion but also why people join such a movement.

Clearly, though, internal disunity is not the only important issue to consider when discussing the emergence of a millenarian movement. Surely ethnic identity can play an important role in the formation of a millenarian ideology. For example, in the Taki Onkoy Rebellion in colonial Peru, paradise was promised for those who embraced indigenous customs.[13] This meant the destruction of the Spanish colonial economy and society and the murder of all Spaniards. The emphasis was on things Andean, because "unless the natives withdrew their willingness to appease the Europeans, they would collaborate in their own destruction."[14]

In addition to this ethnic component, religious belief can also encourage the formation of a millenarian ideology. In fact, in Brazil the Catholicism practiced by those isolated from the organized church contains a millenarian view of history, in that people await "the arrival of the Antichrist, the Apocalypse, the Day of Judgement, and Heaven on Earth for the few who will be saved."[15] The Contestado rebels were certainly aware of the legend of the Portuguese king Sebastião, who, after his death in the Crusades, would return to create heaven on earth. Indeed, much reference was made to Sebastião, and José Maria was to return to the Contestado with the king and his army (see chapter 6).

The presence of such "raw material" undoubtedly contributed to the emergence of the "Speaking Cross" millenarian phase of the Caste War. According to Nancy Farriss, the Maya often adopted Christian symbols, yet ascribed different meanings to them. The Speaking Cross, she argues, "is probably taken from Christian rather than pre-Colombian iconography." The Cross represented, however, indigenous saints and deities the Maya could no longer publicly worship. The practice of an idol "speaking" can be traced to pre-Colombian practices.[16]

Farriss's arguments illustrate the importance of both religious and ethnic identity in the formation of a millenarian movement. Nevertheless, ethnic identity and religious belief do not, in and of themselves, explain the origins of millenarian movements. After all, the Caste War of Yucatán was not initially a millenarian movement, even though these elements were already in place. Likewise, the prophet João Maria wandered through the Contestado region years before José Maria, yet no millenarian movement emerged at that time.

Millenarianism and
the History of the Old Republic

A new emphasis on the history of rural Brazil, on peasants and the pressures and divisions associated with the capitalist transition, revises our understanding of millenarianism in the Old Republic. Focusing on changes in production and in patron-client relations better explains not only the appeal of millenarian leaders such as Padre Cícero and Antonio Conselheiro, but the internal dynamics of their movements as well. It also promises to revise our understanding of the history of the Old Republic by placing a new emphasis on the rural to urban continuum in national politics.

In the case of Joaseiro, for example, we can now recognize the importance of the obvious, yet virtually unexplored, split among followers of Padre Cícero. Indeed, it was the "masses" that gave the Joaseiro movement its millenarian character, for they, and *not* the clergy and educated laity who suppported Padre Cícero, believed that the miracle signaled the end of the world.[17] The decline of the regional cattle-ranching economy and the switch to sugar and cotton production (which was then threatened by droughts) meant that landowners "were either unwilling or unable to provide the rural population with jobs and protection."[18] In this case, pilgrims likely interpreted the 1889 "miracle" in millenarian terms because of extensive changes in both the material and cultural realms. Thus, while Padre Cícero promised material benefits of food and shelter, his paternalistic actions also revitalized the culture of patron-client relations now on the wane.[19]

Millenarianism was thus more than a simple vehicle of peasant protest against declining material conditions. It was also more than a political battle among local and regional elites. Nevertheless, explaining millenarianism in material and cultural terms also tells us a great deal about the political history of Brazil in the Old Republic. It encourages us to look beyond battles among political and economic elites to the interactions between members of the upper and lower classes, and between the city and the countryside.[20] As such, the events, both local and national, that sparked millenarian movements highlight the need for research in local, interior archives and not just in the largest state and national collections.[21]

Peasants rebelled because of threats to their existence, threats frequently initiated or at least supported by urban-based economic and political elites. On the other hand, the union of tens of thousands of peasants from north to south, and their oftentimes violent resistance to the armies of the nation, no doubt contributed as much as urban events to the shift towards militarism and authoritarianism, the decline of Jacobin leaders, and the repression of popular protest in the early years of the Old Republic.[22] Government fear of rural millenarian movements led to some of Brazil's largest military encounters since the Paraguayan War, and out of these battles emerged army officers whose calls for intervention in urban politics would shape the history of Brazil in the 1920s and beyond.[23] The study of millenarianism exposes this rural-urban continuum in the history of the Old Republic.

A Final Thought

The complexities involved in the study of millenarian movements should come as no surprise to scholars, for the complexities and confusion of such studies merely mirror the historical reality of societies in transformation. They mirror the historical reality of millenarian movements themselves. Inevitably, scholars attempting to explain such events simplify not only the process, but the outcome as well. By assuming, for example, that "backward" and "superstitious" peasants are unable to mobilize in a "modern" fashion, the scholar ignores the complex intersection of material, social, and spiritual issues, and argues instead that millenarianism is almost "natural" among peasants.

It turns out that at least one "backward" survivor of the Contestado Rebellion much more willingly admits to the confusing, and contradictory, nature of millenarian movements. In 1985 Rosa Paes de Farias, crippled by blindness and her nearly 100 years of age, just faintly resembled the teenage girl who proudly sewed the magical uniforms of the elite *Pares de França* (Peers of France) rebel guard. And what was the millenarian movement in which she participated? "Well," sighed Rosa, "people in the camps always spoke of order, order, order; but people were dying all around." Yet today she still believes in God, for "there is no other way." But what was the *santa religião?* Here Rosa wearily responded that "no one knows exactly what *fanatismo* was."[24]

Notes

In the citation of archival material, volume number, book number, date, and page number are given whenever possible. In addition, the following abbreviations are used throughout the note section.

AC	Fundação Getúlio Vargas, Rio de Janeiro, Arquivo Setembrino de Carvalho
AN	Arquivo Nacional, Rio de Janeiro
APP	Arquivo Público do Paraná, Curitiba, Secretaria de Obras Públicas e Colonização
ASC	Arquivo do Estado de Santa Catarina, Florianópolis
BL	Forbes Collection, Baker Library, Harvard University
BMAIC	Brazil, Ministério da Agricultura, Indústria e Comércio
BMVOP	Brazil, Ministério da Viação e Obras Públicas
BN	Biblioteca Nacional, Rio de Janeiro, Arquivo George Percival Farquhar
CCRI	Canoinhas, Santa Catarina, Cartório de Registro de Imóveis
CNCRI	Campos Novos, Santa Catarina, Cartório de Registro de Imóveis
CNST	Campos Novos, Santa Catarina, Segundo Tabelinato
IP	Irani Produções
PC	Paróquia de Canoinhas, Santa Catarina
PG	Paraná, Governador
PPGE	Paraná, Procurador Geral do Estado
PSB	Paróquia de Senhor Bom Jesus da Coluna, Rio Negro, Paraná
PSI	Paraná, Secretaria do Interior
PSOPC	Paraná, Secretaria de Obra Públicas e Colonização
RPCRC	Rio Negro, Paraná, Cartório de Registro de Casamento
RPCRI	Rio Negro, Paraná, Cartório de Registro de Imóveis
RPCRN	Rio Negro, Paraná, Cartório de Registro de Nascimento
RPCCC	Rio Negro, Paraná, Cartório Civil e Comércio
SCG	Santa Catarina, Governador

SCSG-A   Santa Catarina, Secretaria Geral
SCSG-B   Santa Catarina, Secretário Geral
SDVOPA   Santa Catarina, Directoria de Viação, Obras Públicas e Agricultura
SDVTOP   Santa Catarina, Diretoria de Viação, Terras e Obras Públicas
UPCRI   União de Vitória, Paraná, Cartório de Registro de Imóveis, Primeiro Ofício

1 The Contestado Rebellion

1. Interview with Rosena Francisca de Proença, near Curitibanos, Santa Catarina, 24 Apr. 1985; Rosena is a member of the Crespo family and lived, as an infant, in the rebel camp described in this section. IP, videotaped interview with João Paes de Farias, Lebon Régis, Santa Catarina, 1985.

2. Maurício Vinhas de Queiroz, *Messianismo e conflito social: a Guerra Sertaneja do Contestado, 1912–1916*, 3d ed. (São Paulo, 1981), 77–83; Maria Isaura Pereira de Queiroz, *O messianismo no Brasil e no mundo*, 2d ed. (São Paulo, 1976), 271–74.

3. Vinhas de Queiroz, *Messianismo*, 77–83; Pereira de Queiroz, *O messianismo*, 271–74. João Maria roamed through the Paraná–Santa Catarina countryside in the 1890s. In addition to his healing abilities, he was also a famous seer. According to one elderly resident of the region, João Maria predicted in the 1890s that (a) men would fly, (b) cars would run without horses, and (c) Brazil would become a much studied country; IP, videotaped interview with Manoel Batista dos Santos, Timbó Grande, Santa Catarina, 1985.

4. Vinhas de Queiroz, *Messianismo*, 82.

5. The attempt by the messianic leader Antonio Conselheiro to establish a holy city in the interior of the Brazilian state of Bahia led to a prolonged and bloody war with the Brazilian army in the 1890s. Brazilians were kept informed of the rebellion by Euclydes da Cunha's accounts in the *O Estado de São Paulo* (São Paulo) newspaper and later in his book *Rebellion in the Backlands* (Chicago, 1944). Local newspaper accounts of José Maria are full of references to the Canudos affair. See, for example, *A Notícia* (Lajes, Santa Catarina), 9 Nov. 1912, and *A Folha do Comércio*, 30 Oct. 1912.

6. Vinhas de Queiroz, *Messianismo*, 90–93; Demerval Peixoto, *Campanha do Contestado: episódios e impressões*, 2d ed. (Rio de Janeiro, 1920), 127–28; *O Estado de São Paulo*, 25 Oct. 1912.

7. Vinhas de Queiroz, *Messianismo*, 104–15.

8. Ibid.; Pereira de Queiroz, *O Messianismo*, 272.

9. IP, videotaped interview with João Paes de Farias.

10. The Peers of France were Charlemagne's twelve most trusted men. According to legend, they were heroic fighters, each able to defeat 100 Moors single-handedly. In Portuguese the word for peer is *par*, which also means two, or a pair. The rebels misunderstood the twelve Peers of France to mean twelve pairs, therefore twenty-four men formed their elite guard. For more

information on the *Pares de França*, see Pereira de Queiroz, *O messianismo*, 277. The information on the *Pares de França* at Taquaraçu comes from Rosa Paes de Farias, who, as a young woman living in Taquaraçu, sewed their white outfits. In a bit of self-serving praise, Rosa attributed the rebel victory to the magical power of the Peers' clothing. IP, videotaped interview with Rosa Paes de Farias. An interview with Benjamin Scoz, a soldier with the attacking force at Taquaraçu, confirmed Rosa's information on the dress of the *Pares de França* and their role in the battle. Interview with Benjamin Scoz, Lajes, Santa Catarina, 24 Apr. 1985.

11. Twelve soldiers were later imprisoned for their desertions at Taquaraçu; ASC, "Ofícios do Corpo de Segurança, 1914."

12. Interview with Benjamin Scoz. The army account of the massacre was reported in *O Diário da Tarde* (Curitiba, Paraná), 10 Feb. 1914. Walter F. Piazza, *Santa Catarina: sua história* (Florianópolis, 1983), 592; Vinhas de Queiroz, *Messianismo*, 129–32.

13. *O Dia* (Florianópolis, Santa Catarina), 1 Apr. and 16 Apr. 1914; Santa Catarina, Governador, *Mensagem do Governador Vidal Ramos, 1914*, 6–8.

14. *O Diário da Tarde*, 7, 11, and 12 Sept. 1914; AC, General Fernando Setembrino de Carvalho to G. Carneiro, 17 Sept. 1914; BL, "Conference WCF[orbes] with Mr. Dapples," 28 Jan. 1915, 1:184; BL, "Report from W. F. Nolting–December," 18 Feb. 1916, vol. 4; Herculano Teixeira d'Assumpção, *A campanha do Contestado*, 2 vols. (Belo Horizonte, 1917–18), 1:17–19; José Cleto da Silva, "Apontamentos sobre o movimento fanático," *Boletim do Instituto Histórico, Geográfico, e Etnográfico Paranaense* 28(1976): 62–63; Vinhas de Queiroz, *Messianismo*, 169–72.

15. Assumpção, *A campanha do Contestado*, 1:297–98. Vinhas de Queiroz argues that the rebels controlled roughly 3 percent of the national territory of Brazil; *Messianismo*, 177.

16. Ibid.; Zélia de Andrade Lemos, *Curitibanos na história do Contestado*, 2d ed. (Curitibanos, Santa Catarina, 1983), 121.

17. As a result of the September attacks, the Brazil Railway line running through the region was closed to all service for one week. After that the line opened to military traffic only. It was not until four months later that passenger service resumed but with only one train a week, and that train stopped only at those stations guarded by federal troops. *O Diário da Tarde*, 18 Dec. 1914; Peixoto, *Campanha do Contestado*, 2d ed., 507.

18. For the best treatment of Padre Cícero, see Ralph della Cava, *Miracle at Joaseiro* (New York, 1970).

19. José Cleto da Silva, *Apontamentos históricos de União de Vitória, 1768–1933* (Curitiba, 1933), 132.

20. The best single source for the day-to-day operations of the Carvalho expedition is Peixoto, *Campanha do Contestado*, 2d ed.

21. Ibid., 470–71.

22. Ibid., 476–77. The information on the giving away of children comes from IP, videotaped interview with dona Olga (?), Três Barras, Santa Catarina,

1985. Dona Olga was in her youth at the time of the rebellion and witnessed the suffering of the rebel mothers who surrendered in Três Barras.

23. Peixoto, *Campanha do Contestado*, 2d ed., 540–41, 550, and 553.

24. IP, videotaped interview with Manoel Batista dos Santos.

25. Assumpção, *A campanha do Contestado*, 2:387–88; Peixoto, *Campanha do Contestado*, 2d ed., 630–31, 636, and 765; *O Diário da Tarde*, 5 Apr. 1915.

26. Cost figures for the war come from a speech by General Setembrino de Carvalho, cited in *A Folha do Comércio*, 22 July 1915; the U.S. dollar figure is calculated from exchange rates found in Thomas Holloway, *Immigrants on the Land* (Chapel Hill, 1980), 181. For a detailed account of the last months of the rebellion, see Todd A. Diacon, "Capitalists and Fanatics: Brazil's Contestado Rebellion, 1912–1916," Ph.D. diss., University of Wisconsin–Madison, 1987, 29–32.

27. José Octaviano Pinto Soares, *Guerra em sertões Brasileiros* (Rio de Janeiro, 1931), 127–28; *O Estado* (Florianópolis, Santa Catarina), 17 Dec. 1916; interview with Benjamin Scoz.

28. Assumpção, *A campanha do Contestado*, 1:41–47 and 183; Lemos, *Curitibanos*, 42–44; Piazza, *Santa Catarina*, 653–77.

29. Piazza, *Santa Catarina*, 580–85.

30. Ibid., 580–85, 597–600; IP, videotaped interview with Orti Machado, Canoinhas, Santa Catarina, 1985 (Machado is a local historian); *O Libertador* (Campos Novos, Santa Catarina), 9 Jan. 1910; *A Região Serrana* (Lajes, Santa Catarina), 12 Sept. 1909.

31. Romário Martins, *Documentos comprobatórios dos direitos do Paraná na questão de limites com Sta. Catarina* (Rio de Janeiro, 1915); Pereira de Queiroz, *O messianismo*, 271–72.

32. Peixoto, *Campanha do Contestado*, 2d ed., 59; Marli Auras, *Guerra do Contestado: a organização da irmandade cabocla* (Florianópolis, 1984), 26.

33. Da Cunha, *Rebellion in the Backlands*; Mario Vargas Llosa, *The War of the End of the World* (New York, 1985).

34. For more on the complexities of nation building, see Florencia E. Mallon, "Introduction," *Latin American Perspectives* 48 (Winter 1986): 3–17, and Todd A. Diacon, "Down and Out in Rio de Janeiro: Urban Poor and Elite Rule in the Old Republic," *Latin American Research Review* 25, no. 1 (Jan. 1990): 243–52.

35. Ralph della Cava, "Brazilian Messianism and National Institutions: A Reappraisal of Canudos and Joaseiro," *Hispanic American Historical Review* 47, no. 3 (Aug. 1968): 402–20; della Cava, *Miracle at Joaseiro*. Robert M. Levine, while discussing other factors, also concentrates on the relationship between millenarianism and politics; " 'Mud Hut Jerusalem': Canudos Revisited," *Hispanic American Historical Review* 68, no. 3 (Aug. 1988): 525–72. The same holds true for da Cunha, *Rebellion in the Backlands*.

36. The miracle of 1889 refers to Padre Cícero's claim that as he administered communion the host "miraculously transformed itself into blood,

unquestionably held to be the blood of Christ"; della Cava, *Miracle at Joaseiro*, 1.

37. Vinhas de Queiroz, *Messianismo*; Rui Facó, *Cangaceiros e fanáticos* (Rio de Janeiro, 1963); Noel Nascimento, "Canudos, Contestado, e fanatismo religioso," *Revista Brasiliense* 44 (Nov.–Dec. 1961): 62–67; Bernard Siegel, "The Contestado Rebellion, 1912–1916: A Case Study in Brazilian Messianism and Regional Dynamics," in *The Anthropology of Power*, ed. R. Fogelson and R. Adams (New York, 1977); Nelson Thomé, *Trem de ferro: história da ferrovia no Contestado*, 2d ed. (Florianópolis, 1983).

38. E. J. Hobsbawm, *Primitive Rebels* (New York, 1959). It is to Hobsbawm that we owe thanks for stressing the importance of studying social movements emerging from the transition to capitalism. He has been criticized, however, for his belief in the inevitable evolution of "premodern" movements into something more "progressive," such as urban-based worker rebellions. For a cogent critique, see James C. Scott, *Weapons of the Weak: Everyday Forms of Peasant Resistance* (New Haven, 1985), 273.

39. In 1984 an estimated 162,230 rural Santa Catarina residents were without secure access to land; Comissão Pastoral de Terra de Santa Catarina, "Em S.C. não é diferente," *Cheiro da Terra* 5, no. 32 (Sept.–Oct. 1984): 6.

40. Comissão Pastoral de Terra de Santa Catarina, "Acampamentos e ocupações," *Cheiro da Terra* 5, no. 32 (Sept.–Oct. 1984): 7, and "Sobressalto no campo," *Veja* (12 June, 1985): 80–82.

41. Norman Cohn, *The Pursuit of the Millennium: Revolutionary Millenarians and Mystic Anarchists of the Middle Ages* (New York, 1970), 21. For a further definition of millenarianism, see Yonina Talmon, "Millenarianism," *International Encyclopedia of the Social Sciences*, vol. 10 (New York, 1968), 354.

42. For a ground-breaking analysis of both the material and cultural contexts of Brazilian millenarianism, see Patricia R. Pessar, "Unmasking the Politics of Religion: The Case of Brazilian Millenarianism," *Journal of Latin American Lore* 7, no. 2 (1981): 255–78.

2 The Contestado
Backwater Economy, Patriarchal Society

1. The Contestado region included portions of Paraná and Santa Catarina. For the purpose of this discussion, however, I am concentrating on Santa Catarina. To emphasize Paraná in the discussions on industrial development, population figures, and infrastructure levels would distort the picture, given the size of the state. Such figures would include data from northern and central Paraná, areas far more developed than the southern portion of the state. In socioeconomic terms then, southern Paraná was much closer to Santa Catarina.

2. Reginald Lloyd, W. Feldwick, and R. T. Delaney, *Twentieth-Century Impressions of Brazil* (London, 1913), 619, 622, 785, 788, 933, 993, and 1043; Fredrick A. Molitor, *Report on the Railway Properties in Southern Brazil*

Leased, Owned, or Controlled by the Brazil Railway Company (privately printed, 1915), 12; Thomas W. Merrick and Douglas H. Graham, *Population and Economic Development in Brazil: 1800 to the Present* (Baltimore, 1979), 31, 119; Idaulo José Cunha, *Evolução econômico-industrial de Santa Catarina* (Florianópolis, 1982), 37.

3. Molitor, *Report*, 20; Cunha, *Evolução*, 82–83. Molitor and Cunha obtained these figures from the Centro-Industrial of Brazil. Neither explains the criteria used to define what is meant by an "industry." Nevertheless, the criteria used is, one can assume, internally consistent. The information on German immigrant industries comes from Piazza, *Santa Catarina*, 404–6.

4. Molitor, *Report*, 21; see also Piazza, *Santa Catarina*, 551–60, 596.

5. Auguste de Saint-Hilaire, *Viagem à província de Santa Catharina, 1820* (São Paulo, 1936), 43.

6. Piazza, *Santa Catarina*, 336; Romário Martins, *Quantos somos e quem somos* (Curitiba, 1941), 96–97, 99–100. Railroad population estimates are from Molitor, *Report*, 34; export figures are from Piazza, *Santa Catarina*, 440.

7. Piazza, *Santa Catarina*, 169–70; Vinhas de Queiroz, *Messianismo*, 21–23; Romário Martins, *História do Paraná* (São Paulo, 1939), 310; Lemos, *Curitibanos*, 34; Stanley J. Stein, *Vassouras: A Brazilian Coffee County, 1850–1900* (Princeton, 1985), 92.

8. Piazza, *Santa Catarina*, 170–74.

9. Martins, *História do Paraná*, 408–9; *A cidade e o município do Rio Negro* (Curitiba, 1924).

10. Lemos, *Curitibanos*, 69–75. The Palmas figures are from Piazza, *Santa Catarina*, 380–83. For documents that mention the creation of various *fazendas* in the Palmas area, see APP, "Medição das terras requeridas por Absalão Antonio Carneiro," 1897, and "Medição das terras requeridas por Absalão Antonio Carneiro e outros," 23 May 1900. The *processo* of one Manoel Lourenço de Araujo stated that the land he owned had been cultivated since 1851; APP, "Medição das terras requeridas por Manoel Lourenço de Araujo."

11. The information on Canoinhas comes from IP, videotaped interview with Orti Machado. Population figures are from Piazza, *Santa Catarina*, 362.

12. The information found in this section comes from Sílvio Coelho dos Santos, *Indios e brancos no sul do Brasil* (Florianópolis, 1973), esp. 18–154.

13. ASC, SDVTOP, "Requerimentos de concessões de terras públicas," vol. 179, 9 May 1918, 16.

14. Jules Henry quoted in Coelho dos Santos, *Indios e brancos*, 37.

15. Coelho dos Santos, *Indios e brancos*, 39.

16. The quote comes from APP, "Medição das terras requeridas por Antonio dos Santos Carneiro, Manoel dos Santos Carneiro e Maria Prudencia de Souza," 9 Sept. 1899. The attacks against the Campo Alto *fazenda* were reported in *O Trabalho* (Curitibanos, Santa Catarina), 3 Dec. 1907. Information on the 1906 attack comes from da Silva, *Apontamentos históricos*, 88. The Curitibanos attack was reported in *A Notícia*, 14 Dec. 1912.

17. In 1970 it was estimated the 1,800 Xokleng lived on three reservations in Santa Catarina. See Coelho dos Santos, *Indios e brancos*, 79–154.

18. Vinhas de Queiroz, *Messianismo*, 26–31; Piazza, *Santa Catarina*, 585–86; Duglas Teixeira Monteiro, *Os errantes do novo século* (São Paulo, 1974), 19–36; Brasil Pinheiro Machado, "Formação da estrutura agrária tradicional dos Campos Gerais," *Boletim da Universidade do Paraná*, no. 3 (June 1963): 4–25. According to Piazza (447) slaves formed 23 percent of the Santa Catarina population in 1810, 16 percent in 1856, and 9 percent in 1872; in the Lajes municipality (176, 402) slaves formed 21 percent of the population in 1808, and 13 percent in 1851.

19. In addition to the works mentioned, see also James Slade, "Cattle Barons and Yeoman Farmers: Land Tenure, Division, and Use in a County in Southern Brazil, 1711–1889," Ph.D. diss., Indiana University, 1971; Joseph L. Love, *Rio Grande do Sul and Brazilian Regionalism, 1882–1930* (Stanford, 1971).

20. This inflation of land claims, and the purchase of "excess" lands by *fazendeiros*, is examined in detail in chapter 4.

21. APP, "Medição das terras requeridas por José Antonio Carneiro," 29 Oct. 1898; "Medição das terras requeridas por João Simeão Carneiro e outros," 16 June 1900; "Medição das terras requeridas por Antonio dos Santos Carneiro, Manoel dos Santos Carneiro e Maria Prudencia de Souza," 9 Sept. 1899; "Medição das terras requeridas por Absalão Antonio Carneiro e outros," 23 May 1900; "Medição das terras requeridas por Absalão Carneiro," 2 Apr. 1898 (?).

22. APP, "Medição das terras requeridas por Nicolau Bley Netto"; RPCRI, "Registro de terras," book 123, 1895, 47–48; RPCCC, "Inventário de Cel. João Pacheco dos Santos Lima," 12 Aug. 1907. The publication referred to is the book *A cidade e o município de Rio Negro*.

23. See notes 21 and 22. The "old-timer claim" comes from an interview with Cipriano Rodrigues de Moraes (age seventy-five at the time of the interview), Fraiburgo, Santa Catarina, 26 Apr. 1985. See also Vinhas de Queiroz, *Messianismo*, 30.

24. SCSG-A, *Relatório 1907*, 78–79; Piazza, *Santa Catarina*, 599–608; Vinhas de Queiroz, *Messianismo*, 31.

25. APP, "Medição de terras requeridas por Nicolau Bley Netto"; RPCCC, "Inventário de Cel. João Pacheco dos Santos Lima," 12 Aug. 1907; *A cidade e o município de Rio Negro*.

26. The information on *erva mate* production comes from Eduardo Heinz, *O matte ou chá do Paraná* (Curitiba, 1909), 13. Information on the Pacheco brothers comes from *A cidade e o município de Rio Negro*.

27. SCSG-A, *Relatório 1907*, 78–79; PSOPC, *Relatório 1913*, 52. The quote is from *O Trabalho*, 3 July 1910.

28. Vinhas de Queiroz, *Messianismo*, 26–41; Machado, "Formação," 11–18. For information on the *camaradas*, see the various *processos* in APP.

29. Interview with Francisco Calistro Pacheco dos Santos Lima, Rio Negro, Paraná, 27 Feb. 1985; Vinhas de Queiroz, *Messianismo*, 30.

30. APP, "Medição das terras requeridas por Antonio dos Santos Carneiro, Manoel dos Santos Carneiro e Maria Prudencia de Souza," 9 Sept. 1899; "Medição das terras requeridas por João Simeão Carneiro e outros," 16 June 1900.

31. Vinhas de Queiroz, *Messianismo*, 28–31.

32. Mario Góngora, *Origen do los inquilinos de Chile central* (Santiago, Chile, 1960), 36–42, 74, 99–102, and 113–17.

33. Interview with Francisco Pacheco; APP, "Medição das terras requeridas por Manoel Lourenço de Araujo," no date 1896?; APP, "Medição das terras requeridas por Arthur de Paula e Souza" (includes documents from 1899–1905); APP, "Medição das terras requeridas por Absalão Antonio Carneiro e outros," 23 May 1900.

34. Interview with Francisco Pacheco; IP, videotaped interview with José Maria Gomes, Lebon Régis, Santa Catarina, 1985; interview with João Rupp Sobrinho, Campos Novos, Santa Catarina, 9 May 1985. The literature on the Contestado Rebellion does not mention the existence of two different types of *camaradas*.

35. Stuart B. Schwartz, "Elite Politics and the Growth of a Peasantry in Late Colonial Brazil," in *From Colony to Nation: Essays on the Independence of Brazil*, ed. A. J. R. Russell Wood (Baltimore, 1975), 133–54.

36. APP, "Medicão das terras requeridas por Nicolau Bley Netto"; "Medição das terras requeridas por Manoel Lourenço de Araujo," 20 Dec. 1899.

37. ASC, SDVTOP, "Requerimentos de concessões de terras públicas," vol. 182, book 183, 2 Oct. 1918, 193; vol. 92, 26 Oct. 1905; and vol. 136, 21 Nov. 1911, 168.

38. APP, "Medição das terras requeridas por João Carneiro e outros," 6 June 1900; SCSG-A, *Relatório 1903*, 13.

39. Vinhas de Queiroz, *Messianismo*, 30. On patron-client relations, and the need for protection, see the various contributions in *Friends, Followers, and Factions: A Reader in Political Clientelism*, ed. Steffen W. Schmidt, Laura Guasti, Carl H. Landé, and James C. Scott (Berkeley and Los Angeles, 1977).

40. ASC, SDVTOP, "Requerimentos de concessões de terras públicas," vol. 136, 21 Nov. 1911, 68; vol. 133 (1911), 90.

41. IP, videotaped interview with Baldo Ricardo da Silva, Canoinhas, Santa Catarina, 1985; interview with Benjamin Scoz.

42. Emília Viotti da Costa, *Da monarquia à república: momentos decisivos*, 3d ed. (São Paulo, 1985), 141; Warren Dean, "Latifundia and Land Policy in Nineteenth-Century Brazil," *Hispanic American Historical Review* 51 (Nov. 1971): 606–25.

43. Dean, "Latifundia," 608–9. The land documents referred to are from ASC, SDVTOP, "Requerimentos de concessões de terras públicas."

44. Interview with João Rupp Sobrinho. João, the grandson of Henrique, spoke of how people would come from miles around to look at his grandfather's stove.

45. These figures come from CNST, "Livro de Terras," books 9–15 and 17.

The dollar amount is based on an average of the exchange rates of the era as found in Holloway, *Immigrants on the Land*, 181.

46. Lemos, *Curitibanos*, 179–81.

47. Vinhas de Queiroz, *Messianismo*, 175–76; APP, "Medição das terras requeridas por Arthur de Paula e Souza" (includes documents from 1899–1905); UPCRI, various land sale records from 1897–1912. Unfortunately, the general trend in the Contestado was to not mention the area of a purchase in the land documents; usually the documents mention only the location of the land, the price paid, and any buildings on the property.

48. Vinhas de Queiroz, *Messianismo*, 175–76; da Silva, *Apontamentos históricos*, 79, 81, 84, and 104.

49. IP, videotaped interview with Rufino Ferreira da Silva, Fraiburgo, Santa Catarina, 1985.

50. Monteiro, *Os errantes*, 37–49; Vinhas de Queiroz, *Messianismo*, 43–48.

51. George M. Foster, "The Dyadic Contract in Tzintzuntzen, II: Patron-Client Relationship," *American Anthropologist* 65 (1963): 1280–94; S. N. Eisenstadt and L. Roniger, *Patrons, Clients, and Friends* (Cambridge, 1984); James C. Scott, *The Moral Economy of the Peasant* (New Haven, 1976). See also Schmidt et al., *Friends, Followers, and Factions*.

52. George M. Foster, "The Dyadic Contract: A Model for the Social Structure of a Mexican Village," *American Anthropologist* 63 (1961): 1173–92; Douglas A. Chalmers, "Parties and Societies in Latin America," in Schmidt et al., *Friends, Followers, and Factions*, 401–21.

53. Wayne A. Cornelius, "Leaders, Followers and Official Patrons in Urban Mexico," in Schmidt et al., *Friends, Followers and Factions*, 332–53; Clifford Geertz, "The Changing Role of Cultural Brokers: The Javanese Kijaji," *Comparative Studies in Society and History* 2 (1960): 228–49; Sydel F. Silverman, "Patronage and Community-Nation Relationships in Central Italy," in Schmidt et al., *Friends, Followers and Factions*, 293–304; Abner Cohen, "The Social Organization of Credit in a West African Cattle Market," in Schmidt et al., *Friends, Followers and Factions*, 233–41.

54. Florencia E. Mallon, *The Defense of Community in Peru's Central Highlands* (Princeton, 1983), and "Murder in the Andes: Patrons, Clients, and the Impact of Foreign Capital, 1860–1922," *Radical History Review* 27 (1983): 79–98.

55. Scott, *Weapons of the Weak*, 306.

56. Marcel Mauss, *The Gift*, trans. Ian Cunnison (New York, 1967), 1.

57. Pierre Bourdieu, *Outline of a Theory of Practice*, trans. Richard Nice (Cambridge, 1977), 5.

58. E. Bradford Burns, *The Poverty of Progress* (Berkeley and Los Angeles, 1980), 87.

59. James C. Scott and Benedict J. Kerkvliet, "How Traditional Rural Patrons Lose Legitimacy: A Theory with Special Reference to Southeast Asia," in Schmidt et al., in *Friends, Followers, and Factions*, 440.

60. Eisenstadt and Roniger, *Patrons, Clients, and Friends*, 49.

61. Scott, *Weapons of the Weak*, 335.

62. Ibid., 336, 329–30. Here, of course, Scott is rejecting the idea of a dominant hegemony. This argument is made possible, however, only by ignoring the role religion plays in the lives of the Malay villagers he studies. The few mentions of Islamic religious feasts dwell on material exchanges between rich and poor and not on how these practices may sanctify social relations. See Alba Zaluar, *Os homens de deus, um estudo dos santos e das festas no catolicismo popular* (Rio de Janeiro, 1983); Michael W. Foley, "Organizing, Ideology, and Moral Suasion: Political Discourse and Action in a Mexican Town," *Comparative Studies in Society and History* 32, no. 3 (July 1990): 458.

63. Monteiro, *Os errantes*, 13–14.

64. Interview with Francisco Pacheco dos Santos; APP, "Medição das terras requeridas por Manoel Lourenço de Araujo," 20 Dec. 1899.

65. Compare this situation to that of the western highlands of Puerto Rico in the nineteenth century. There, as noted by Laird Bergard, disease and war decimated the Taino Indian population after conquest. As opposed to the Contestado then, this lack of an Indian threat left Puerto Rican *agregados* free to "simply leave for other areas"; Bergard, *Coffee and the Growth of Agrarian Capitalism in Nineteenth-Century Puerto Rico* (Princeton, 1983), 50.

66. The information about Albuquerque comes from *A Folha do Comércio*, 20 Sept. 1916, 1. For the Vieira incident, see *O Diário da Tarde*, 11–15 Dec. 1914.

67. ASC, SDVTOP, "Requerimentos de concessões de terras públicas," vol. 74, Feb. 1900, 121–23.

68. Interviews with Benjamin Scoz and Francisco Pacheco dos Santos; Peixoto, *Campanha do Contestado*, 2d ed., 786.

69. For a detailed study of patrons in the Old Republic, see Linda Lewin, *Politics and Parentela in Paraíba* (Princeton, 1987).

70. In her work on the role of free labor in Espírito Santo, Maria Sylvia de Carvalho Franco discusses the patron-client tie and argues that clients did play patrons against one another. As an example of this, she cites the case of a particular *agregado* who worked for one landowner but lived on the land of another *fazendeiro*; Carvalho Franco, *Homens livres na ordem escravocrata* (São Paulo, 1969), 93.

71. *A Notícia*, 20 July 1912, 2; *A Vanguarda* (Campos Novos, Santa Catarina), 15 Aug. 1908, 2. Because he studies peasants alive today, Scott has uncovered numerous examples of what he terms "everyday resistance" in Malaysia. Examples include work stoppages, petty theft, and the destruction of livestock, all of which, although not collective action, nevertheless "are *intended* [author's emphasis] to mitigate or deny claims . . . made on that class [the peasantry] by superordinate classes." Scott, *Weapons of the Weak*, 290, 249, and 256–71.

72. Maria Isaura Pereira de Queiroz, "Messiahs in Brazil," *Past and Present* 31 (July 1965): 69–70.

73. *A cidade e o município do Rio Negro;* Stein, *Vassouras.*

74. Lemos, *Curitibanos,* 149–50; Pereira do Queiroz, "Messiahs in Brazil," 70.

75. Monteiro, *Os errantes,* 37–49.

76. Interview with João Rupp Sobrinho.

77. *A Notícia,* 13 Jan. 1912, 1.

78. Góngora, *Origen,* 74, 99–102, and 113–17.

79. Amaury de Souza, "The Cangaço and the Politics of Violence in Northeast Brazil," in *Protest and Resistance in Angola and Brazil,* ed. Ronald H. Chilcote (Berkeley and Los Angeles, 1972), 110; Maria Isaura Pereira de Queiroz, "O coronelismo numa interpretação sociológica," in *O Brasil republicano,* 3d ed., Tomo III, ed. Boris Fausto (São Paulo, 1982), 1:170.

80. Pereira de Queiroz, "O coronelismo," 171; de Souza, "Cangaço," 116. For a similar argument about an earlier era in Brazil, see Patricia Ann Aufderheide, "Order and Violence: Social Deviance and Social Control in Brazil, 1780–1840," Ph.D. diss., University of Minnesota, 1976, esp. chapter 5.

81. Vargas Llosa, *The War of the End of the World,* esp. 189–92; although this book is based on historical events, it is a work of fiction and thus does not represent a concrete case.

82. Ibid., 160.

83. Monteiro, *Os errantes,* 37–49.

84. Ibid., 57–70; Vinhas de Queiroz, *Messianismo,* 29–30.

85. S. W. Mintz and E. R. Wolf, "An Analysis of Co-parenthood (*compadrazgo*)," *Southwestern Journal of Anthropology* 6, no. 4 (1950): 341.

86. Ibid., 353–54.

87. Ibid., 355–64.

88. Antonio Augusto Arantes Neto, "A sagrada família—una análise estrutural de compadrío," Tese de Mestrado, Departamento de Ciências Sociais, Faculdade de Filosofia, Letras, e Ciências Humanas, Universidade de São Paulo, 1970, 8.

89. Stephen Gudeman, "Spiritual Relationships and Selecting a Godparent," *Man* 10 (1975): 221.

90. Raymond T. Smith, "Introduction," in *Kinship Ideology and Practice in Latin America,* ed. Raymond T. Smith (Chapel Hill, 1984), 20.

91. Stephen Gudeman and Stuart B. Schwartz, "Cleansing Original Sin: Godparenthood and the Baptism of Slaves in Eighteenth-Century Bahia," in Smith, *Kinship Ideology and Practice,* 55.

92. Arantes Neto, "A sagrada família," 7 and 11; Gudeman and Schwartz, "Cleansing Original Sin," 35.

93. M. Bloch and S. Gudeman, "*Compadrazgo,* Baptism and the Symbolism of a Second Birth," *Man* 16 (1981): 378.

94. Ibid.; Arantes Neto, "A sagrada família," 7, 11, and 22; Gudeman, "Spiritual Relationships," 225.

95. Bloch and Gudeman, "*Compadrazgo,*" 376.

96. Arantes Neto, "A sagrada família," 32.
97. Bloch and Gudeman, "Compadrazgo," 380–81.
98. Ibid., 384.
99. Arantes Neto, "A sagrada família," 11; Juan M. Ossio, "Cultural Continuity, Structure, and Compadrazgo," in Smith, Kinship Ideology and Practice, 121–22.
100. Scott, Moral Economy; E. P. Thompson, "The Moral Economy of the English Crowd in the Eighteenth Century," Past and Present 50 (Feb. 1971): 76–136; Eric R. Wolf, Peasant Wars of the Twentieth Century (New York, 1969).
101. Thompson, "English Crowd," 79.
102. Scott, Moral Economy, 42.
103. Gudeman and Schwartz, "Cleansing Original Sin," 40–43.
104. Ibid., 41.
105. Ibid.
106. Ibid., 40–43.
107. Henry Koster, quoted in Gudeman and Schwartz, "Cleansing Original Sin," 42.
108. Eul Soo Pang, In Pursuit of Honor and Power: Noblemen of the Southern Cross in Nineteenth-Century Brazil (Tuscaloosa, 1988), 142–43. Pang writes that "the ritual parentela in the world of the slaves is yet to be studied, but evidence suggests that the status of a child's mother—her standing within the plantation or ranch as well as the existence of a carnal relationship with the owner—determined the availability of free godparents for her offspring."
109. PSB, "Registro de Batismo."
110. PSB, book 22, no. 12, 1915. This child baptized was the daughter of Gaspar Torres Pereira and Estevelina Pacheco Pereira. The godparents were Antonio dos Santos Pacheco and Maria Elisa Bley.
111. PSB, no. 315, 5 June 1910, and no. 673, 1 Nov. 1911; RPCRN, book 6, 6 Aug. 1909, 63, and book 9, 30 July 1910, 4.
112. PPGE, Relatório 1910, 70; the quote comes from the report of Hugo Gutierrez Simas, Promotor Público of Rio Negro.
113. Monteiro, Os errantes, 58; interview with Francisco Pacheco dos Santos.
114. PSB, "Registro de Batismo," book 20, no. 54, 23 Feb. 1913; RPCRC, book 6, 16 Mar. 1912, 79. The term lavrador does not necessarily mean one was a peasant. Lavradores could indeed hold significant amounts of land. In this case, however, I believe the lavrador mentioned was a peasant. In the same records one man is listed as an "abonado natural," that is, a large landowner. If this lavrador had owned a sizable amount of land, then I am assuming that he too would have been listed as an "abonado natural."
115. PSB, "Registro de Batismo," book 21, no. 345, 26 Apr. 1914; RPCRC, book 1, 1914, 14.
116. Interview with Sebastião Calomeno, Curitibanos, Santa Catarina, 25

Apr. 1985. Sebastião's uncle was killed by the rebel leader Adeodato in 1915. Adeodato's father had been an *agregado* of this uncle.

117. Interview with João Rupp Sobrinho; interview with Francisco Pacheco dos Santos.

118. *O Diário da Tarde*, 8 Jan. 1914, 5.

119. Soares, *Guerra em sertões Brasileiros*, 48–49.

120. Ibid., 49.

121. IP, videotaped interview with Rufino Ferreira da Silva, Fraiburgo, Santa Catarina, 1985.

122. Interview with Francisco Pacheco dos Santos.

123. APP, "Medição das terras requeridas por Absalão Antonio Carneiro," 1897.

124. Ibid.

125. Interview with Francisco Pacheco dos Santos.

126. *A cidade e o município do Rio Negro*.

127. In 1914, *O Diário da Tarde* reported that the patron Bonifácio Papudo had constructed a chapel where services, celebrations, and dances were held; 17 Sept. 1914. Near Rio Negro, "in 1920 Elibio [Ferreira de Chagas Braz] ordered constructed, at his own cost, the church of N.S. da Piedade, where . . . masses, marriages, and baptisms are celebrated"; *A cidade e o município do Rio Negro*.

128. Zaluar, *Os homens de deus*, 68–77; Pessar, "Unmasking the Politics of Religion," 256–60.

129. Pessar, "Unmasking the Politics of Religion," 261.

130. Peixoto, *Campanha do Contestado*, 2d ed., 561–63.

3 Capitalists and Colonists

1. AN, W. C. Forbes to Charles A. Gauld, 27 Nov. 1950, Arquivo Farquhar, AP21-Caixa 1.

2. *O Trabalho*, 3 Dec. 1910.

3. Molitor, *Report*, 132.

4. AN, Percival Farquhar, "Resumo do Programa Percival Farquhar ao organizar a Brazil Railway Company," 1942, Arquivo Farquhar, AP21-Caixa 1; Thomé, *Trem de Ferro*, 73; BL, Charles E. Perkins to W. H. Grant, vol. 20.

5. For the board of directors, see AN, Farquhar, "Resumo do Programa," 2–3. For the holdings of the Brazil Railway Company, see Molitor, *Report*, 125. For the creation of a monopoly, see Molitor, *Report*, 32, and also *Brazil Ferro-Carril* (Rio de Janeiro), 12 Dec. 1912, 292. In this issue *Brazil Ferro-Carril* examined the uproar the creation of the Farquhar trust produced in Brazil. For its part, the magazine condemned Farquhar's monopoly in the south, complaining of the control it gave over "the richest, most prosperous, most fertile, and most civilized areas of the country."

The Madeira-Marmoré Railroad, built in the Amazon jungle near Bolivia, was designed to profit from the rubber boom of the late nineteenth and early twentieth centuries. After great human and material expense, the line opened in 1912, just as the rubber boom turned to bust. For more information see Charles A. Gauld, *The Last Titan Percival Farquhar: American Entrepreneur in Latin America* (Stanford, 1964), 126–59; Francisco Foot Hardman, *Trem fantasma: a modernidade na selva* (São Paulo, 1988).

6. BMVOP, *Relatório 1915*, 1:128–30; Molitor, *Report*, 82–87; AN, Farquhar, "Resumo do Programa," 3.

7. Thomé, *Trem de ferro*, 53; BMVOP, *Relatório 1914*, 129, AN.

8. Ibid.; Molitor, *Report*, 85–86.

9. Molitor, *Report*, 85–86; BMVOP, *Relatório 1908*, 339–43; Thomé, *Trem de ferro*, 59 and 95.

10. The quote is from Molitor, *Report*, 86. See also Molitor, *Report*, 433–34; BMVOP, *Relatório 1915*, 128–30; *Brazil Ferro-Carril*, 7 Sept. 1912, 212; Hortêncio de Alcântara, *A questão de terras entre a União e o Paraná* (Curitiba, 1954), 4.

11. Da Silva, *Apontamentos históricos*, 80–87.

12. The quote is from Thomé, *Trem de ferro*, 58; BMVOP, *Relatório 1906*, 558–60; da Silva, *Apontamentos históricos*, 99–100.

13. BMVOP, *Relatório 1909*, 353; *A Região Serrana*, 28 Nov. 1909; da Silva, *Apontamentos históricos*, 100; AN, "Tomada de contas da E.F. São Paulo–Rio Grande," Arquivo do Ministério dos Transportes, Maço 108, #1327, 1910, AN.

14. BMVOP, *Relatório 1911*, 251; Thomé, *Trem de ferro*, 103–4. Thomé writes that a flood destroyed the hastily built wooden bridge on May 29, 1911. Until a new bridge was completed in 1912, the passengers were forced to cross the Uruguay River on large wooden rafts.

15. Thomé, *Trem de ferro*, 110 and 114; BMVOP, *Relatório 1909*, 2:343; Molitor, *Report*.

16. BMVOP, *Relatório 1911*, 105–7; SCSG, *Relatório 1915*, 191–92, and *Relatório 1916*, 258–59.

17. AN, "A Companhia E. Ferro S. Paulo–Rio Grande requer prorogação de prazo para a construcção da Linha de S. Francisco," Arquivo do Ministério dos Transportes, Maço 202, #10275, 1913, AN.

18. AN, Forbes to Gauld, 27 Nov. 1950, Arquivo Farquhar.

19. AN, "Explicação dos direitos de propriedade que assistem aos vários grupos de portadores de obrigações sobre todos os haveres do Brazil Railway Company," Arquivo Farquhar, AP21-Caixa 1, 1942; "Brazil Railway Company," *Brazil Ferro-Carril*, 5, no. 83 (Dec. 1914): 395; Ruy Wachowicz, "O comércio da madeira," (copy at the ASC), 322–25. Wachowicz writes that H. Weinmaster, the director of the Southern Brazil Lumber Company (a subsidiary of Brazil Railway), wished to blow up key bridges during the 1930 revolution to prevent Vargas's troops from reaching Rio de Janeiro. AN, Bender, Hamlyn, and Company, London, to Esmael de Oliveira Maia, 22 Aug. 1940 (English trans. of Decree 2436), Arquivo Farquhar, AP21-Caixa 2. Vargas justified the nationalization on the grounds that the company failed to meet its loan payments to foreign banks, "thereby causing, over a long period, discontent and harmful confusion to the public credit."

20. SCSG-B, *Relatório 1911*, 109–10. The Brazil Railway Company was

not the first to note the revenue potential of the southern forests. In 1871 André Rebouças founded the Companhia Florestal Paranaense to exploit the pine reserves of Paraná. Opposition from a powerful local family eventually forced Rebouças to abandon his plans. See Richard Graham, *Britain and the Onset of Modernization in Brazil* (Cambridge, 1968), 194.

21. BN, Percival Farquhar, "The Southern Brazil Lumber and Colonization Company," I-33, 12, 15.

22. Percival Farquhar, quoted in Gauld, *Last Titan*, 216.

23. BL, W. C. Forbes, "Southern Brazil Lumber and Colonization Company," vol. 16.

24. BL, Brazil Railway Company, "Report of Proceedings of Meetings of Bondholders," 20 May 1915, 23:7. For the going price for land, see the land records at RPCRI, especially livro 3.

25. Brazil Railway Company, *Annual Report 1910* (London, 1911), 11, and *Annual Report 1911* (London, 1912), 7; *A Região Serrana*, December 1911, 3.

26. Gauld, *Last Titan*, 217.

27. Clayton S. Cooper, *The Brazilians and Their Country* (n.p., 1917), 219.

28. Ibid.; BL, Nolting to W. C. Forbes, 22 Jan. 1916, vol. 4.

29. PSOPC, *Relatório 1911*, 13.

30. Brazil Railway Company, *Report 1911*, 9. One local story tells of a man who suffered a serious arm injury during one morning of work. Instead of receiving immediate attention, the man was left in an office until the end of the day, until someone took him to Canoinhas to see a doctor. (Personal communication with Ênio Staub.)

31. Thomé, *Trem de ferro*, 131.

32. BL, Nolting to W. C. Forbes, 25 Jan. 1917, vol. 7.

33. Emília Viotti da Costa, *Da senzala à colonia*, 2d ed. (São Paulo, 1982), esp. 3–101; Viotti da Costa, *Da monarquia à república*, esp. 139–61, and 228–47; Holloway, *Immigrants*; Warren Dean, *Rio Claro: A Brazilian Plantation System, 1820–1920* (Stanford, 1976).

34. Viotti da Costa, *Da senzala à colonia*, 100; Holloway, *Immigrants*, 36–44.

35. Viotti da Costa, "Política das terras no Brasil e nos Estados Unidos," in *Da monarquia à república*, 139–61.

36. Ibid., 140.

37. PG, *Relatório do Governador Augusto Machado d'Oliveira*, 15 Sept. 1884.

38. *Boletim colonial agricola do Paraná* (Curitiba) (May–July 1908). This statement was printed on a flyer inserted in the journal.

39. PG, *Relatório do Governador Joaquim d' Almeida Faria Sobrinho, 1888*, 26. For more on the history of racial thought in Brazil, see Thomas E. Skidmore, *Black Into White* (New York, 1974).

40. PSOPC, *Relatório 1908*, 23 and *Relatório 1909*, 26–27; Paraná, Ministério da Viação e Obras Públicas, *Boletim 1909*, 237.

41. State-sponsored colonization in Santa Catarina only occurred in areas

removed from the Contestado zone. For this reason no mention of Santa Catarina colonization appears in this chapter. One should remember, however, that many of the areas colonized by Paraná are now part of Santa Catarina—as a result of the 1916 border accord.

42. PSOPC, *Relatório 1907*, 56–60; Paraná, *Relatório apresentado ao Dr. João Baptista da Costa Carvalho Filho*, 28 Oct. 1895, 39.

43. PSOPC, *Relatório 1908*, 23, and *Relatório 1909*, 25–28.

44. PSOPC, *Relatório 1909*, 26–27, and *Relatório 1910*, 21–28. Other records detail the specific land purchases around Lucena. In May 1905, for example, José Jasiniewski of Lucena purchased 164 hectares near the colony. In May 1907, Augusto Kuchler and others purchased 1,195 hectares. For more examples see APP, "Portaria," 29 Aug. 1910.

45. PSOPC, *Relatório 1912*, 18.

46. PSOPC, *Relatório 1910*, 27.

47. PSOPC, *Relatório 1904*, 20.

48. PSOPC, *Relatório 1906*, 20–21.

49. PSOPC, *Relatório 1908*, 19.

50. PSOPC, *Relatório 1909*, and *Relatório 1912*, 27–28.

51. PSOPC, *Relatório 1907*, 48–50, 59–60; *Relatório 1910*, 29–30; *Relatório 1911*, 13; *Boletim colonial agrícola do Paraná* (May–July 1908): 337–38.

52. Martins, *Quantos somos e quem somos*, 107 and 114–15.

53. BMVOP, *Relatório 1910*, 229.

54. Ibid., 248.

55. PSOPC, *Relatório 1909*, 133–34; Martins, *Quantos somos e quem somos*, 114–15.

56. *A Vanguarda*, 15 Sept. 1908. In 1908 one *milreis* equalled US $0.31. Thus, a 10-*alqueire* (approx. 25-hectare) plot sold for US $77.50. Exchange information taken from Holloway, *Immigrants*, 181.

57. *O Trabalho*, 18 Apr. 1908.

58. Ibid.

59. Molitor, *Report*, 427.

60. BL, W. C. Forbes to Joint Bondholders Committee, 21 Jan. 1916, vol. 21.

61. Molitor, *Report*, 433–34.

62. AN, Farquhar, "Resumo do Progama," 11.

63. Ibid., 12.

64. Brazil Railway Company, *Annual Report, 1912* (London, 1913), 10.

65. The question of existing claims, and the conflicts they created, is discussed in the next chapter.

66. BL, "Brazil Development and Colonization Company," vol. 18; Molitor, *Report*, 431–32; Gauld, *Last Titan*, 212; AN, Farquhar, "Resumo do Programa," 12–13; BL, W. C. Forbes, "Narrative Report of the Receiver of the Brazil Railway Company to the Court of Maine," 3 Dec. 1914, 24:36; *O Diário da Tarde*, 2 Jan. 1914; da Silva, "Apontamentos sobre o movimento

fanático"; BL, Brazil Railway, Paris, to W. C. F[orbes] (telegram), 2 Feb. 1917, vol. 7.

4 The Deadly Triumvirate
State Power, the Brazil Railway Company and Local Landowners in the Contestado

1. All quotes come from SDVTOP, "Requerimentos de concessões de terras públicas," vol. 114, book 113, 8 Sept. 1908, 221–27.
2. A Região Serrana, 11 Apr. 1909. The newspaper reprinted the text of Ramos's telegram.
3. Emília Viotti da Costa, The Brazilian Empire: Myths and Histories (Chicago, 1985), 79.
4. Ibid., 81. The recent work of Stuart Schwartz addresses the thorny question of the primary function of landownership in Brazil. He finds it difficult to separate economic power and social prestige but notes that because colonial planters were denied true titles of nobility, landownership and economic performance were especially important in that they created the conditions that allowed planters to lead a noblelike life-style. Stuart B. Schwartz, Sugar Plantations in the Formation of Brazilian Society (Cambridge and New York, 1985), 245–94.
5. Viotti da Costa, Brazilian Empire, 81.
6. Celso Furtado, Economic Development of Latin America, 2d ed. (Cambridge, 1976), 42–43.
7. Viotti da Costa, Brazilian Empire, 80.
8. Thomas E. Skidmore and Peter H. Smith, Modern Latin America (New York and Oxford, 1984), 157. For more on the export economy, see João Manoel Cardoso de Mello and Maria da Conceição Tavares, "The Capitalist Export Economy in Brazil, 1884–1930," in The Latin American Economies: Growth and the Export Sector, 1880–1930, ed. Roberto Cortés Conde and Shane J. Hunt (New York, 1985).
9. Viotti da Costa, Brazilian Empire, 79.
10. Ibid., 80. Other factors also regulated the rhythm of land privatization. In an extractive economy, such as that of the Amazon region during the rubber boom, commercial control was more important than landownership, thereby limiting the need for privatization of land. See Barbara Weinstein, The Amazon Rubber Boom, 1850–1920 (Stanford, 1983).
11. APP, "Medição das terras requeridas por Absalão Antonio Carneiro," 1897.
12. Santa Catarina, Collecção de leis do estado de Santa Catarina (Florianópolis, 1895), 48–52.
13. Ibid., 52.
14. Sources for table 2: SDVTOP, Relatório 1907, 3; SCSG-B, Relatório 1909, 90–91; SCSG-B, Relatório 1910, 175–76; SCSG-B, Relatório 1911, 112–14, SCSG-B, Relatório 1912; SCSG-B, Relatório 1914, 178; SCG, Men-

sagem do Governador Felippe Schmidt, 1917, 25; SDVTOP, *Relatório 1919*, 26; SDVOPA, *Relatório 1920*, 38–41; SDVOPA, *Relatório 1923*, 62.

15. Santa Catarina land area and population figures are from BMAIC, *Annuário Estatistico do Brazil, 1908–1912* (Rio de Janeiro, 1916), 1:251–53 and 344.

16. Montiero, *Os errantes*.

17. Vinhas de Queiroz, *Messianismo*, 65.

18. Reprinted in *O Libertador*, 9 Feb. 1910, 2.

19. SDVTOP, *Relatório 1907*, 27.

20. SCSG-B, *Relatório 1912*, 110–12.

21. SDVTOP, *Relatório 1907*, 26–28.

22. *A Região Serrana*, 3 May, 9 May, 26 Sept., 31 Oct., and 7 Nov. 1909; *A Folha do Comércio*, 30 July 1914; ASC, SDVTOP, "Requerimentos de concessões de terras públicas," 178:35–37, 13 Nov. 1918.

23. *O Libertador*, 9 Feb. 1910.

24. APP, "Medição das terras requeridas por João Carneiro e outros," 6 June 1900.

25. SCSG-B, *Relatório 1904*, 93.

26. SCSG-B, *Relatório 1912*, 110–12.

27. PSOPC, *Relatório 1912*, 15.

28. PSOPC, *Relatório 1913*, 44.

29. ASC, SDVTOP, "Requerimentos de concessões de terras públicas," vol. 92; vol. 133, 90; vol. 175, book 176.

30. Ibid., 129:68.

31. Ibid., 159:49.

32. Ibid., 156:16.

33. See chapter 3.

34. PSOPC, *Relatório 1906*, 21–22.

35. PSOPC, *Relatório 1910*, 27–28.

36. PSOPC, *Relatório 1913*, 43.

37. *A cidade e o município de Rio Negro*.

38. *A Vanguarda*, 1 May 1908.

39. ASC, "Ofícios das intendências municipais," 1907.

40. IP, videotaped interview with João Paes de Farias, site of the Santa Maria redoubt, near Fraiburgo, Santa Catarina, 1985. João is the son of Chico Ventura, one of the main leaders of the Contestado Rebellion. He was fourteen years old when the rebellion began, and he served as a drummer boy for the rebels. During this interview, in which João guided the Irani Produções team through the old redoubt, his face drew tight and his voice quivered when asked about the availability of land before the outbreak of the rebellion.

41. Brazil Railway Company, *Annual Report 1912*, 10. A study funded by the state of Paraná in 1954 found that the Brazil Railway Company received over 700,000 hectares in land concessions from the federal government; see Hortêncio de Alcântara, *A questão de terras*, 5.

42. SCG, *Mensagem 1912*, 121–22; PPGE, *Relatório 1913*, 93–95; Alcân-

tara, *A questão de terras*, 5. The state of Paraná did not officially recognize the Brazil Railway concession until 1917.

43. *A Vanguarda*, 15 July 1909; *O Libertador*, 24 Dec. 1909, 24 Sept. 1910, and 9 Feb. 1910.

44. *A Vanguarda*, 1 Oct. 1910, 3. For company surveys, see the various *processos* included in APP.

45. "Edital," *A Vanguarda*, 3 Sept. 1910, 6.

46. Monteiro, *Os errantes*, 31; Vinhas de Queiroz, *Messianismo*, 72.

47. *O Libertador*, 9 Aug. 1911, 3. This announcement appeared in the following six issues of the newspaper.

48. APP, "Medição das terras no logar 'Lageado do Leãozinho' concedidas à Companhia de Estrada de Ferro São Paulo-Rio Grande," 8 May 1911; "Medição das terras no logar 'Rio Uruguay,' " 23 May 1911; "Medição das terras no logar 'Rio de Peixe,' " 2 Jan. 1912.

49. Rosângela Cavallazzi da Silva, "Terras públicas e particulares: o impacto do capital estrangeiro sobre a institucionalização da propriedade privado (um estudo da 'Brazil Railway Company' no meio oeste catarinense)," Tese de Mestrado, Universidade Federal de Santa Catarina, 1983.

50. Quoted in Ibid., 61–62.

51. Quoted in Ibid., 62.

52. Demerval Peixoto, *Campanha do Contestado: episódios e impressões* (Rio de Janeiro, 1916), 1:71. Peixoto's book should be subtitled "The Formation of the 'Tenente' Mentality." In this work he assumes a nationalistic stance, criticizing foreign activities in Brazil, and the fact that the federal government gave foreign corporations special business concessions. He also complains of the lack of modern weapons with which to fight the rebels and the complete lack of modern scientific military training. These were the very concerns of the young, nationalistic officers, the "Tenentes," so important in Brazil during the 1920s and 1930s. For more on the *Tenentes* see John D. Wirth, "Tenentismo in the Brazilian Revolution of 1930," *Hispanic American Historical Review* 44, no. 2 (May 1964): 161–79; José Augusto Drummond, *O movimento tenentista: a intervenção política dos oficiais jovens (1922–1935)* (Rio de Janeiro, 1986); Frank D. McCann, "The Formative Period of Twentieth-Century Brazilian Army Thought, 1900–1922," *Hispanic American Historical Review* 44, no. 2 (Nov. 1984): 737–65.

53. Peixoto, *Campanha do Contestado*, 2d ed., 561–62.

54. PSOPC, *Relatório 1913*, 40–41.

55. Interview with Benjamin Scoz.

56. Brazil Railway Company, *Annual Report 1919* (London, 1920), 43.

57. APP, "Medição das terras no logar 'Jangada' concedidas a Companhia de Estrada de Ferro São Paulo-Rio Grande," 2 June 1911. The following discussion is based on information contained in this source.

58. BL, "Southern Brazil Lumber and Colonization Company," vol. 16.

59. RPCRI, "Livro de Notas," 29:73–75; RPCRI, "Registro de terras," book 3, nos. 99, 100, and 101, 37.

60. The information for this discussion comes from APP, "Medição do

terreno 'São Sebastião de Bom Retiro' por the So. Brazil Lumber Company,"
1910.

61. ASC, SDVTOP, "Requerimentos de concessões de terras publicas,"
vol. 187, book 188, 16 Dec. 1918, 143. The quote comes from vol. 160, 17
Nov. 1916, 10.

62. PG, *Mensagem do Governador Dr. Calvacanti de Albuquerque,
Fevereiro 1, 1913*, 19–20; O Trabalho, 23 Oct. 1909.

63. The EFSPRG lawyer is quoted in Cavallazzi da Silva, "Terras Públicas," 51; Farquhar is quoted in Gauld, *Last Titan*, 216. See also BL, W. C.
Forbes, "Memorandum," vol. 17, 15 Mar. 1915, 5.

64. *A Vanguarda*, 1 July 1910, 1.

65. This information comes from a compilation of the entries found in the
CNCRI (Proprietária: Légia Santos Brizola), book 3A (1908–24). The dollar
amount is a very rough estimate. It is impossible to determine exactly in
what year land sales were made at Erval d'Oeste, due to delays in the land
registration process.

66. According to the suit, Rupp planned to "vender os mattos que lhe
pertencem à Companhia S.Paulo–Rio Grande," and thus the company pro-
tested "contra quaisquer alienações que o Sr. Rupp pretenda fazer, das suas
terras, enquanto não fizer o pagamento daquella quantia." *O Libertador*, 9
May 1910, 4. See also 24 Jan. 1910 and 9 Feb. 1910 issues.

67. Ibid., 24 Sept. 1910, 1.

68. In Campos Novos, the first mention of a Stephanes purchase at Rio
Bonito is in a March 1913 land registration. The last mention of a Stephanes
sale is in 1924. According to local residents, these registration dates are
misleading, for long delays usually occurred between the sale of a property
and the registration of that sale. Two examples in Campos Novos documents
point to such delays. First, EFSPRG colonization of land near Campos Novos
began in 1910–11. In the municipal records, however, the first company
colonization registration does not appear until 1920. Second, in one 1921
registration Henrique Rupp is listed as the buyer of a property at Erval
d'Oeste, but he died in 1915. These delays make it difficult to detail the exact
time frame of Stephanes' actions in the Peixe River area. See interviews with
João Rupp Sobrinho and Légia Santos Brizola, Campos Novos, Santa Catarina, 9 May 1985, and various entries in CNCRI, book 3A.

69. CNCRI, book 3A, no. 223, 8 Mar. 1913, and 414, 11 Oct. 1914; CNST,
"Livro de Terras," book 28, 23 Nov. 1912, 35–36, and book 31, 5–6.

70. CNCRI, book 3A, nos. 525–28, 3 Feb. 1919; nos. 561–66, 8 July 1919;
and no. 567, 20 Aug. 1919.

71. Ibid., nos. 589 and 596, 8 Dec. 1919, and nos. 2681–83, 26 Apr. 1924.

72. Da Silva, *Apontamentos históricos*, UPCRI, book 3, no. 188, 4 Aug.
1909, 49.

73. APP, "Medição das terras requeridas por Arthur de Paula e Souza"
(documents from 1899–1905).

74. CCRI, book 3C, no. 1608, 17 May 1898, and no. 1609, 21 Sept. 1898; UPCRI, book 3, nos. 457–58 and 460–64.

75. UPCRI, book 3, nos. 459, 465, and 620–21.

76. *A Folha de Comércio,* 25 Oct. 1912, 1; UPCRI, book 3C, nos. 6–11, 11 Aug. 1908, 2.

77. RPCCC, "Inventário de Coronel João Pacheco dos Santos Lima," 12 Aug. 1907; RPCRI, "Registro de terras," book 3, nos. 47–48, 5 Aug. 1904, 20. *Coronel* Pacheco left 6,500 hectares to his wife Leocádia and between 240 and 480 hectares to his children, Adelaide, João Filho, Bemvindo, Maria da Conceição, Bemvinda, Leocádio, Antonia, Firmino, Pedro, Rivadávia, Leocádia, and Joaquina.

78. RPCRI, "Registro de terras," book 3, no. 72, 5 June 1908, 29, no. 83, 10 Mar. 1909, 32, and no. 102, 24 Aug. 1910, 37. Leocádio went on to command a group of civilian fighters (*vaqueanos*) during the Contestado Rebellion. He died in one of the rebellion's last battles.

79. RPCCC, "Inventário de Coronel João Pacheco"; RPCRI, "Registro de terras," book 3, 23 Oct. 1907; nos. 93, 97, and 98, 15 Jan. 1910, 35–37; no. 103, 14 Sept 1910, 38; no. 114, 22 Apr. 1911, 42.

80. APP, "Medição das terras requeridas por Aleixo Gonçalves de Lima," 12 Dec. 1898.

81. APP, "Medição de terras requeridas por Firmino e Pedro Pacheco dos Santos Lima," 7 Jan. 1912.

82. On 17 November 1913, Aleixo Gonçalves served as the *padrinho* to the infant Waldemiro, son of José Gonçalves de Lima and Francelina de Assis. The ceremony took place at the Igreja Matriz in Canoinhas. PC, "Registro de Batismo," no. 486, 17 Nov. 1913. For information on Gonçalves's title, see note 80.

83. UPCRI, book 3, 21 Nov. 1896 (this is the registration of São Roque by the inheritors of the João Cardoso Paes Carneiro–Maria dos Passos Ferreira estate). For more on the Carneiro and Araujo families, see chapter 2.

84. UPCRI, book 3, no. 144, 21 July 1909, 44 (this is the registration of the São Roque sale by Camargo). The quotes come from a Camargo speech to the Paraná Chamber of Deputies, reprinted in *O Diário da Tarde,* 21 Feb. 1914.

85. The information on the *erva mate* contract comes from BL, "Nolting to W. C. Forbes," vol. 4, 22 Jan. 1916; Camargo's quote is from *O Diário da Tarde,* 21 Feb. 1914.

86. Captain João Teixeira de Matos Costa quoted in Peixoto, *Campanha do Contestado,* 2d ed., 229–30. Elias de Moraes quoted in Soares, *Guerra em sertões Brasileiros,* 95. According to Contestado historian Zélia de Andrade Lemos, a large number of the rebels at the "Bom Sossego" redoubt were "antigo posseiros, trabalhadores de erva mate [que] andavam já de quareles com os fazendeiros ricos . . . Artur de Paula e Souza e Fabrício Vieira"; *Curitibanos,* 116.

87. *O Diário da Tarde,* 9 Oct. 1914.

88. Interview with Francisco Pacheco dos Santos.

5 Progress and Anarchy

1. *A Vanguarda*, 1 June 1908.
2. Ibid., 1 June 1910.
3. This photograph is in the possession of Dario de Almeida Prado of Florianópolis, Santa Catarina.
4. *O Libertador*, 9 Nov. 1909.
5. *A Vanguarda*, 15 Apr. and 1 June 1910; *A Região Serrana*, 29 May 1910.
6. "O relatório do Coronel Albuquerque, January 2, 1910," reprinted in *O Trabalho*, 3 May 1910.
7. *A Vanguarda*, 16 July 1910.
8. psopc, *Relatório 1908*, 19.
9. Assumpção, *A campanha do Contestado*, 1:163–70; Martins, *Quantos somos e quem somos*, 96–100; Piazza, *Santa Catarina*, 531, 600, and 602; scsg-b, *Relatório 1902*; psi, *Relatório 1908*. The 1914 figure comes from Assumpção, a soldier in the federal forces. Figures from 1902 and 1906 come from Santa Catarina and Paraná, respectively.
10. asc, Ofícios das intendências municipais (Campos Novos, 1904–13).
11. scsg-b, *Relatório 1910*, 50.
12. scsg-b, *Relatório 1912*, 39.
13. asc, sdvtop, "Requerimentos de concessões de terras públicas," vol. 74, 19 Feb. 1900, 121–23.
14. Ibid., vol. 175, 5 Dec. 1911 and 10 Apr. 1912, 116–21.
15. Ibid., vol. 174, 19 Feb. 1900, 121–23.
16. *O Libertador*, 9 Nov. 1909.
17. Various government *relatórios* from the construction era mention the shortage of workers. See for example, bmvop, *Relatório 1912*, 102; and an, "A companhia E. Ferro S. Paulo-Rio Grande requer prorogação de prazo para a construcção da linha de S. Francisco," Arquivo do Ministério do Transportes, Maço 202, #10275, 1913.
18. This 96 to 120 *milreis* per month wage (depending on the number of days actually worked) compares with the following salaries in Rio de Janeiro in 1906: unskilled laborer—107 *milreis*; bricklayer—195 *milreis*; carpenter—198 *milreis*. Source: Eulália Maria Lahmeyer Lobo and Eduardo Navarro Stotz, "Flutuações cíclicas da economia, condições de vida e movimento operário—1880 a 1930," *Revista Rio de Janeiro* 1, no. 1 (Sept.–Dec. 1985): 74.
19. bmvop, *Relatório 1907*, 1:557–60, and *Relatório 1909*, 2:352; *O Libertador*, 9 Feb. 1910. The 8,000 figure comes from Thomé, *Trem de ferro*, 95. One local newspaper placed the late-1909 workforce at over 6,000; see *A Região Serrana*, 28 Nov. 1909.
20. *A Região Serrana*, 4 Apr. 1909; ppge, *Relatório 1912*.
21. *O Trabalho*, 18 July 1908; asc, Ofícios das intendências municipais (Canoinhas), vol. 3, 1912.
22. Interview with Benjamin Scoz; newspaper quote from *A Vanguarda*, 15 Dec. 1910; mortality estimate from *A Folha do Comércio*, 6 Apr. 1914. A

typical example of the violence in the area was the case of Manoel Constant-ino, a Portuguese track worker living near Erval d'Oeste. In 1912 he murdered the Spaniard Adolpho Álvarez during a violent argument and wounded a man who came to the latter's aid. Local authorities later arrested Constantino. See *A Vanguarda*, 1 July 1912.

23. Aufderheide, "Order and Violence," 7–8; for more on marginality, see also 84–101.

24. *A Vanguarda*, 1 Nov. 1910. The first complaint against the EFSPRG administration appeared in the Campos Novos newspaper *O Libertador*. In its 9 February 1910 edition, the newspaper reprinted a telegram sent to Florianópolis by a local judge complaining of the activities of the EFSPRG police force.

25. *A Vanguarda*, 15 Dec. 1910. The quote complaining of security force violence and the passivity of the local population is as follows: "Antes de tudo deve-se crer que uma das principaes atribuições da polícia da estrada de ferro fosse acautelar a vida de todo o indivíduo contra qualquer perigo, evitando greves, assaltos ou distúrbios, sendo livre de dúvida que aonde existe uma força armada e alerta não desenro-lar-se-a tactos bárbaros de que dizem, são testimunhas as margens do Rio do Peixe e grande parte do povo sem energia que tudo presencia estáctico sem dar um signal de vida em desaffronta de seu semelhante barbaramente esquartejado ou fusilado."

26. Cooper, *Brazilians and Their Country*, 219–20.

27. IP, videotaped interview with Baldo Ricardo da Silva. Da Silva, ninety-three years old at the time of this interview, lived in Canoinhas during the Contestado Rebellion. He remembered *caboclos* trading *erva mate* for goods at a store in Canoinhas. Vinhas de Queiroz also writes of *caboclos* trading *erva mate* for goods; see *Messianismo*, 65.

28. Interview with Benjamin Scoz; Vinhas de Queiroz, *Messianismo*, 65. One contemporary observer noted, "In general, those occupied with the collection of *mate* are those laboring and immigrant classes . . . from which, in connection with their agricultural work, they derive their liveli-hood"; Heinz, *O mate ou chá de Paraná*, 11.

29. Molitor, *Report*, 280–82; *A Região Serrana*, 23 June and 26 Sept. 1909.

30. *A Notícia*, 3 Aug. and 5 Oct. 1912.

31. For example, João Pereira de Camargo of Curitibanos warned "todos quantos costumam invadir os campos e mattos de sua dita fazenda, caçando, melando, pondo criações e mesmo transitando, que d'ora em diante não consente continuarem commetindo taes abusos"; *O Trabalho*, 25 May 1913. Five years earlier F. F. d'Almeida of Campos Novos placed a similar notice, prohibiting anyone from breaking ground and planting crops on his Invernada do Leão *fazenda*; *A Vanguarda*, 15 Aug. 1908.

32. *O Libertador*, 24 Jan. 1910.

33. *A Notícia*, 3 Aug. 1912.

34. Eric Wolf quoted in Silverman, "Patronage and Community-Nation Relationships," 293.

35. Ibid., 294. As an example of something that is not a critical issue, Silverman writes that a merchant who brings the latest fashions to town is not a broker.

36. Vitor Nunes Leal, *Coronelismo, enxada, e voto,* 3d ed. (São Paulo, 1976), 251–53. Many large landowners became *coronéis* (*coronels*) when they led National Guard units during the monarchy. Today the term denotes a political boss.

37. Ibid., 253.

38. Maria Isaura Pereira de Queiroz, "O coronelismo," 160.

39. Leal, *Coronelismo,* 225–30.

40. *O Trabalho,* 5 Feb. 1909. In a similar election, the "official" candidate in the Campos Novos municipal superintendent race of 1910 received 335 votes to only 1 vote for the opposition candidate. See *A Vanguarda,* 1 Jan. 1911.

41. See the various "registro de terras" documents contained in APP.

42. Stein discusses the use of labor gangs to harvest coffee in the Paraíba Valley after abolition; *Vassouras,* 264–65.

43. *O Diário da Tarde,* 17 Sept. 1914.

44. SDVTOP, *Relatório 1907,* 20; PSOPC, *Relatório 1913,* 52.

45. *O Trabalho,* 3 June 1910.

46. BMVOP, *Relatório 1912,* 102. The quote comes from AN, "A Companhia E. Ferro S. Paulo-Rio Grande requer prorogação de prazo para a construcção da linha de S. Francisco," Arquivo do Ministério dos Transportes, Maço 202, #10275, 1913. See also Peixoto, *Campanha do Contestado,* 2d ed., 9.

47. Karl Marx, *Capital* (International Publishers, 1967), 1:359–68.

48. Monteiro, *Os errantes,* 43.

49. Ruy Wachowicz, "O comércio da madeira e a atução da Brazil Railway no sul do Brasil," photocopy located in the Arquivo Público de Santa Catarina.

50. For the Contestado, Monteiro and Thomé rely on Vinhas de Queiroz for their information on labor brokerage. For his part, Vinhas de Queiroz only briefly mentions the contracting of laborers for track construction. He notes only that workers were divided into gangs headed by *tarfeiros* (contractors), who were responsible for paying the wages of the workers. See Vinhas de Queiroz, *Messianismo,* 70–71; Monteiro, *Os errantes,* 43; and Thomé, *Trem de ferro,* 89.

In the general literature on railroads in Brazil, Robert Mattoon provides the greatest amount of information on construction workers and labor contractors. In his dissertation, "The Companhia Paulista de Estradas de Ferro, 1868–1900: A Local Railway Enterprise in São Paulo, Brazil" (Yale, 1971), Mattoon briefly notes the shortages of unskilled labor that the company faced beginning in the 1860s. He also briefly mentions labor contractors but provides no information on who they were or how they contracted the members of their work gangs (see 196–98). Other books and articles (too numerous to mention here) completely ignore the unskilled labor aspect of railroad construction.

51. Interview with Benjamin Scoz; *O Trabalho*, 18 July 1908; *O Diário da Tarde*, 15 Dec. 1914.

52. Wachowicz, "O comércio de madeira," 314.

53. For details on the activities of Rupp and Arthur de Paula e Souza, see chapter 4.

54. *O Trabalho*, 3 June and 18 July 1910.

55. Ibid., 13 Jan. 1911.

56. Ibid.

57. ASC, "Ofícios dos juizes de direito" (Campos Novos), 1909; *O Libertador*, 9 Nov. 1909; Thomé, *Trem de ferro*, 96.

58. ASC, "Ofícios dos juizes de direito" (Campos Novos), 1909.

59. Vinhas de Queiroz, *Messianismo*, 71. The author writes that "como eram baixos os preços tabelados pela estrada, [Vacariano] teve prejuízo e não pode pagar os seus operários. Comprometido com eles, associou-se a outros indivíduos e assaltou o pagador Henrique Baomi."

60. *O Libertador*, 9 Nov. 1909. On the revenge motive, the newspaper wrote that "Por esse facto [that Stengel had paid the contract workers himself] digno de louvor, os 'gravidos' empreiteiros, accostumados a viverem a custa de calotes e do suor dos pobres trabalhadores, revoltaram-se contra o digno chefe da construcção e segundo parece auxiliam a quadrilha de salteadores."

61. *A Vanguarda*, 1 Nov. 1910.

62. For the elite view, see *O Libertador*, 9 Feb. 1910, and *A Vanguarda*, 1 Nov. and 15 Dec. 1910. For the nonelite view, see the interview with Benjamin Scoz.

63. See the beginning of this chapter for details on security force activities.

64. *O Trabalho*, 23 Feb. and 18 July 1910; Peixoto, *Campanha do Contestado*, 2d ed., 71.

65. Peixoto, *Campanha do Contestado*, 2d, ed., 71–72.

66. Monteiro, *Os errantes*, 210.

67. Florencia Mallon, "Murder in the Andes," 79–98.

68. Here it is fruitful to compare political brokerage with labor brokerage. As political brokers, Contestado *coronéis* continued to be important until the end of the First Republic. This was because regional and national officials repeatedly relied upon them to deliver votes in various elections. As labor brokers, however, their usefulness to extralocals ended once sufficient labor had been delivered to the ERFSPRG.

6 Millenarianism and the Crisis of Subsistence

1. Vinhas de Queiroz, *Messianismo*, 77–88; *A Região Serrana*, 15 Dec. 1912.

2. The Amaro and Gomez quotes are found in Assumpção, *A campanha*

do Contestado, 1:79 and 361. The rebel leader's quote comes from a letter reprinted in Fernando Setembrino de Carvalho, *Relatório apresentado ao Gral. de Divisão José Caetano de Farias* (Rio de Janeiro, 1916), 13.

3. After breaking with his father, Dom João VI of Portugal, Dom Pedro I became the emperor of Brazil in 1822. He was followed by his son, Dom Pedro II, who ruled until 1889, when a military plot overthrew him and established the Republic. Roderick J. Barman, *Brazil: The Forging of a Nation, 1798–1852* (Stanford, 1988); Skidmore and Smith, *Modern Latin America*, 146–54.

4. *A história do Imperador Carlos Magno e os doze Pares de França* (São Paulo, no date). This is the version that was read by José Maria.

5. *A Folha do Comércio*, 26 Mar. 1914.

6. Vinhas de Queiroz, *Messianismo*, 114.

7. "Sr. Rufino," quoted in Monteiro, *Os errantes*, 161.

8. The holy army of St. Sebastian refers to Dom Sebastião, king of Portugal, who died fighting the Moors in 1578. Out of his death began the millenarian belief that the king would return to Portugal to liberate the country from Spanish domination. In the Contestado this legend of Dom Sebastião mixed with that of St. Sebastian, the Christian saint from Roman times and the patron saint of many local Contestado chapels. Monteiro, *Os errantes*, 107–11; Vinhas de Queiroz, *Messianismo*, 108–11; Pereira de Queiroz, *O messianismo*, 100–103.

9. IP, videotaped interview with José Maria Gomes. José heard Euzébio make this claim the night the latter set out for Taquaraçu.

10. Interview with Benjamin Scoz.

11. IP, videotaped interview with João Paes de Farias.

12. Quoted in Assumpção, *A campanha do Contestado*, 2:295. It was Assumpção himself who interviewed this prisoner.

13. IP, videotaped interview with Rosa Paes de Farias, Lebon Régis, Santa Catarina, 1985.

14. The prayer is quoted in Assumpção, *A campanha do Contestado*, 2:305–9.

15. Testimony of Maria Alves Moreira, quoted in Monteiro, *Os errantes*, 129.

16. IP, videotaped interview with Manoel Batista dos Santos.

17. Peixoto, *Campanha do Contestado*, 2d ed., 698, 703–4, and 769.

18. IP, videotaped interview with Manoel Batista dos Santos. Numerous interviews with ex-rebels confirm Manoel's description of *a forma*. See also Monteiro, *Os errantes*, 128–30, and Assumpção, *A campanha do Contestado*, 1:78–79.

19. Interview with David Gabriel Riveira, Lebon Régis, Santa Catarina, 26 Apr. 1985. IP, videotaped interview with Salvador Batista do Santos, Timbó Grande, Santa Catarina, 1985; videotaped interview with Rosa Paes de Farias; and videotaped interview with João Paes de Farias.

20. Interview with Rosália Maria de Castro, São João de Timbozinho, Santa Catarina, 25 Apr. 1985; IP, videotaped interview with Manoel Batista dos Santos; Monteiro, *Os errantes*, 131–33.

21. Vinhas de Queiroz, *Messianismo*, 151–52.

22. IP, videotaped interview with João Paes de Farias; Assumpção, *A campanha do Contestado*, 1:78.

23. Interview with Rosália Maria de Castro.

24. Pereira de Queiroz, *O messianismo*, 278–81.

25. Ibid., 281; Monteiro, *Os errantes*, 133.

26. Monteiro, *Os errantes*, 133.

27. Ibid.

28. Interview with Rosália Maria de Castro. Rosália herself married in the rebel redoubt of Caraguatá.

29. Pereira de Queiroz, *O messianismo*, 278. Pereira de Queiroz claims that soldiers eventually destroyed these ledgers.

30. This story was told by Rosindo Paes de Farias, son of the condemned man and grandson of Chico Ventura. As for Chico Ventura, Rosindo, Chico's son João Paes de Farias, and daughter Rosa Paes de Farias all mentioned that he was a dedicated believer in the religion. Rosália Maria de Castro also mentioned Chico's devotion. IP, videotaped interview with Rosindo Paes de Farias, Timbó Grande, Santa Catarina, 1985; and videotaped interviews with João Paes de Farias and Rosa Paes de Farias. Interview with Rosália Maria de Castro.

31. José Vieira da Rosas, "Reminiscências da campanha do Contestado," photocopy at ASC, 1918, 24–25; Vinhas de Queiroz, *Messianismo*, 120–21.

32. Peixoto, *Campanha do Contestado*, 2d ed., 65.

33. Vinhas de Queiroz, *Messianismo*, 90.

34. Peixoto, *Campanha*, 125. *A Folha do Comércio* reported in a similar fashion the meeting between Gualberto and José Maria's emissaries; 30 Oct. 1912.

35. IP, videotaped interview with Rosa Paes de Farias.

36. *A Folha do Comércio*, 10 Feb. 1914.

37. IP, videotaped interviews with Rosa Paes de Farias and João Paes de Farias. In my conversations with locals about the rebellion, talk always turned to the destruction of army graves.

38. Peixoto, *Campanha do Contestado*, 2d ed., 165; Assumpcão, *A campanha do Contestado*, 1:261.

39. The note was reprinted in *O Diário da Tarde*, 21 Oct. 1914.

40. Assumpção, *A campanha do Contestado*, 1:261.

41. Vinhas de Queiroz, *Messianismo*, 164.

42. Ibid., 111.

43. Peixoto, *Campanha do Contestado*, 2d ed., 448; Assumpção, *A campanha do Contestado*, 1:229.

44. IP, videotaped interviews with Rosa Paes de Farias and João Paes de Farias; interviews with David Gabriel Riveira and Rosália Maria de Castro.

45. The quote is from Peixoto, *Campanha do Contestado*, 2d ed., 71. For more on Moraes's political connections see *O Trabalho*, 23 Feb., 18 July, and 13 Nov. 1910. The national version of the Republican party, founded in 1871, agitated for the end of the Brazilian monarchy. When this occurred in 1889,

the party became the dominant political force in the country. This means that the rebel leader Elias de Moraes was once a member of a political party that opposed the monarchy.

46. Peixoto discusses the letter, written in August 1914, in *Campanha do Contestado*, 2d ed., 71–72.

47. Interview with Rosália Maria de Castro.

48. Vinhas de Queiroz, *Messianismo*, 134–35; Lemos, *Curitibanos*, 112.

49. *O Diário da Tarde*, 17 Sept. 1914; IP, videotaped interviews with Orti Machado and Baldo Ricardo da Silva.

50. *O Diário da Tarde*, 16, 17, and 27 July 1914.

51. *A Folha do Comércio*, 14 Jan. 1915; Vinhas de Queiroz, *Messianismo*, 218.

52. *O Diário da Tarde*, 27 July 1914. The quote comes from Tavares's letter, which is reprinted in Peixoto, *Campanha do Contestado*, 2d ed., 467. See also Vinhas de Queiroz, *Messianismo*, 214–15.

53. *O Diário da Tarde*, 20 Jan. 1915. Wolland was, for a time, in contact with the core of the movement's leadership. Indeed, it seems that the virgin Maria Rosa confirmed his entrance into the movement. For a time he led a group of rebels on a series of strikes in the Canoinhas area. According to *O Diário da Tarde*, he was twenty-two years old and a German citizen. See also Vinhas de Queiroz, *Messianismo*, 155–56. Wolland's comments upon his capture contrasted sharply with the actions of other captured rebels, who proclaimed their allegiance to José Maria throughout brutal interrogations.

54. Nascimento, "Canudos, Contestado, e fanatismo religioso," 64.

55. Ibid., 65. For a similar view, see Rui Facó, *Cangaceiros e fanáticos*.

56. Interview with Rosália Maria de Castro (São João de Timbozinho, Santa Catarina), 25 Apr. 1985; IP, videotaped interview with Maria de Jesus Pedroso, Timbó Grande, Santa Catarina, 1985; IP, videotaped interviews with Rosa Paes de Farias and João Paes de Farias; interview with Cipriano Rodrigues de Moraes.

57. For a brief discussion of the scholarly debate over this tension, see Patricia R. Pessar, "Unmasking the Politics of Religion," 272–74.

58. Ibid., 273.

59. Clifford Geertz, *The Interpretation of Cultures* (New York, 1973), 126–27.

60. Ibid., 129.

61. Ibid., 126.

62. Ibid.

63. Interviews with Sebastião Calomeno, João Rupp Sobrinho, and Francisco Pacheco dos Santos.

64. Zaluar, *Os homens de deus*, 258–74; Pessar, "Unmasking the Politics of Religion," 255–78; Todd A. Diacon, "The Search for Meaning in an Historical Context: Popular Religion, Millenarianism, and the Contestado Rebellion," *Luso Brazilian Review* (forthcoming).

65. Peixoto, *Campanha do Contestado*, 2d ed., 561–63; *A cidade e o município de Rio Negro*.

66. The utility of Geertz's ethos–world view system to explain the emergence of a combined material and spiritual crisis, and its applicability to millenarianism, was first suggested by Steve J. Stern in his unpublished paper, "On the Social Origins of Millennial Movements: A Review and a Proposal," 1974.

67. I first proposed this idea of the external-internal continuum in Todd A. Diacon, "The Contestado and the Caste War of Yucatan: Secular and Religious Responses to Crisis Situations," Master's thesis, University of Wisconsin-Madison, 1983, esp. 18–19. By the use of the term "secular movement," I mean a movement which seeks to defend a threatened society's own religious and secular institutions *without* calling for a religious transformation and a transformation of the rebels' own life-style.

68. Pessar, "Unmasking the Politics of Religion," 256.

69. For more on the relationship between an internal crisis of values and millenarianism, see Diacon, "Contestado Movement," esp. 13–20, and Stern, "Social Origins." See also Victor Turner, *Dramas, Fields, and Metaphors: Symbolic Action in Human Society* (Ithaca, N.Y., 1974).

70. For examples of millenarian imagery, see Cohn, *Pursuit of the Millennium*; Pereira de Queiroz, *O messianismo*; Anthony F. C. Wallace, "Revitalization Movements," *American Anthropologist* 58 (1956): 264–81; Byran R. Wilson, "Millennialism in Comparative Perspective," *Comparative Studies in Society and History* 6 (1963): 93–114.

71. See chapter 5 and RPCRI, "Registro de terras," livro 3, nos. 91, 96, 111, 118, 119, and 138.

72. For a similar argument concerning patrons and their responsibilities to their clients, see Monteiro, *Os errantes*, 43–49.

73. Pessar, "Unmasking the Politics of Religion," 256.

74. *A Folha do Comércio*, 26 Mar. 1914.

75. Assumpção, *A campanha do Contestado*, 1:306–7. As an "exception that proves the rule" to this argument about the threat to subsistence, women as managers of the household economy, and their eagerness to join the movement, we have the case of the parents of Cipriano Rodrigues de Moraes. His father, a sizable landowner and cattle rancher, *"ficou loco para a santa religião"* ("he got religion") and joined the movement *against* the wishes of his wife. She did not want to join, according to Cipriano, because she wished to maintain her comfortable life on the *fazenda*. She cried the whole time they lived in the redoubts. Interview with Cipriano Rodrigues de Moraes.

More complicated is the case of dona Dúlcia, the wife of *fazendeiro* and eventual rebel leader Elias de Moraes. We know that one day she abandoned her home and joined the rebellion *ahead* of her husband. Most influential in her decision to join, no doubt, was the fact that she was a *comadre* to the rebel leader Euzébio Ferreira dos Santos. In fact, the existence of *compadre* ties with those already in the movement led many others to join the rebellion; Lemos, *Curitibanos*, 12. For more on the importance of *compadre* ties, see Peixoto, *Campanha do Contestado,* 2d ed., 592, and Vinhas de Queiroz, *Messianismo,* 134–35 and 154.

76. Pessar, "Unmasking the Politics of Religion," 267–68.

77. *A história do Imperador Carlos Magno e os Pares de França,* 120; see also 142 and 162 for references to Charlemagne's paternalism.

78. IP, videotaped interview with João Paes de Farias.

79. Letter from Elias de Moraes to Capt. João Teixeira de Matos Costa, 1914, reprinted in Soares, *Guerra em sertões Brasileiros,* 95.

80. IP, videotaped interview with Rosa Paes de Farias.

81. For more on these attacks, see *O Diário da Tarde,* 23 Oct. 1914 and 5 Jan. 1915, and *A Folha do Comércio,* 28 Dec. 1914.

82. *O Diário da Tarde,* 16 June, 14 and 29 Sept., and 9 Oct. 1914; Lemos, *Curitibanos,* 116.

83. Monteiro, *Os errantes,* 70–75.

84. Molitor, *Report,* 45.

85. Linda Lewin, "The Oligarchical Limitations of Social Banditry in Brazil: The Case of the 'Good' Thief Antonio Silvino," *Past and Present* 82 (Feb. 1979), 138.

86. Peixoto, *Campanha do Contestado,* 2d ed., 294.

87. Ibid., 297.

7 Conclusion
The Power of the Millenarian Call

1. For a detailed analysis of the Caste War, see Diacon, "Contestado Movement," 44–86. See also Nelson Reed, *The Caste War of Yucatán* (Stanford, 1964).

2. Nancy M. Farriss, *Maya Society Under Colonial Rule: The Collective Enterprise of Survival* (Princeton, 1984), 12–18.

3. Ibid., 96–103, 167, 183–85, 263, and 272–85. Farriss notes that during the colonial era in Yucatán, "Indians of whatever rank were to remain firmly and unequivocably within the Indian universe. They would learn some Spanish ways, but only as outsiders seeking to maneuver through the thicket of Spanish administrative judicial systems in order to defend their communities' interests. And because their identity and interests remained firmly embedded within the Maya world, they [the Spanish administrative judicial systems] served as barriers to, rather than conduits of, Spanish cultural influence" (103).

4. Ibid., 367–70; Diacon, "Contestado Movement," 49–51.

5. Diacon, "Contestado Movement," 51–53.

6. Farriss, *Maya Society,* 183–84 and 263.

7. This version of the role of the indigenous elite in the rebellion differs from the interpretation of Victoria Reifler Bricker in *The Indian Christ, The Indian King* (Austin, 1981). Bricker argues that a much more "ladinoized" indigenous elite *joined* the Caste War only after blind *ladino* vengeance following a local massacre *forced* them to abandon *ladino* society (98–99).

For more on my views on this topic, see Diacon, "Contestado Movement," 61–65.

8. Diacon, "Contestado Movement," 66–68.

9. The "preachings of the Cross" were recorded by the Maya and have been translated by Bricker in *The Indian Christ, the Indian King*, 187–205.

10. The ideas of external pressures, village solidarity, and nonmillenarian responses to a crisis situation could be fruitfully applied to the Zapatista movement during the Mexican Revolution. For the classic work on Zapata, see John R. Womack, *Zapata and the Mexican Revolution* (New York, 1968).

11. In his analysis of the sixteenth-century Taki Onqoy millenarian rebellion in colonial Peru, Steve J. Stern presents a case where local elites cooperated with the colonizers to the detriment of fellow villagers; *Peru's Indian Peoples and the Challenge of Spanish Conquest* (Madison, 1982), 51–71.

12. Geertz, *Interpretation of Cultures* (New York, 1973); Steve J. Stern, "Social Origins."

13. Stern, *Peru's Indian Peoples*, 51–71.

14. Ibid., 56.

15. Pessar, "Unmasking the Politics of Religion," 261.

16. Farriss, *Maya Society*, 315.

17. Della Cava, *Miracle at Joaseiro*, 37–40. Della Cava acknowledges this split in the movement but does not explain its origins or importance.

18. Pessar, "Unmasking the Politics of Religion," 263.

19. Much more research is needed on the specifics of the Joaseiro case. For an early and especially cogent argument concerning Padre Cícero's paternalism see Ibid., 265–72.

20. Recent works on the Old Republic tend to focus on elites or the popular classes, but not both. See Jeffrey D. Needell, *A Tropical Belle Epoque: Elite Culture and Society in Turn-of-the-Century Rio de Janeiro* (Cambridge, 1987); Steven Topik, *The Political Economy of the Brazilian State, 1889–1930* (Austin, 1987). Other works do focus on relations between classes but do not discuss how events in the countryside may have shaped these relations. See José Murilo de Carvalho, *Os bestializados: o Rio de Janeiro e a república que não foi* (São Paulo, 1987); June E. Hahner, *Poverty and Politics: The Urban Poor in Brazil, 1870–1920* (Albuquerque, 1986).

21. None of the works cited in the previous note include substantial archival evidence drawn from repositories located outside of the cities of Rio de Janeiro and São Paulo. Similar divisions exist in the recent histories of the Brazilian empire. For works that focus mainly on urban-based political and economic elites, see Barman, *Brazil*; Pang, *In Pursuit of Honor and Power*. For works that do integrate the rural and urban histories of the imperial period, see Thomas Flory, *Judge and Jury in Imperial Brazil: State Control in Imperial Brazil, 1808–1871* (Austin, 1981); Fernando Uricoechea, *The Patrimonial Foundations of the Brazilian Bureaucratic State* (Berkeley and Los Angeles, 1980); Richard Graham, *Patronage and Politics in*

Nineteenth-Century Brazil (Stanford, 1990). Graham's study focuses precisely on the rural-to-urban continuum via an interesting argument concerning the mediating role of patronage. Nevertheless, neither this book nor any of the other histories of the empire include significant amounts of archival evidence drawn from archives beyond Rio de Janeiro and Bahia. The history of "the rest of Brazil" thus remains to be written.

22. Murilo de Carvalho argues that urban unrest in Rio de Janeiro, culminating in the 1904 Revolta Contra Vacina, sparked the narrowing of citizens' rights in Brazil. I am arguing that reaction to rural millenarian movements first set this process in motion. See Carvalho, *Os bestializados*, esp. 37–41.

23. I speak here of the *tenente* movement. The history of the Contestado Rebellion written by the soldier Dermeval Peixoto is full of the kinds of complaints and growing nationalism that marked the *tenentes'* interventionist philosophy; *Campanha do Contestado*, 2d ed. For more on the Contestado Rebellion and state building, see Todd A. Diacon, "Private Power and Public Action: A Case Study of State and Society Relations in the Brazilian Old Republic," paper presented to the 56th Annual Meeting of the Southern Historical Association, New Orleans, 1 Nov. 1990.

24. IP, videotaped interview with Rosa Paes de Farias.

Bibliography

Interviews

Most of my interviews were conducted with the help of the Irani Produções film documentary team—Ênio Staub, Jurandir Pires de Camargo, Sérgio Antônio Flores, and Dario de Almeida Prado, Jr. Videotaped interviews conducted only by Irani Produções are indicated by the presence of the company's name in the citation. Interviews in which I personally participated do not mention the company.

Brizola, Légia Santos. Campos Novos, Santa Catarina, 9 May 1985. Owner of the Campos Novos Cartório de Registro de Imóveis.

Calomeno, Sebastião (b. 1905). Curitibanos, Santa Catarina, 25 Apr. 1985. Nephew of the *fazendeiro* killed by his own *agregado*, the rebel leader Adeodato.

Castro, Rosália Maria de (b. 1895). São João de Timbozinho, Santa Catarina, 25 Apr. 1985. Lived and married in a rebel camp.

Gomes, José Maria (b. 1893). Lebon Régis, Santa Catarina, videotaped by Irani Produções, 1985. Son of a *fazendeiro*, he grew up with the rebel leader Adeodato.

Machado, Orti. Canoinhas, Santa Catarina, videotaped by Irani Produções, 1985. Local historian.

Moraes, Cipriano Rodrigues de (b. 1910). Fraiburgo, Santa Catarina, 26 Apr. 1985. Family joined the rebellion when he was an infant.

Olga, dona (?) (b. 1904). Três Barras, Santa Catarina, videotaped by Irani Produções, 1985. Lifelong resident of Três Barras; witnessed the surrender of the starving rebels.

Pacheco dos Santos, Francisco Calistro. Rio Negro, Paraná, 27 Feb. 1985. Grandson of *coronel* João Pacheco and member of the powerful Pacheco family of Rio Negro.

Paes de Farias, João (b. 1899). Lebon Régis, Santa Catarina, videotaped by Irani

Produções, 1985. Son of rebel leader Chico Ventura and drummer boy for the rebels.

Paes de Farias, Rosa (b. 1891). Lebon Régis, Santa Catarina, videotaped by Irani Produções, 1985. Daughter of rebel leader Chico Ventura and seamstress for the elite Peers of France guard.

Paes de Farias, Rosindo. Timbó Grande, Santa Catarina, videotaped by Irani Produções, 1985. Grandson of rebel leader Chico Ventura.

Pedroso, Maria de Jesus. Timbó Grande, Santa Catarina, videotaped by Irani Produções, 1985. Family joined the rebellion when she was an infant.

Proença, Rosena Francisca de. Curitibanos, Santa Catarina, 24 Apr. 1985. Lived in the Santa Maria redoubt.

Riveira, David Gabriel (b. 1899?). Lebon Régis, Santa Catarina, 26 Apr. 1985. Lived with his family in the Santa Maria and Timbó Grande redoubts.

Rupp Sobrinho, João. Campos Novos, Santa Catarina, 9 May 1985. Grandson of Henrique Rupp, the municipal official and powerful landowner from Campos Novos, Santa Catarina.

Santos, Manoel Batista dos (b. 1903). Timbó Grande, Santa Catarina, videotaped by Irani Produções, 1985. Lived as a boy in a series of rebel redoubts.

Santos, Salvador Batista dos (b. 1895?). Timbó Grande, Santa Catarina, videotaped by Irani Produções, 1985. Brother of Manoel; lived with family in redoubts.

Scoz, Benjamin (b. 1891). Lajes, Santa Catarina, 24 Apr. 1985. Member of the 54th Caçadores force; participated in several attacks against the rebels.

Silva, Baldo Ricardo da (b. 1902). Canoinhas, Santa Catarina, videotaped by Irani Produções, 1985. Resident of Canoinhas during the Contestado Rebellion; witnessed the surrender of many rebels.

Silva, Rufino Ferreira (b. 1903). Fraiburgo, Santa Catarina, videotaped by Irani Produções, 1985. Lived as a boy in the rebel redoubts.

Archival Sources, Brazil

Arquivo Nacional (AN), Rio de Janeiro

Arquivo do Ministério dos Transportes, Maço 108, #1327. "Tomada de contas da E. F. São Paulo–Rio Grande." 1910.

Arquivo do Ministério dos Transportes, Maço 202, #10275. "A Companhia E. Ferro S. Paulo–Rio Grande requer prorogação de prazo para a construcçao da Linha de S. Francisco." 1913.

Arquivo Farquhar, AP21-Caixa 1. "Explicação dos direitos de propriedade que assistem aos vários grupos de portadores de obrigações sobre todos os haveres do Brazil Railway Company," 1942.

Arquivo Farquhar, AP21-Caixa 1. Percival Farquhar, "Resumo do Programa Percival Farquhar ao organizar a Brazil Railway Company," 1942.

Arquivo Farquhar, AP21-Caixa 1. W. C. Forbes to Charles A. Gauld. 27 Nov. 1950.

Arquivo Farquhar, AP21-Caixa 2. Bender, Hamlyn, and Company, London, to Esmael de Oliveira Maia. 22 Aug. 1940.

Arquivo Público do Paraná (APP),
Curitiba, Secretaria de Obras Públicas e Colonização

"Medição das terras no logar 'Jangada' concedidas à Companhia de Estrada de Ferro São Paulo–Rio Grande." 2 June 1911.
"Medição das terras no logar 'Lageado do Leãozinho' concedidas à Companhia de Estrada de Ferro São Paulo–Rio Grande." 8 May 1911.
"Medição das terras no logar 'Rio do Peixe' concedidas à Companhia de Estrada de Ferro São Paulo–Rio Grande." 2 Jan. 1912.
"Medição das terras no logar 'Rio Uruguay' concedidas à Companhia de Estrada de Ferro São Paulo–Rio Grande." 23 May 1911.
"Medição das terras requeridas por Absalão Antonio Carneiro." 1897.
"Medição das terras requeridas por Absalão Carneiro." 2 Apr. 1898.
"Medição das terras requeridas por Absalão Carneiro e outros." 23 May 1900.
"Medição das terras requeridas por Alexio Gonçalves de Lima." 12 Dec. 1898.
"Medição das terras requeridas por Antonio dos Santos Carneiro, Manoel dos Santos Carneiro e Maria Prudencia de Souza." 9 Sept. 1899.
"Medição das terras requeridas por Arthur de Paula e Souza." (Includes documents from 1899–1905.)
"Medição das terras requeridas por Firmino e Pedro Pacheco dos Santos Lima." 7 Jan. 1912.
"Medição das terras requeridas por João Carneiro e outros." 6 June 1900.
"Medição das terras requeridas por João Simeão Carneiro e outros." 16 June 1900.
"Medição das terras requeridas por José Antonio Carneiro." 29 Oct. 1899.
"Medição das terras requeridas por Manoel Lourenço Araujo." 20 Dec. 1899.
"Medição das terras requeridas por Manoel Lourenço Araujo." No date.
"Medição das terras requeridas por Nicolau Bley Netto." No date.
"Medição do terreno 'São Sebastião de Bom Retiro' por the So. Brazil Lumber Company." 1910.
"Portaria."

Arquivo do Estado de Santa Catarina (ASC), Florianópolis

Directoria de Viação e Obras Públicas. "Requerimentos de concessões de terras públicas."
"Ofícios das intendências municipais."
"Ofícios do Corpo de Segurança, 1914."
"Ofícios dos juizes de direito" (Campos Novos).
"Relatório apresentado de Campos Novos pelo Superintendente Municipal Juventude Sobrinho" (Campos Novos). 7 Jan. 1916.
Vieira da Rosas, José. "Reminiscências da campanha do Contestado." Photocopy, 1918.

Biblioteca Nacional (BN), Rio de Janeiro

Arquivo George Percival Farquhar, 1-33, 12, 15. Percival Farquhar, "The Southern Lumber and Colonization Company." No date.

Fundação Getúlio Vargas, Rio de Janeiro

Arquivo Setembrino de Carvalho (AC). General Setembrino de Carvalho to G. Carneiro. 17 Sept. 1914.

Local Archives, Brazil

Campos Novos, Santa Catarina. Cartório de Registro de Imóveis. "Livro de terras."
Campos Novos, Santa Catarina. Segundo Tabelionato. "Livro de terras."
Canoinhas, Santa Catarina. Cartório de Registro de Imóveis. "Registro de Imóveis."
Paróquia de Canoinhas. Canoinhas, Santa Catarina. "Registro de batismo."
Paróquia de Senhor Bom Jesus de Coluna. Rio Negro, Paraná. "Registro de batismo."
Rio Negro, Paraná. Cartório Civil e Comércio. "Inventário do Coronel João Pacheco dos Santos Lima." 12 Aug. 1907.
Rio Negro, Paraná. Cartório de Registro de Casamento. "Registro de casamento."
Rio Negro, Paraná. Cartório de Registro de Imóveis. "Livro de Notas."
Rio Negro, Paraná. Cartório de Registro de Imóveis. "Registro de terras."
Rio Negro, Paraná. Cartório de Registro de Nascimento. "Registro de nascimento."
União da Vitória, Paraná. Cartório de Registro de Imóveis. Primeiro Ofício. "Registro de terras."

Archival Sources, United States

Forbes Collection, Baker Library (BL), Harvard University

"Brazil Development and Colonization Company." Vol. 18.
Brazil Railway, Paris, to W. C. F[orbes]. Vol. 7, 7 Feb. 1917.
Brazil Railway Company, "Report of Proceedings of Meetings of Bondholders." Vol. 23, 20 May 1915.
Charles E. Perkins to W. H. Grant. Vol. 20.
"Conference WCF[orbes] with Mr. Dapples." Vol. 1, 28 Jan. 1915.
Nolting to W. C. Forbes. Vol. 4, 22 Jan. 1916.
Nolting to W. C. Forbes. Vol. 7, 25 Jan. 1917.
"Report from W. F. Nolting-December." Vol. 4, 18 Feb. 1916.
W. C. Forbes to Joint Bondholders Committee. Vol. 21, 21 Jan. 1916.

W. C. Forbes, "Memorandum." Vol. 17, 15 Mar. 1915.
W. C. Forbes, "Narrative Report of the Receiver of the Brazil Railway Company to the Court of Maine." Vol. 24, 3 Dec. 1914.
W. C. Forbes, "Southern Brazil Lumber and Colonization Company." Vol. 16.

Newspapers and Periodicals

Boletim colonial agrícola do Paraná (Curitiba, Paraná).
Brazil Ferro-Carril (Rio de Janeiro).
O Diário da Tarde (Curitiba, Paraná).
O Estado (Florianópolis, Santa Catarina).
A Folha do Comércio (Florianópolis, Santa Catarina).
O Libertador (Campos Novos, Santa Catarina).
A Notícia (Lajes, Santa Catarina).
A Região Serrana (Lajes, Santa Catarina).
O Trabalho (Curitibanos, Santa Catarina).
A Vanguarda (Campos Novos, Santa Catarina).

Published Primary Sources

Assumpção, Herculano Teixeira d'. *A campanha do Contestado,* 2 vols. Belo Horizonte, 1917–18.
Brazil, Ministério da Agricultura, Indústria, e Comércio. *Annuário Estatistico do Brasil, 1908–1912,* vol. 1. Rio de Janeiro, 1916.
Brazil, Ministério da Viação e Obras Públicas. *Relatório,* various years (1907–12, 1914–15). Rio de Janeiro.
Brazil Railway Company. *Annual Report,* various years (1910–12, 1919). London.
Carvalho, Fernando Setembrino de. *Relatório apresentado ao Gral. de Divisão José Caetano de Farias.* Rio de Janeiro, 1916.
Molitor, Fredrick A. *Report on the Railway Properties in Southern Brazil Leased, Owned, or Controlled by the Brazil Railway Company.* Privately printed, 1915. (A copy is on file at the Baker Library, Harvard University.)
Peixoto, Demerval. *Campanha do Contestado: episódios e impressões.* Rio de Janeiro, 1916; 2d ed., 1920.
Paraná, Governador. *Mensagem do Governador Dr. Calvacanti de Albuquerque, Fevereiro 1, 1913.* Curitiba, 1914.
———. *Relatório do Governador Augusto Machado d'Oliveira, 1884.* Curitiba, 1885.
———. *Relatório do Governador Joaquim d'Almeida Faria Sobrinho, 1888.* Curitiba, 1889.
Paraná, Ministério de Viação e Obras Públicas. *Boletim 1909.* Curitiba.
Paraná, Procurador Geral do Estado. *Relatório,* various years (1910, 1912). Curitiba.

Paraná, Secretaria de Obras Públicas e Colonização. *Relatório*, various years (1904, 1906–13). Curitiba.
———. *Relatório apresentado ao Dr. João Baptista da Carvalho Filho.* Curitiba.
Paraná, Secretaria do Interior. *Relatório 1908.* Curitiba, 1909.
Saint-Hilaire, Auguste de. *Viagem à província de Santa Catharina, 1820.* São Paulo, 1936.
Santa Catarina. *Collecção de leis do estado de Santa Catarina.* Florianópolis, 1895.
Santa Catarina, Directoria de Viação, Obras Públicas e Agricultura. *Relatório*, various years (1920, 1923). Florianópolis.
Santa Catarina, Directoria de Viação, Terras e Obras Públicas. *Relatório*, various years (1907, 1919). Florianópolis.
Santa Catarina, Governador. *Mensagem, 1912.* Florianópolis, 1913.
———. *Mensagem do Governador Vidal Ramos, 1913.* Florianópolis, 1914.
———. *Mensagem do Governador Vidal Ramos, 1914.* Florianópolis, 1915.
———. *Mensagem do Governador Felippe Schmidt, 1917.* Florianópolis, 1918.
Santa Catarina, Secretaria Geral. *Relatório*, various years (1903, 1907, 1911, 1913, 1915). Florianópolis.
Santa Catarina, Secretário Geral. *Relatório*, various years (1902, 1904, 1907, 1909–12, 1914). Florianópolis.

Secondary Sources

Alcântara, Hortêncio de. *A questão de terras entre a União e o Paraná.* Curitiba, 1954.
Arantes Neto, Antonio Augusto. "A sagrada família—una análise estrutural de compadrío." Tese de Mestrado, Departamento de Ciências Sociais, Faculdade de Filosofia, Letras e Ciências Humanas, Universidade de São Paulo, 1970.
Auras, Marli. *Guerra do Contestado: a organização da irmandade cabocla.* Florianópolis, 1984.
Barkun, Michael. *Disaster and the Millenium.* New Haven, 1974.
Barman, Roderick J. *Brazil: The Forging of a Nation, 1798–1852.* Stanford, 1988.
Bergard, Laird. *Coffee and the Growth of Agrarian Capitalism in Nineteenth-Century Puerto Rico.* Princeton, 1983.
Bloch, M., and S. Gudeman. "*Compadrazgo*, Baptism and the Symbolism of a Second Birth." *Man* 16 (1981): 376–86.
Bordieu, Pierre. *Outline of a Theory of Practice.* Trans. Richard Nice. Cambridge, 1977.
Bricker, Victoria Reifler. *The Indian Christ, The Indian King.* Austin, 1981.
Burns, E. Bradford. *The Poverty of Progress.* Berkeley and Los Angeles, 1980.
Cardoso de Mello, João Manoel, and Maria Conceição Tavares. "The Capitalist Economy in Brazil, 1884–1930." In *The Latin American Economies:*

Growth and the Export Sector, 1880–1930, ed. Roberto Cortés Conde and Shane J. Hunt (82–136). New York, 1985.

Carvalho, José Murilo de. *Os bestializados: o Rio de Janeiro e a república que não foi*. São Paulo, 1987.

Carvalho Franco, Maria Sylvia de. *Homens livres na ordem escravocrata*. São Paulo, 1969.

Cavallazzi da Silva, Rosângela. "Terras públicas e particulares: o impacto do capital estrangeiro sobre a institucionalização do propriedade privado (um estado da 'Brazil Railway Company' no meio oeste catarinense)." Tese de Mestrado, Universidade Federal de Santa Catarina, 1983.

A cidade e o município de Rio Negro. Curitiba, 1924.

Cohen, Abner. "The Social Organization of Credit in a West African Cattle Market." In *Friends, Followers, and Factions: A Reader in Political Clientelism*, ed. Steffen W. Schmidt, Laura Guasti, Carl H. Landé, and James C. Scott (233–41). Berkeley and Los Angeles, 1977.

Cohn, Norman. *The Pursuit of the Millennium: Revolutionary Millenarians and Mystic Anarchists of the Middle Ages*, 3d ed. New York, 1970.

Comissão Pastoral de Terra de Santa Catarina. "Em S.C. não é diferente." *Cheiro da Terra* 5, no. 32 (Sept.–Oct. 1984): 6.

———. "Acampamentos e ocupações." *Cheiro da Terra* 5, no. 32 (Sept.–Oct. 1984): 7.

Cooper, Clayton S. *The Brazilians and Their Country*. N.p., 1917.

Cornelius, Wayne A. "Leaders, Followers, and Official Patrons in Urban Mexico." In *Friends, Followers, and Factions: A Reader in Political Clientelism*, ed. Steffen W. Schmidt, Laura Guasti, Carl H. Landé, and James C. Scott (332–53). Berkeley and Los Angeles, 1977.

Cunha, Euclydes da. *Rebellion in the Backlands*. Trans. Samuel Putnam. Chicago, 1944.

Cunha, Idaulo José. *Evolução econômico-industrial de Santa Catarina*. Florianópolis, 1982.

Da Silva, José Cleto. *Apontamentos históricos da União da Vitória*. Curitiba, 1933.

———. "Apontamentos sobre o movimento fanático." *Boletim do Instituto Histórico, Geográfico, e Ethnográfico Paranaense* 28 (1976): 49–64.

Dean, Warren. "Latifundia and Land Policy in Nineteenth-Century Brazil." *Hispanic American Historical Review* 51 (Nov. 1971): 606–25.

———. *Rio Claro: A Brazilian Plantation System, 1820–1920*. Stanford, 1976.

Della Cava, Ralph. *Miracle at Joaseiro*. New York, 1970.

De Souza, Amaury. "The Cangaço and Politics of Violence in Northeast Brazil." In *Protest and Resistance in Angola and Brazil*, ed. Ronald H. Chilcote (109–31). Berkeley and Los Angeles, 1972.

Diacon, Todd A. "Capitalists and Fanatics: Brazil's Contestado Rebellion, 1912–1916." Ph.D. dissertation, University of Wisconsin–Madison, 1987.

———. "The Contestado Movement and the Caste War of Yucatán: Secular and Religious Responses to Crisis Situations." Master's Thesis, University of Wisconsin–Madison, 1983.

———. "Down and Out in Rio de Janeiro: Urban Poor and Elite Rule in the Old Republic." *Latin American Research Review* 25, no. 1 (Jan. 1990): 243–52.

———. "Private Power and Public Action: A Case Study of State and Society Relations in the Brazilian Old Republic." Paper presented at the 56th Annual Meeting of the Southern Historical Association, New Orleans, 1 Nov. 1990.

———. "The Search for Meaning in an Historical Context: Popular Religion, Millenarianism, and the Contestado Rebellion." *Luso Brazilian Review* (forthcoming).

Drummond, José Augusto. *O movimento tenentista: a intervenção política dos oficiais jovens (1922–1935)*. Rio de Janeiro, 1986.

Eisenstadt, S. N., and L. Roniger. *Patrons, Clients, and Friends*. Cambridge, 1984.

Facó, Rui. *Cangaceiros e fanáticos*. Rio de Janeiro, 1963.

Farriss, Nancy M. *Maya Society under Colonial Rule: The Collective Enterprise of Survival*. Princeton, 1984.

Flory, Thomas. *Judge and Jury in Imperial Brazil, 1808–1871*. Austin, 1981.

Foley, Michael W. "Organizing, Ideology, and Moral Suasion: Political Discourse and Action in a Mexican Town." *Comparative Studies in Society and History* 32, no. 3 (July 1990): 455–87.

Foster, George M. "The Dyadic Contract: A Model for the Social Structure of a Mexican Village." *American Anthropologist* 63 (1961): 1173–92.

———. "The Dyadic Contract in Tzintzuntzen, II: Patron-Client Relationship." *American Anthropologist* 65 (1963): 1280–94.

Furtado, Celso. *Economic Development of Latin America*, 2d ed. Cambridge, 1976.

Gauld, Charles A. *The Last Titan Percival Farquhar: American Entrepreneur in Latin America*. Stanford, 1964.

Geertz, Clifford. "The Changing Role of Cultural Brokers: The Javanese Kijaji." *Comparative Studies in Society and History* 2 (1960): 228–49.

———. *The Interpretation of Cultures*. New York, 1973.

Góngora, Mario. *Origen de los inquilinos de Chile central*. Santiago, 1960.

Graham, Richard. *Britain and the Onset of Modernization in Brazil*. Cambridge, 1968.

———. *Patronage and Politics in Nineteenth-Century Brazil*. Stanford, 1990.

Gudeman, Stephen. "Spiritual Relationships and Selecting a Godparent." *Man* 10 (1975): 221–37.

Gudeman, Stephen, and Stuart B. Schwartz. "Cleansing Original Sin: Godparenthood and the Baptism of Slaves in Eighteenth-Century Bahia." In *Kinship Ideology and Practice in Latin America*, ed. Raymond T. Smith (35–58). Chapel Hill, 1984.

Hahner, June E. *Poverty and Politics: The Urban Poor in Brazil, 1870–1920.* Albuquerque, 1986.
Hardman, Francisco Foot. *Trem fantasma: a modernidade na selva.* São Paulo, 1988.
Heinz, Eduardo, *O matte ou chá do Paraná.* Curitiba, 1909.
A história do Imperador Carlos Magno e os doze Pares de França. São Paulo, n.d.
Hobsbawm, E. J. *Primitive Rebels.* New York, 1959.
Holloway, Thomas. *Immigrants on the Land.* Chapel Hill, 1980.
Leal, Vitor Nunes. *Coronelismo, enxada, e voto,* 3d ed. São Paulo, 1976.
LeGrand, Catherine. "Perspectives for the Historical Study of Rural Politics and the Colombian Case: An Overview." *Latin American Research Review* 12, no. 1 (1977): 7–36.
Lemos, Zélia de Andrade. *Curitibanos na história do Contestado,* 2d ed. Curitibanos, 1983.
Levine, Robert M. "'Mud Hut Jerusalem': Canudos Revisited." *Hispanic American Historical Review* 68, no. 3 (Aug. 1988): 525–72.
Lewin, Linda. "The Oligarchical Limitations of Social Banditry in Brazil: The Case of the 'Good' Thief Antonio Silvino." *Past and Present* 82 (Feb. 1979): 116–46.
———. *Politics and Parentela in Paraíba.* Princeton, 1987.
Lloyd, Reginald, W. Feldwick, and R. T. Delaney. *Twentieth-Century Impressions of Brazil.* London, 1913.
Lobo, Eulália Maria Lahmeyer, and Eduardo Navarro Stotz. "Flutuações cíclas de economia, condições de vida e movimento operário—1880 a 1930." *Revista Rio de Janeiro* 1, no. 1 (Sept.–Dec. 1985): 61–86.
Love, Joseph L. *Rio Grande do Sul and Brazilian Regionalism, 1882–1930.* Stanford, 1971.
Machado, Brasil Pinheiro. "Formação da estrutura agrária tradicional dos Campos Gerais." *Boletim da Universidade do Paraná* 3 (June 1963).
McCann, Frank D. "The Formative Period of Twentieth-Century Brazilian Army Thought, 1900–1922." *Hispanic American Historical Review* 44, no. 2 (Nov. 1984): 737–65.
Mallon, Florencia E. *The Defense of Community in Peru's Central Highlands.* Princeton, 1983.
———. "Murder in the Andes: Patrons, Clients, and the Impact of Foreign Capital, 1860–1922." *Radical History Review* 27 (1983): 79–98.
———. "Introduction." *Latin American Perspectives* 48 (Winter 1986): 3–17.
Martins, Romário. *Documentos comprobatórios dos direitos do Paraná na questão de limites com Sta. Catarina.* Rio de Janeiro, 1915.
———. *História do Paraná.* São Paulo, 1939.
———. *Quantos somos e quem somos.* Curitiba, 1941.
Marx, Karl. *Capital,* vol. 1. International Publishers, 1967.
Mattoon, Robert. "The Companhia Paulista de Estradas de Ferro, 1868–1900:

A Local Railway Enterprise in São Paulo, Brazil." Ph.D. dissertation, Yale University, 1971.

Mauss, Marcel. *The Gift.* Trans. Ian Cunnison. New York, 1967.

Merrick, Thomas W., and Douglas H. Graham. *Population and Economic Development in Brazil: 1800 to Present.* Baltimore, 1979.

Mintz, S. W., and E. R. Wolf. "An Analysis of Co-parenthood (*Compadrazgo*)." *Southwestern Journal of Anthropology* 6, no. 4 (1950): 341–68.

Monteiro, Duglas Teixeira. *Os errantes do novo século.* São Paulo, 1974.

Nascimento, Noel. "Canudos, Contestado, e fanatismo religioso." *Revista Brasiliense* 44 (Nov.–Dec. 1961): 62–67.

Needell, Jeffrey D. *A Tropical Belle Epoque: Elite Culture and Society in Turn-of-the-Century Rio de Janeiro.* Cambridge, 1987.

Ossio, Juan M. "Cultural Continuity, Structure, and *Compadrazgo.*" In *Kinship Ideology and Practice in Latin America,* ed. Raymond T. Smith (118–46). Chapel Hill, 1984.

Pang, Eul Soo. *In Pursuit of Honor and Power: Noblemen of the Southern Cross in Nineteenth-Century Brazil.* Tuscaloosa, 1988.

Pereira de Queiroz, Maria Isaura. "O coronelismo numa interpretação sociológica." In *O Brasil republicano,* 3d ed., ed. Boris Fausto (III:1:153–90). São Paulo, 1982.

———. *La guerre sainte au Brésil: Le movement messianique du Contestado.* São Paulo, 1957.

———. "Messiahs in Brazil." *Past and Present* 31 (July 1985): 62–86.

———. *O messianismo no Brasil e no mundo,* 2d ed. São Paulo, 1976.

Pessar, Patricia R. "Unmasking the Politics of Religion: The Case of Brazilian Millenarianism." *Journal of Latin American Lore* 7, no. 2 (1981): 255–78.

Piazza, Walter F. *Santa Catarina: sua história.* Florianópolis, 1983.

Reed, Nelson. *The Caste War of Yucatán.* Stanford, 1964.

Santos, Sílvio Coelho dos. *Índios e brancos no sul do Brasil.* Florianópolis, 1973.

Friends, Followers, and Factions: A Reader in Political Clientelism. Berkeley and Los Angeles, 1977.

Schwartz, Stuart B. "Elite Politics and the Growth of a Peasantry in Late Colonial Brazil." In *From Colony to Nation: Essays on the Independence of Brazil,* ed. A. J. R. Russell Wood. Baltimore, 1975.

———. *Sugar Plantations in the Formation of Brazilian Society.* New York, 1985.

Scott, James C. *The Moral Economy of the Peasant.* New Haven, 1976.

———. *Weapons of the Weak: Everyday Forms of Peasant Resistance.* New Haven, 1985.

Scott, James C., and Benedict J. Kerkvliet. "How Traditional Rural Patrons Lose Legitimacy: A Theory with Special Reference to Southeast Asia." In *Friends, Followers, and Factions: A Reader in Political Clientelism,* ed. Steffen W. Schmidt, Laura Guasti, Carl H. Landé, and James C. Scott (439–58). Berkeley and Los Angeles, 1977.

Siegel, Bernard. "The Contestado Rebellion, 1912–1916: A Case Study in Brazilian Messianism and Regional Dynamics." In *The Anthropology of Power*, ed. R. Fogelson and R. Adams (325–36). New York, 1977.

Silverman, Sydel F. "Patronage and Community-Nation Relationships in Central Italy." In *Friends, Followers, and Factions: A Reader in Political Clientelism*, ed. Steffen W. Schmidt, Laura Guasti, Carl H. Landé, and James C. Scott (293–304). Berkeley and Los Angeles, 1977.

Skidmore, Thomas E. *Black Into White*. New York, 1974.

Skidmore, Thomas E., and Peter H. Smith. *Modern Latin America*. New York and Oxford, 1984.

Slade, James. "Cattle Barons and Yeoman Farmers: Land Tenure, Division, and Use in a County in Southern Brazil, 1711–1889." Ph.D. dissertation, Indiana University, 1971.

Smith, Raymond T. "Introduction." In *Kinship Ideology and Practice in Latin America*, ed. Raymond T. Smith (3–34). Chapel Hill, 1984.

Soares, José Octaviano Pinto. *Guerra em sertões brasileiros*. Rio de Janeiro, 1931.

"Sobressalto no campo." *Veja* (12 June 1985): 80–82.

Stein, Stanley J. *Vassouras: A Brazilian Coffee County, 1850–1900*. Boston, 1958; Princeton, 1985.

Stern, Steve J. "On the Social Origins of Millenial Movements: A Review and Proposal." Unpublished paper, 1974.

———. *Peru's Indian Peoples and the Challenge of Spanish Conquest*. Madison, 1982.

Talmon, Yonina. "Millenarianism." *International Encyclopedia of the Social Sciences* (10:349–62). New York, 1968.

Thomé, Nelson. *Trem de ferro: história da ferrovia no Contestado*, 2d ed. Florianópolis, 1983.

Thompson, E. P. "The Moral Economy of the English Crowd in the Eighteenth Century." *Past and Present* 50 (Feb. 1971): 76–136.

Topik, Steven. *The Political Economy of the Brazilian State, 1889–1930*. Austin, 1987.

Turner, Victor. *Dramas, Fields, and Metaphors: Symbolic Action in Human Society*. Ithaca, 1974.

Uricoechea, Fernando. *The Patrimonial Foundations of the Brazilian Bureaucratic State*. Berkeley and Los Angeles, 1980.

Vargas Llosa, Mario. *The War of the End of the World*. Trans. Helen R. Lane. New York, 1985.

Vinhas de Queiroz, Maurício. *Messianismo e conflito social*, 3d ed. São Paulo, 1981.

Viotti da Costa, Emília. *The Brazilian Empire: Myths and Histories*. Chicago, 1985.

———. *Da senzala à colonia*, 2d ed. São Paulo, 1982.

———. *Da monarquia à república: momentos decisivos*, 3d ed. São Paulo, 1985.

Wachowicz, Ruy. "O comércio da madeira e a atução da Brazil Railway no sul do Brasil." Photocopy located at the Arquivo Público de Santa Catarina, Brazil.

Wallace, Anthony F. C. "Revitalization Movements." *American Anthropologist* 58 (1956): 264–81.

Weinstein, Barbara. *The Amazon Rubber Boom, 1850–1920.* Stanford, 1983.

Wilson, Byran R. "Millenialism in Comparative Perspective." *Comparative Studies in Society and History* 6 (1963): 93–114.

Wirth, John D. "Tenentismo in the Brazilian Revolution of 1930." *Hispanic American Historical Review* 44, no. 2 (May 1964): 161–79.

Wolf, Eric R. *Peasant Wars of the Twentieth Century.* New York, 1969.

Womack, John R. *Zapata and the Mexican Revolution.* New York, 1968.

Zaluar, Alba. *Os homens de deus: um estudo dos santos e das festas no catolicismo popular.* Rio de Janeiro, 1983.

Index

About the Author

Todd A. Diacon is Assistant Professor of History at the University of Tennessee, Knoxville, Tennessee.

Library of Congress Cataloging-in-Publication Data

Diacon, Todd A.

Millenarian vision, capitalist reality : Brazil's Contestado
Rebellion, 1912–1916 / Todd A. Diacon.

p.   cm.

Includes bibliographical references and index.

ISBN 0–8223–1157–7 (cloth). — ISBN 0–8223–1167–4 (paper)

1. Brazil—History—Contestado Insurrection, 1912–1916.
2. Millennialism—Brazil—History—20th century. 3. Paraná (Brazil
: State)—History. 4. Santa Catarina (Brazil : State)—History.
I. Title.

F2537.D52   1991

981'.05—dc20
                                                          91–521
                                                           CIP